# The New Foreign Policy

# NEW MILLENNIUM BOOKS IN INTERNATIONAL STUDIES

### Titles in the Series
*Global Backlash* edited by Robin Broad
*Globalization and Belonging* by Sheila Croucher
*The Global New Deal*, 2nd ed., by William F. Felice
*The Information Revolution and World Politics* by Elizabeth C. Hanson
*Sword & Salve* by Peter J. Hoffman and Thomas G. Weiss
*International Law in the 21st Century* by Christopher C. Joyner
*Elusive Security* by Laura Neack
*International Negotiation in a Complex World*, 3rd ed., by Brigid Starkey, Mark A. Boyer, and Jonathan Wilkenfeld
*Global Politics as if People Mattered*, 2nd ed., by Mary Ann Tétreault and Ronnie D. Lipschutz
*Military-Civilian Interactions*, 2nd ed., by Thomas G. Weiss

# The New Foreign Policy

## Complex Interactions, Competing Interests

### Third Edition

Laura Neack

ROWMAN & LITTLEFIELD PUBLISHERS, INC.
Lanham • Boulder • New York • Toronto • Plymouth, UK

Published by Rowman & Littlefield Publishers, Inc.
A wholly owned subsidiary of
The Rowman & Littlefield Publishing Group, Inc.
4501 Forbes Boulevard, Suite 200, Lanham, Maryland 20706
www.rowman.com

10 Thornbury Road, Plymouth PL6 7PP, United Kingdom

British Library Cataloguing in Publication Information Available

**Library of Congress Cataloging-in-Publication Data**
The new foreign policy : complex interactions, competing interests / Laura Neack. — Third edition.
pages cm. — (New millennium books in international studies)
Includes bibliographical references and index.
ISBN 978-1-4422-2006-5 (cloth : alk. paper) — ISBN 978-1-4422-2007-2 (pbk. : alk. paper) — ISBN 978-1-4422-2008-9 (electronic) 1. International relations—Philosophy. 2. International relations—History—21st century I. Title.
JZ1305.N424 2013
327.101—dc23
2013014864

Printed in the United States of America

# Contents

# Preface

This is the third edition of *The New Foreign Policy*. This third edition is subtitled *Complex Interactions, Competing Interests* to indicate the inherent messiness in the subject matter before we distill it into understandable parts. This book attempts to describe and discuss what analysts and scholars think they know about foreign policy and to describe and discuss the "stuff" of foreign policy for countries from around the globe.

The third edition contains new scholarship and cases, but chapter 1 still begins with the Tangled Tale of Tibet, and chapter 10 still tells the Tangled Tale of Pinochet. In between, some of the old cases from previous editions remain but are updated, and some new cases appear. Some of the new case material is in short form, some in extended discussion. The chapter descriptions below include some—but not all—of the cases explored. The book uses a level-of-analysis approach to organizing the material.

Chapters 2, 3, and 4 focus on the individual level of analysis. In chapter 2, the focus is on rational actors and rational decision making for a first take on the individual level of analysis. In a second take, chapter 3 turns to cognitive and personality studies on the beliefs, perceptions, and misperceptions of national decision makers. Chapter 3 includes a new, preliminary attempt to construct the operational code of German chancellor Angela Merkel to understand her reaction to the Eurozone debt crisis.

In chapter 4, the subject is small-group decision-making dynamics. The primary case discussed here involves an analysis of the Iranian supreme leader's inner circle on the issue of nuclear negotiations with the West. This is updated through the end of 2012. A new case included in chapter 4 explores how the American decision to use military force abroad is supposed to be controlled by multiple autonomous groups acting together. According to the Constitution, the executive and legislative branches share this authority, but in practice the US Congress tends to vacate its authority to the president. The issue of targeted assassinations of terrorists by the Obama administration is discussed in this context.

Chapters 5, 6, and 7 are set at the state level of analysis. Chapter 5 analyzes the impact of national self-image and culture on foreign policy choices. Some of the new case study material presented in this chapter compares and contrasts the antimilitarist national cultures of Germany and Japan. Chapter 6 examines the impact of domestic politics on foreign policy. The primary case material here concerns domestic political competition between Palestinian leaders and how this competition contributed to a Palestinian civil war and three wars with Israel since the Palestinian legislative elections. Chapter 7 begins with a case study on the apparent belligerence of the Canadian public, media, and leadership in defending Canadian sovereignty in the Arctic. This chapter discusses the complicated relationship between public opinion, elites, interest groups, and media on states' foreign policies.

Chapters 8 and 9 shift the focus to the international system level of analysis. These chapters have been dramatically revised from the second edition. Since the last edition went to press, it has become clear that the international system will remain unipolar for the foreseeable future. This has important consequences for the foreign policies of the states near the "top" of the hierarchy of states. Chapter 8 discusses "great power" as a general concept and then discusses the grand strategy of the singular great power, the United States. The building of the post–World War II US-constructed international order is discussed, along with the unipolar American grand strategies of presidents from George H. W. Bush through Barack Obama. Chapter 9 then delves into what we can expect of the foreign policies of China and Russia as potential balancers and competitors to the United States; major power allies France and Britain; rising powers India and Brazil; middle powers Canada, Australia, and Indonesia; and client state Saudi Arabia. Finally, chapter 10 focuses on the rise of nonstate actors and linkage actors starting with the case of the Tangled Tale of Pinochet. This chapter ends with a new case study on the Egyptian Revolution as another demonstration of linkage actors and their impact on the foreign (and domestic) policies of states.

As with previous editions, I am most grateful for the continued support of the editorial board of the New Millennium Books in International Studies series from Rowman & Littlefield. Series coeditor Eric Selbin has been especially kind and always available. Susan McEachern, editorial director for history, international studies, and geography at Rowman & Littlefield, keeps her insightful eye tuned to growing this series, and Susan's constant support for this title and its many editions is greatly appreciated. Great thanks to Carolyn Broadwell-Tkach and Janice Braunstein for overseeing the production of this third edition. Thanks also go to the foreign policy students I've taught over many years at Miami University, and the foreign policy students around the world who were and are the reasons for this book.

*Chapter One*

# Introduction: The New Foreign Policy

## IN THIS CHAPTER

- The Tangled Tale of Tibet
- The New Foreign Policy
- Defining the Subject: Foreign Policy
- Selecting Entrance Points: Levels of Analysis
- Worldviews and Theories
- The Bridge between International and Comparative Politics
- A New Millennium
- Back to the Tangled Tale of Tibet
- Chapter Review

## CASES FEATURED IN THIS CHAPTER

- The tangled relations between Tibet, China, and the United States.
- The impact of the Cold War on the development of the comparative study of foreign policy.

## THE TANGLED TALE OF TIBET

Our starting point is 1989 at the top of the world—Tibet. In 1989, the tenth Panchen Lama, one of two of the highest leaders of Tibetan Buddhism, died under mysterious circumstances in his monastery. By Buddhist tradition, the soul of the Panchen Lama would be reincarnated, returning to Earth to teach others the path to enlightenment. Also according to Buddhist tradition, the former friends and teachers of the late Panchen Lama would begin a series of divinations designed to determine where he would be reincarnated so they could locate the living Buddha and ensure his proper religious training and preparation.

What does this have to do with *The New Foreign Policy*? This is one entrance point into a tangled tale that involves many countries strong and weak, key international figures, transnational human rights and religious groups, the United Nations, and even Hollywood. We could open the tale years earlier—decades and centuries earlier—or in the US presidential election campaign of 2000. If we fast-forwarded to 2007, we would find the Dalai Lama in Washington, D.C., receiving a Congressional Gold Medal while the Chinese government registered its anger over congressional meddling in Chinese internal affairs.

Changing the starting point would change the issues somewhat, but the tangled nature of the tale would not change, nor would its entanglement in the foreign relations of some powerful **states**. Indeed, the fate of Tibetan Buddhism is inextricably enmeshed in the foreign policy choices of several important countries and presents us with a perfect case study for starting our discussion of *The New Foreign Policy*.

Back to the story. In early 1995, the Panchen Lama search party narrowed its search to a short list of boys, in and outside Tibet, and assembled photos and evidence to present to the highest holy figure in Tibetan Buddhism, the Dalai Lama. The search party would offer its opinion on which boy was most likely to be the reincarnate lama. The Dalai Lama would make the final decision on the recognition of the eleventh Panchen Lama, taking into account the evidence and opinion of the search party. So here's where we'll bring foreign policy in—at this time, the Dalai Lama was the spiritual and political **leader** of the government of Tibet in exile. The Dalai Lama and his government reside in Dharamsala in northern India, where they sought refuge from the Chinese occupation of Tibet. The Chinese army invaded Tibet in 1950 in order to incorporate it into the new communist **regime**, or, as the Chinese explain it, the Chinese army entered Tibet in order to liberate its people. By 1959, brutal Chinese efforts to eradicate Buddhism and the culture of the Tibetan people and to suppress a Tibetan uprising against Chinese authorities caused the Dalai Lama to flee Tibet in the hope of maintaining in sanctuary some semblance of the true Tibet. Of course, this is not the story the Chinese government told—then or now.

Regardless of whether one takes the position that Tibet was part of China for centuries or that Tibet was always independent, since 1950 Tibet has been part of the country called the People's Republic of China. From the time he fled Tibet, the Dalai Lama has frustrated and angered the Chinese government because of his work for the liberation of his people and culture. The Chinese government long maintained that the Dalai Lama encouraged dangerous "splittism" aimed at dismembering the country of China. Since his flight from Tibet, the Dalai Lama had been accorded head-of-state treatment by governments around the world, including the executive and legislative branches of the US government, and had been praised and supported by international human rights and religious freedom groups. As an advocate of nonviolence, the Dalai Lama was awarded the Nobel Peace Prize in 1989. Further, the Dalai Lama's government in exile is located in the territory of one of China's main competitors—India. In chapter 9, we will discuss Chinese-Indian relations; Tibet and the Dalai Lama remain central to unresolved disputes between these countries over borders and territorial claims.

The Panchen Lama chose to be reincarnated inside Tibet. Worried about the reaction of the Chinese authorities, the Dalai Lama carefully weighed the options about announcing who the reincarnate lama was. In April 1995, the Dalai Lama decided to name the boy to start the process of his training and preempt any efforts by the Chinese to thwart the process. The Chinese government formed its own naming team and chose a different boy as the reincarnation. In December, the Chinese government (which is officially atheist) staged a grand ceremony at which its designee assumed the position of the eleventh Panchen Lama. The Dalai Lama's choice, Gedhun Choekyi Nyima, and his family disappeared into Chinese custody and have not been seen since the spring of 1995. The Dalai Lama, human rights groups such as Amnesty International, and religious groups declared the boy to be the world's youngest political prisoner. The Chinese government would only say that Gedhun Choekyi Nyima "is where he is supposed to be."[1]

How does this tale become a foreign policy issue? The Chinese government declared many times that this tale or any tale about Tibet should never be a foreign policy issue, since it involves the domestic affairs of China. As a foreign ministry spokesperson said in 1993 regarding Tibet, "The business of the United States should be addressed by the American people, and the business of the Chinese people should be handled by the Chinese people."[2] But the domestic affairs of any given country can often be the source of dispute with—or an opportunity ripe for manipulation by—other countries. How and to what extent the tale of the Panchen Lama gets entwined in foreign policy depends on the decisions and actions taken and the power held by various actors in various countries. Let's switch sites and see how this plays out.

Let's move our story back a few years. Ever since the Chinese government's violent crackdown on the prodemocracy demonstrators in Tiananmen Square on June 3, 1989, the George H. W. Bush (Bush 1) administration had been subjected to criticism for its policy toward China. A few months prior to Tiananmen, the Chinese had used violence to quell an uprising in Lhasa, Tibet. The violence in Tibet did not garner much **public** attention in the United States. On Tiananmen, Bush's view was that the best way to influence China and end human rights violations there in the longer term was to remain constructively engaged with China, offering incentives rather than disincentives to change.

A majority in the US Congress disagreed with **constructive engagement**, as did human rights and religious interest groups in US society. When the president vetoed a tough sanctions bill to punish China, congressional critics decided to place human rights conditions on the yearly renewal of China's **most favored nation (MFN)** trading status.[3] Constructive engagement remained US policy for the remainder of the Bush 1 administration, but the 1992 presidential election would keep a prosanctions coalition alive and hopeful.

After meeting with members of Congress and leaders of various interest groups opposed to the Bush 1 China policy, Democratic presidential candidate Bill Clinton came out in favor of attaching human rights conditions to any future granting of MFN status to China. Clinton announced his position: "I do not want to isolate China . . . but I believe our nation has a higher purpose than to coddle dictators and stand aside from the global movement toward democracy."[4] This statement was repeated many times by Clinton on the campaign trail. Upon Clinton's election, Chinese authorities signaled their unhappiness with the results of the US election by suspending further human rights talks. But the complexities of the China policy soon became clear to the president-elect, who announced a moderated view in late November 1992: "We have a big stake in not isolating China, in seeing that China continues to develop a market economy. . . . But we also have to insist, I believe, on progress in human rights and human decency."[5]

Before his inauguration, Clinton hosted several conferences in his hometown of Little Rock, Arkansas, to clarify key issues for the new administration. At the economic conference, the chief operating officer of toy manufacturer Mattel raised worries about Mattel's ability to stay on top of the world toy market if human rights conditions were attached to renewing China's MFN status. Voices within the United States—such as the aircraft and wheat industries—and voices outside the United States—such as the governments of Japan and Hong Kong—similarly urged Clinton to back away from his campaign stand on China.

Right before the Clinton inauguration, two groups of Democratic senators visited China and Tibet in December 1992 and January 1993 at the invitation of the Chinese government. This Chinese effort to influence the domestic political debate within the United States—and thereby shape US foreign policy in the new administration—reaped some benefits, as several of the senators declared that it would be shortsighted to link trade and human rights.

A new US policy on China was formulated in 1993 by the new administration in which the president, acting under executive orders authority, attached some pro–human rights conditions to the US-Chinese relationship, but not on trade issues. This compromise policy was hammered out through talks on many levels between administration officials and various members of Congress, with their respective domestic interest groups engaged behind the scenes. The compromise allowed voices on both sides to be partially satisfied and partially dissatisfied (this being the nature of compromise). Farm and business groups and their supporters in Congress were glad to keep trade off this particular table, while human rights groups and their congressional supporters were glad to see some official pronouncement privileging human rights and **democracy**. Even in this age of **globalization**, where market forces seemed to drive so much international activity, it appeared that key noneconomic values would remain central to US foreign policy. At the signing ceremony for the executive order, leaders of human rights groups, business leaders, prodemocracy Chinese students, and members of the Tibetan government in exile stood behind President Clinton.[6] The president warned that the next year's renewal of MFN status would be subject to human rights conditions and conditions designed to curtail Chinese weapons sales (an increasingly troublesome issue). Concurrently, anti-Chinese demonstrations in Lhasa, Tibet, were being ended forcefully by the Chinese military.

There were some in the Clinton administration and Congress who favored a tough China policy for reasons other than Tibet or the treatment of the Tiananmen prodemocracy advocates. Chinese weapons sales to "rogue" states were causing worries among some security analysts. Adding to these worries, in October 1993, the Chinese conducted an underground nuclear weapon test. In response, Clinton ordered the Department of Energy to prepare for its own test.

The compromise China policy would not last, and the threat about the following year would not be carried out. Internal divisions within the Clinton administration—reflecting divisions in American society—led to a reevaluation of policy over the following year. "On the one side were the economic agencies, Treasury, Commerce, and the National Economic Council (NEC), who favored developing ties with China and pursuing human rights concerns only secondarily. . . . On the other side were State Department officials . . . who favored continuing a tough stance on human rights."[7] The economic agencies gained the upper hand on the issue, with support from corporate leaders and increasing numbers of members of Congress, all of whom were interested in tapping into China's enormous potential market. This coalition was able to change the Clinton policy and avoid future threats to link MFN status with human rights issues. As Clinton explained the change in policy in May 1994, "**linkage** has been constructive during the last year, but . . . we have reached the end of the usefulness of that policy."[8] Human rights groups went along with this delinking in order not to lose their potential leverage on the rest of the China policy.

By the next year, 1995, the controversy over the reincarnation of the Panchen Lama came to a climax of sorts with the naming of the two competing "soul boys." That December, as the Chinese-favored Panchen Lama was ceremoniously installed, the Chinese government also sentenced a prominent democracy advocate to fourteen years in prison. These events caused some members of Congress and human rights groups to attempt to force a Clinton policy reassessment on trade with China. Yet even in the face of this pressure, the deputy US trade representative reassured all that the president's previous decision to delink MFN status and human rights remained unchanged. Although human rights problems in China might temper the climate of talks somewhat, the president was committed to helping China gain entry into the World Trade Organization, unless, the trade rep warned, the Chinese leaders continued to make no progress on opening their markets. There will be more on this tangled tale at the end of this chapter.

## THE NEW FOREIGN POLICY

This saga demonstrates several important observations about foreign policy that will be explored in detail in this book:

- Foreign policy is made and conducted in complex domestic and international environments.
- Foreign policy often results from the work of coalitions of interested domestic and international actors and groups.
- Foreign policy issues are often linked and delinked, reflecting the strength of various parties and their particular concerns.
- The "stuff" of foreign policy derives from issues of domestic politics as well as foreign relations.
- Foreign policy analysis needs to be multilevel and multifaceted in order to confront the complicated sources and nature of foreign policy.

How each of these key features pertains to the Tangled Tale of Tibet is summarized below.

*Foreign policy is made and conducted in complex domestic and international environments.* The Tangled Tale of Tibet illustrates that decision makers—here, Bill Clinton and the members of his administration in charge of China policy—operate in at least two different environments, domestic and international. Bill Clinton the candidate was focused primarily on the domestic environment, with very little serious attention paid to the international environment. Bill Clinton the newly elected president had to give attention to both the domestic and international environments. Robert Putnam has described this situation that national leaders find themselves in as a "two-level," "dual," or **"nested" game.**[9] Leaders cannot afford to focus exclusively on one level but must try to play both to some advantage. Sometimes issues on one level will cause a leader to put greater emphasis there, and sometimes leaders will use issues on one level to pursue goals in the other, but no leader can afford to ignore the reality of this nested game.

*Foreign policy often results from the work of coalitions of interested domestic and international actors and groups.* Coalitions are, by nature, in constant flux. The coalition of interests and groups that might get a politician elected is not necessarily the coalition that will get that leader's programs legislated or executed. Leaders come to power "owing" some groups, yet often intent on "wooing" others. As the environments shift, issues and coalitions shift. Leaders often need to pay more attention to those who form the opposition—trying to entice them into forming policy coalitions to get favored programs passed—than to their loyal constituents. The human rights and religious groups inside the United States and human rights and democracy advocates outside the United States (such as the Tibetan government in exile, Chinese students studying in the United States, and the governments of other countries) could not pose any significant threat to the Clinton presidency if Clinton were to "water down" his China policy somewhat. Indeed, we might say that these groups needed the Clinton presidency more than the Clinton presidency needed them—especially the coalition of non-US actors who were not very "powerful" international actors. In order to pursue his broader list of goals—both domestic and international—Clinton needed to garner key support from groups that opposed linking trade with human rights.

*Foreign policy issues are often linked and delinked, reflecting the strength of various parties and their particular concerns.* Because of the "nested game" leaders play and the necessity of building various policy coalitions, issues cannot help but be linked and delinked. Politics is a game of bargaining and compromising, and this involves trade-offs. The politics of foreign policy making is sometimes no different than the politics of domestic policy making. Although the Chinese government insisted that human rights should not be linked to trade issues, by this very demand China made it clear that the United States could not hope to achieve its goals vis-à-vis China unless it quit talking about human rights. That is, the Chinese linked favorable relations with the United States on a broad array of issues to the requirement that human rights stay off the table. The Chinese government and the US domestic interests that wanted entrance into the potential Chinese market commanded the greatest influence over the Clinton policy, and this informal "coalition" was able to win the day and get trade policy delinked from human rights. The domestic and international groups in favor of using trade as a way to compel China to follow a better human rights standard found themselves with less leverage, perhaps because their issues were more narrowly focused, and so they could not link their desired China policy to other issues over which they had control.

*The "stuff" of foreign policy derives from issues of domestic politics as well as foreign relations.* Despite Chinese insistence that domestic politics was off limits to outsiders, the line between domestic politics and international politics is blurry. Issues go across national borders, and coalitions supporting or opposing certain policies on those issues also form across national borders. Some have called this blurring of the distinction between international and domestic politics "intermestic," combining the words "international" and "domestic" to indicate the combining of issues and interests. Others prefer to use the terms **"transnational actors"** and "transnational forces" to indicate the pursuit of interests across national lines. Since the mid-1990s, some observers have suggested that the line between domestic and international politics is not just blurry but is quickly disappearing because of globalization. Globalization refers to the increasing internationalization of culture and economics. As national markets are increasingly opened to the global market, national cultures similarly are opened to the global culture. National **sovereignty** is eroded in terms of both control of the national economy and—perhaps more importantly—preservation of national culture. When the Clinton administration took human rights conditions off its China trade policy, the justification was that opening up China for trade would open up China for other influences, ultimately changing the behavior of the Chinese government in the way that human rights and democracy groups wanted. Put another way, the Clinton policy was based on the idea that, ultimately, the forces of globalization would compel changes in Chinese human rights behavior, and US policy should facilitate those forces.

Further emphasizing this "intermestic" quality of politics, leaders have been known to use foreign policies to promote domestic agendas, and vice versa. In the US presidential election of 1992, Bush 1 attempted to convince American voters to reelect him—a domestic agenda—by pointing to his foreign policy accomplishments. This can be turned around the other way—sometimes domestic credentials are used to promote foreign policy goals. The Chinese government released political prisoners from time to time as a demonstration of its cooperative nature in order to garner greater US investment, US support for Chinese membership in the World Trade Organization, and international support for hosting the 2008 Olympic Games in Beijing.

## DEFINING THE SUBJECT: FOREIGN POLICY

Before we go any further we need to be clear about our subject: foreign policy. Charles Hermann calls foreign policy a "neglected concept."[10] He asserts, "This neglect has been one of the most serious obstacles to providing more adequate and comprehensive explanations of foreign policy." Hermann thinks that part of the reason for this neglect is that "most people dealing with the subject have felt confident that they knew what foreign policy was."[11] To put it colloquially, we know it when we see it. Ultimately, Hermann defines foreign policy as "the discrete purposeful action that results from the political level decision of an individual or group of individuals. . . . [It is] the observable artifact of a political level decision. It is not the decision, but a product of the decision."[12] Thus, Hermann defines foreign policy as the *behavior* of states.

Hermann rejects the idea that the study of foreign policy is the study of policy, but his is a minority view. Bruce Russett, Harvey Starr, and David Kinsella take an opposite and broader view: "We can think of a policy as a program that serves as a guide to behavior intended to realize the goals an organization has set for itself. . . . Foreign policy is thus a guide to actions taken beyond the boundaries of the state to further the goals of the state."[13] Although these scholars define foreign policy as a program or statement of goals, they also stress that the study of foreign policy must involve study of both the "formulation and implementation" of policy.[14]

Deborah Gerner takes foreign policy further when she defines it as "the intentions, statements, and actions of an actor—often, but not always, a state—directed toward the external world and the response of other actors to these intentions, statements and actions."[15] Gerner combines Hermann's interest in behavior with Russett, Starr, and Kinsella's emphasis on programs or guides. Note that in Gerner's definition the emphasis is on states, but it does not have to be on. Other actors—such as international cause groups, businesses, religions, and so forth—in the international system formulate guidelines and goals that direct their actions toward other international actors. In this book, the emphasis is primarily on states, but other actors will appear from time to time as well.

We will use a broad definition of foreign policy that includes both statements and behaviors or actions. The study of foreign policy, however, needs to consider more than what states declare to be their goals and how they attempt to achieve them. The study of foreign policy needs to consider how certain goals arise and why certain behaviors result. Thus, we will explore the factors that cause a state to declare and embark on a certain foreign policy course. Our emphasis will be on understanding these factors and the processes by which policy (as both statements and behaviors) is made. In summary, the "stuff" of our foreign policy study includes processes, statements, and behaviors.

## SELECTING ENTRANCE POINTS: LEVELS OF ANALYSIS

This book rests on the assertion that studying foreign policy is a complicated undertaking requiring multilevel, multifaceted research. This is not meant to imply, though, that we need to study every foreign policy case in all of its varied aspects. Indeed, this quickly could become an unmanageable task. Instead, foreign policy analysts disaggregate or break down each case into different component parts in order to study and understand select aspects. The knowledge generated by many such studies—studies conducted in the same way, asking the same questions, in similar and different contexts and cases—may begin to accumulate and form a body of knowledge.

As the case of the Tangled Tale of Tibet demonstrates, we can enter a case and study it at many different points. For example, we might want to study the change that occurred in Bill Clinton's stance from the perspective of Bill Clinton the individual decision maker. Was Clinton inclined to see the world through a particular "lens" that altered what he saw to fit what he believed? Did he have some weakly held beliefs about the Chinese, allowing him to be open to new thinking about China policy? Were there key advisors whose opinions shaped his, or did his opinion or preferences shape the views of his closest advisors? Were there some group dynamics at play that gave the economics-focused cabinet members or inner circle of presidential advisors greater leverage over those who privileged human rights? Did this lead to an imbalanced consideration of the policy and, therefore, a policy recommendation that did not leave Clinton much room for choice? We could conduct a study of this case using any of these questions to guide our research. Each of these is posed at the *individual level of analysis*—a focus on individual decision makers, how they make decisions, what perceptions and misperceptions they hold, the ways key decision makers interact in small, top-level groups, and so on.

We might, instead, decide to explore the involvement of interest groups and Congress in the changing nature of the Clinton China policy. We could explore the lobbying of Congress and the executive branch by groups on the pro–human rights and pro-trade sides. We could explore the "turf" problems between the executive and legislative branches in defining the US China policy. We could ask whether the Pentagon, worried about potential Chinese military threats, lobbied the White House and Congress for a certain stand against the Chinese. We could investigate the rise and fall of the fortunes of the pro–human rights groups and the rise of the pro-trade groups, charting their different strategies, arguments, and overall effectiveness. Entering the case in this way involves study at the *state level of analysis*. At the state level, we examine those societal (historical, cultural, religious, economic) and governmental (type of government, division of powers) factors that contribute to the making of foreign policy in a particular state.

If we expanded our focus, we could investigate the following questions: Did changes in the overall **balance of power** between countries in the Asia-Pacific region convince American leaders that accommodating China was the most prudent way to have some influence over China? Were there some international mechanisms for pursuing human rights separately from trade, thus allowing the United States to delink the issues and still pursue both? Was there some consensus among key allies that China would need to be enticed into being a "good international citizen" rather than bullied into such a role? These questions about state versus state, or geostrategic concerns about regional or global power tilts, or states acting through international organizations, are all posed at the *system level of analysis*. The system level explores bilateral (state-to-state) relations, regional issues and interactions, and global issues and multilateral interactions between states. At this level we also consider the role played by regional and **international organizations** and by **nonstate actors** such as transnational **nongovernmental organizations (NGOs)** that have a direct influence on the foreign policies of states.

The levels of analysis are tools—heuristic devices—that help us study our subject. All disciplines employ levels of analysis, although the levels vary depending on the discipline. The levels might be better understood by thinking about the lens on a camera and the detail we desire in our subject. At each level of analysis, we gain a particular view on or understanding of our subject. Our understanding may be quite thorough for that level but will necessarily exclude information that can only be attained using one of the other levels of analysis. When we pose our questions at a single level, we acknowledge that our understanding will be limited. Recall that the case study detailed above revealed complexities across the levels of analysis. Analysis conducted at just one level of understanding will not yield a complete picture. Yet as foreign policy analysts we generally take such a risk and emphasize a single level because we are curious about questions at that level, and perhaps we are convinced that one level gives a better explanation more often than the others. It is also true that choosing to frame our study at a single level helps us better manage what we study. This is an important point that shouldn't be overlooked.

## WORLDVIEWS AND THEORIES

In some important ways, the emphasis on a particular level of analysis is related to what the individual scholar thinks is important. Every one of us holds a view of "how things work" or of "human nature." These views might be very elaborate or very simple, but they set the stage for how we act in the world. These "worldviews" don't have to apply to politics; a personal worldview might explain why your best friend won't talk to you today, how to play the stock market or pick lottery numbers (or whether to bother playing the market or picking lottery numbers at all), or why countries choose peace over war.

The study of foreign policy derives, in large part, from the academic discipline called international relations. There are three worldviews or grand theories that dominate the study of international relations: realism,[16] liberalism,[17] and Marxism.[18] Although there are variants and even disagreements within each of these worldviews, these offer three fairly straightforward explanations of "how things work" in the world. Scholars and foreign policy makers all have identifiable worldviews, although from time to time individuals may use one or the other or borrow key concepts to fit particular circumstances.

An explanation of how something works is also known as a *theory*. We can call realism, liberalism, and Marxism worldviews, traditions, or theories. At their most fundamental level, each offers what we call a *grand theory* of how the world of politics works. A grand theory purports to explain why things are the way they are—or how things *might* be. In this latter sense, theories can be *prescriptions* for action to achieve the desired endpoint.

Theories are also used to help us tell the future, or predict. An explanation of a single incident in the past might be interesting, but it cannot tell us anything about the future. This is a problem for scholars, but even more so for foreign policy makers. Foreign policy makers need to be able to confront new circumstances with decisive, effective responses, and they need to be able to be proactive when planning the course for their countries. Theories about how the world works can help policy makers generalize from the past to new experiences, thereby helping them know which policies to undertake and which to avoid.

When analysts apply their theories about the world to the study of particular aspects of foreign policy—such as why countries form alliances, why countries enter into trade agreements, and why countries ban land mines or why they don't—they offer something of use to policy makers. The explanations of the world that result from these particularized studies are called *midrange theories*. These midrange theories don't claim to explain everything, just selected parts of world politics. In fact, midrange theories tend to do a better job of explaining parts of the world than the grand theories do in explaining the entire world. This should make sense on an intuitive level.

Theories explain the past and help predict the future. With predictive capability, policy makers can plan their own actions. Theories are of no use to analysts or policy makers if they are too particular or overly specified. Theories need to go beyond single instances; they need to generalize across cases, events, incidents, and time frames. That is, theories should help in the development of generic knowledge.

How much do foreign policy makers consider the theories—grand or midrange—of scholars? Scholars around the world sit in foreign ministries (or state departments) and analyze the world and advise their governments. Sometimes these scholars are officeholders—such as US president Woodrow

Wilson, who was a professor of international relations and politics at Princeton University before he was president—or hold key ministerial/cabinet positions. Fernando Henrique Cardoso, the president of Brazil from 1995 to 2003, was a leading international scholar in the Marxist dependency theory tradition studying asymmetrical power relations between rich and poor countries. In Canada, as another example, foreign policy and international relations scholars frequently spend part of their careers in universities and part in the Department of Foreign Affairs and International Trade. Sometimes scholars write syndicated columns for newspapers or host talk shows that are broadcast around their countries and the world. The work of scholars gets translated into the work of foreign policy makers, and that translation happens in many different ways. This is why there is an imperative that foreign policy studies have something to say about the world—something tangible and practical.

Scholars in different traditions or using different theories can examine the same set of events and arrive at different explanations about why those events occurred and how best to deal with similar events in the future. Theories give us different answers to the puzzles of the world because they begin with different starting assumptions, stress different critical variables, and have different ideal endpoints. It is also important to note that an analyst working within a particular tradition will sometimes ignore evidence that another analyst using a different worldview would find indispensable. When a scholar comes up with an answer as to why an event occurred and whether it will occur again, we would be wise to ask: What tradition is this person applying? What factors did this person ignore, disregard, or downplay? Will we imperil our policy if we ignore other potentially important variables?

As foreign policy makers as well as students of foreign policy, we should read every study with caution—with a critical mind—remembering that each scholar's orientation has led her or him to choose some variables over others. We might learn a great deal from this scholar's work, but the things we are not learning might be just as important. We would be wise, then, to critically mix and match our studies, looking for scholars of different orientations to offer us competing explanations that we can assess critically on the path to a more comprehensive understanding of events.

Let's review the dominant grand theories in brief.

## Realism

Classical realists start with a pessimistic view of human nature, and from this they make key assumptions about the "nature" of states and state behaviors. Humans are essentially self-interested and exist in a social condition characterized by the constant struggle to maintain autonomy from other self-interested humans. States also are self-interested actors existing in an **interna-**

**tional system** characterized by the constant struggle to maintain autonomy (sovereignty) from other states.

Whereas in a national society some legal limitations are placed on the ability of individuals to infringe on the autonomy of other individuals, in the international system any "society" that exists is loosely formed with no ultimate guarantor of the sovereignty of states except the states themselves. Indeed, the dominant characteristic of the international system is **anarchy**. Neorealists or structural realists emphasize this, rather than human nature, as the starting point for their explanation of world politics. Because of anarchy, states are compelled to be constantly vigilant, watching out for impositions on their autonomy. The best way to protect a state's autonomy—and thus ensure its survival—is to amass power resources that can be used to deter or defend against other states. All states are similarly motivated and thus can be expected to do what is necessary to survive—sometimes resorting to the use of armed violence against others to capture additional power resources that can be harnessed for the protection of the state. Power itself (or the things that together constitute power, such as military and economic might) is finite in the international system, so whenever a state lays claim to a certain amount of power resources, other states are deprived of those resources. International politics is necessarily conflictual.

The realist perspective is state centered. States and only states are international actors, or the only international actors of note, privilege, and agency. International organizations and nongovernmental actors are only important to study as instruments of states pursuing their own **national interests**. What goes on within a state also is unimportant—or should be unimportant if a state is pursuing its long-term interests—because all states have the same operating motivation. The important topics to study from a realist perspective include the balance of power, globally or regionally, and the grand strategies of major powers and rising competitors (topics discussed in chapters 8 and 9). More recent realist scholarship focuses on whether to balance power or balance threats, whether states should pursue offensive power–increasing strategies or can be content with the status quo, and states' pursuit of relative and contingent gains over others.

Globalization is a process that realists meet with some suspicion. Globalization both poses a serious threat to national autonomy and control and creates interdependencies that impede the pursuit of national interests.

## Liberalism

Liberals start from a different assumption about human nature than do realists and end up with a different view about international politics. Humans, in the liberal view, cherish autonomy but do not assume that their autonomy is threatened by other humans. Instead, humans exist within many networks of relationships that help them achieve collectively what they cannot achieve on their own. Humans who have the opportunity to exercise personal autonomy and self-determination will respect others' rights to the same and will value the social fabric that assists all individuals in self-realization. Just as national society should be built on a political system that respects the rights of individuals and serves the collective will of those individuals, international society should also be founded on principles that respect the rights of individual, self-determining states and serve the **collective good**. International politics, then, is characterized by—or can be characterized by—harmony among international actors. Because of this expectation that the future might find countries in harmony with one another, the liberal view was once called idealism.

Liberals are **pluralists**. They conceptualize politics as the interaction of multiple actors pursuing multiple interests and using different types of resources and methods of interaction (such as bargaining, **coalition building**, arm-twisting, and so on). States, as well as substate and nonstate actors of all sorts, are important in different ways, depending on the issues at hand. Liberals focus on the formation of international law, organizations, and cooperative arrangements of many sorts that regulate and routinize global interactions, as well as on coercive statecraft directed at preserving some greater, collective good such as international peace or the promotion of human rights. Liberals value multiplicity and norms like good **governance** and the **rule of law** that protect and encourage multiplicity.

For liberals, free and open trade between countries can decrease the possibility of conflict between them. Essentially, the argument is that the more people trade, the greater the ties that bind them together. And the more people trade, the more they reap the benefits of trade together. In time, interdependencies and mutual gains will make war and violent conflict less likely, as all countries benefit from—and understand that they benefit from—their open relationships with one another.

**Neoliberal institutionalism** is a variant on liberalism that also sees international cooperation as a natural result of world politics. Unlike liberals, however, neoliberal institutionalists propose that this cooperation comes out of the pursuit of self-interests; thus neoliberals make peace with realists on this issue. Self-interested actors acknowledge that through cooperation with other actors they can achieve more security, wealth, and well-being than through **unilateral** action. Such cooperation is assisted and sustained by multilateral action in international institutions. Rewards and punishments are built into the institutional arrangements of international organizations, relieving states of the worry about whether other states can be trusted. Trust in the benefits of the system (not necessarily trust in other states) is achieved over time over a variety of issues as time and events demonstrate that the institutional arrangement benefits all good actors without discrimination and compels all actors—even the most powerful—to be good partners most of the time. Moreover, over time actors expect that all kinds of international problems are best solved through **multilateralism**.

Globalization is a phenomenon that liberals of all sorts welcome, even as they acknowledge that aspects of globalization need to be tempered in order to accommodate different peoples' concerns and interests.

## Marxism

The Marxist view was established as a critique and response to capitalism. Both of the grand political theories discussed above, realism and liberalism, are compatible with capitalism. Marxism constitutes both a response to the problems inherent to capitalism—an economic system—and a response to realism and liberalism, which chiefly describe political systems.

As with realism and liberalism, there is more to Marxism than will be described here. The foundation of the Marxist view is that the economic organization of a society determines its political and social systems. A society premised on capitalism, with its free market and private ownership of wealth and property, is a society divided into economic and social classes. Essentially, there are two classes—owners and workers. The societal norms and political system built on a capitalist-based economy are designed to maintain the continued profit taking of the owner class. Politics will be dominated by **elite** interests, and the institutions of government will be designed and directed to keeping the workers in an exploited, dependent position in order to preserve and increase the wealth of the owners. An international system based on capitalism is also a system divided into the owners, or the "haves," and the workers, or the "have-nots." The institutions of the rich states—such as their militaries and legal systems—are used to maintain the world capitalist system, which serves elite interests.

Communist or Marxist states attempted to build a different political/social domestic order by instituting an economic system that rejected private ownership and wealth-based social classes. Instead, centrally planned economies were constructed to serve the interests of all citizens—theoretically. These states—primarily the Eastern bloc led by the Soviet Union during the Cold War—attempted to "remove" themselves from the capitalist world system in order to protect themselves from the inherent distortions of that system. The Cold War conflict between the Soviet-led Eastern bloc and the American-led Western bloc was inevitable, according to the Marxist view, as capitalist states would use all means necessary to protect against the existential threat posed by communism.

Despite the collapse of the Soviet Union and the worldwide turn to neoliberal capitalism (a turn even manifested in the remaining communist states of China, Vietnam, and Cuba; North Korea doesn't quite fit any category), the Marxist critique of capitalism remains relevant. During and beyond the Cold War, Marxist discussions of international politics focused on how the world's rich states mobilize their resources and tools of statecraft to maintain and increase their wealth and predominance. International organizations serve as instruments of the rich (called the core or center) states to maintain a world system that remains stratified into the rich few and the poor many on the periphery. Because this view stresses the structure of the world system and the structural determinants of power within the world economic system, it is also referred to as structuralism (but don't confuse it with structural realism!).

A Marxist or structuralist observer might focus on how the policies of international lending agencies keep developing countries submerged in debt and dependent on the core states for trade, new technologies, and investment. Similarly, such an analysis might discuss how the terms attached to international loans coerce developing countries to enact domestic economic policies that increase poverty and human suffering in order to be able to make the service payments on external debt. Marxists also examine the patterns in the use of force—unilaterally and multilaterally—by core states against dependent states as continuing evidence of inevitable class conflict.

In this era of globalization, the Marxist/structuralist perspective on international politics remains an ongoing critique of the problems of a global free-market system. Globalization provokes strong opposition among realists and Marxists alike. Realists reject globalization because, as mentioned above, it erodes national sovereignty. That is, the opening of national borders and markets diminishes the ways in which central governments traditionally exert power. The Marxists reject globalization because there appears to be no safe harbor for poor people in the free-market tsunami. The economic system being globalized is a wide-open liberal economic system; if states want to ride this wave to potential prosperity, they must disengage any "safety net" provisions designed to protect their poor and workers against the free market. Further, there is no countering force to globalization that will ensure a more equitable distribution of power in the system; thus globalization will only increase the structural power of the center at the expense of all others.

These worldviews don't just focus on different actors and issues but also on different levels of analysis. Realists are focused on the state—not on what's "in" the state but on relations between states based on differences in power. Thus realists study foreign policy at the system level—whether bilateral relations, regional, or global. Realists do imagine the calculations of state interests and foreign policy behaviors to be those of a rational economic actor; thus they will study strategic decision making with the caveat that the "individuals" making rational decisions are idealized individuals.

Liberals, being pluralists, focus on all the levels of analysis, depending on the subject of study. Liberals borrow from comparative politics and look at the persons, groups, structures, cultures, and so on within a state that may lead it to take certain foreign policy stands. They may examine the workings of international organizations—which is a system-level international relations interest. They may also explore the interaction of nonstate actors across state boundaries. Or they may look at the **belief sets** or personalities of individuals who form the foreign policy elite.

Marxists look at foreign policy from the system and state levels. At the system level, the asymmetrical relations between states are important. At the state level, Marxists study the common interests of economic elites in one state with the elites in another. For instance, they might study how military-capitalist-industrial interests push states into war. Group politics is important to Marxists, so we can find such explanations of foreign policy posed at the state and system levels.

## Constructivism

Is it true, as the realists say, that the world is a hostile place in which no other state can be trusted and every state must be constantly ready to prey or be preyed upon? Is anarchy a reality that states ignore at their own folly? If we start with realist assumptions about the world, we must go where the realists take us—to a self-help system in which violence is both natural and at times the preferred foreign policy instrument. If we change the starting assumptions, we get to a differently constituted world. This idea has led scholars to use alternative grand theories to understand the world, such as liberalism and Marxism. Of course, all three worldviews present starting assumptions that lead us in certain intended directions.

There is an approach to understanding reality that, although not a grand theory per se, offers an alternative tool for analysis. This approach is called **constructivism**. Constructivists argue that there is no more-or-less objective social reality, but instead reality is socially constructed from society's perceptions of it. Society projects a certain understanding of reality onto the world—such as the "reality" of anarchy—and from this projected understanding, different identities and "appropriate" behaviors result. To constructivists, states/societies believe that the international system is anarchic, and then the system they create by their beliefs makes the states self-interested and predatory by necessity. Constructivism can help us understand how certain views of the world have become predominant, but constructivism itself does not offer us an alternative vision of the world.

## THE BRIDGE BETWEEN INTERNATIONAL AND COMPARATIVE POLITICS

The study of foreign policy sits in the subdiscipline of political science known as international relations, although you could say foreign policy sometimes jumps over the fence into the subdiscipline of comparative politics. As a distinct "field" of study, foreign policy analysis is relatively new, coalescing more or less in the mid-1960s. There were, of course, scholars who studied foreign policy before this time, but their pursuit was one of many within the broader studies of international relations and diplomatic history.

The early study of foreign policy, like the study of international relations and comparative politics, reflected academic debates over the proper "ways of knowing" that dominated social science research starting in the 1950s and 1960s. Foreign policy study arose in this era as a bridge between international relations and comparative politics. To understand foreign policy scholarship, we need to consider the development of international relations and comparative politics against real-world politics.

Prior to the twentieth century, Deborah Gerner explains,

> neither foreign policy nor international relations constituted a distinct field. Diplomatic history probably came the closest to what we now label as "foreign policy," and much of what we call international relations came under the rubric of international law, institutional analysis, or history. [19]

Although the post–World War I years marked the strong emergence of the idealist (liberal) worldview and witnessed tangible efforts to incorporate some idealist notions into the newly established League of Nations, the study of international relations and foreign policy was dominated by realism. According to Gerner,

> For the study of foreign policy, this essentially meant the study of the international actions of individual state leaders—frequently monarchs—who were believed to have few constraints on their actions other than those imposed by the external situation. [20]

Real-world events, such as states' nationalistic responses to the Great Depression and the mobilization for World War II, reinforced the appropriateness of the international relations emphasis on political realism. Growing fascism on the European continent, as well as the entrenchment of Soviet-style communism, caused significant out-migration of politics and government scholars. Many of these scholars made their way to the United States, bringing with them "new and often broader perspectives about international relations and foreign policy"[21] than typically had been found in American academic departments studying government and politics.

The study of comparative politics was established in the interwar period as a result of the same exodus of European scholars.[22] "Fascist Italy, Imperialist Japan, and Nazi Germany taught [these scholars] the dangers of mobilized masses from the extreme right end of the spectrum, while the politics of the Soviet Union taught them the dangers of mobilized masses from the left."[23] The new study of comparative politics was normative in its focus, exploring the development of "good" moderate participatory politics as found in the United States and some countries of Western Europe.[24]

In the post–World War II years, this new study of comparative politics coalesced around modernization theory (also called developmental economics), with its emphasis on state and economy building along the path of the Western model. In brief, this model proposed that all countries could develop into advanced industrialized countries with participatory democratic systems if they followed in the established steps of the United States and its Western European friends. Moreover,

> as the Cold War emerged and deepened, the modernization/developmental model became the formula by which Western states, especially the United States, examined, judged, and intervened in developing states to protect them from the dangers of the mass politics of the left (communism) being exported by the Soviet Union.[25]

That is, the political cause and theoretical model that characterized the study of comparative politics was adopted with alacrity by Western policy makers as one of many tools to be used to fight the Cold War.

The politics of the day also influenced the broader study of politics, as Laura Neack, Jeanne Hey, and Patrick Haney explain:

> A principal strategy of the United States in the Cold War involved beating the Soviets through scientific advancements; academics were recruited to this cause. Federal funding for "scientific" research created a strong impetus among social scientists to become more "scientific" (and perhaps less "social" or "historical"). . . . This is also the era in which the majority of departments of politics or governments in the United States turned into departments of political science.[26]

International relations scholars joined this movement in political science, although Gerner tells us that those who focused on foreign policy were temporarily left behind:

> The fields of international relations and foreign policy, which had been intertwined, began to pull apart. International relations—or at least a significant subgroup of researchers represented after 1959 by the International Studies

Association—became more scientific, with a goal of increasing knowledge through statistical tests and rational and dynamic modeling. Foreign policy theorists, however, were slower to adopt the behavioralist approach, and instead tended to continue in the classical tradition [derived from philosophy, history, and law].[27]

As part of this positivist shift in international relations, a team of scholars produced two studies that proved critical to later foreign policy scholarship. In 1954 and 1963, Richard Snyder, H. W. Bruck, and Burton Sapin[28] presented a systematic decision-making framework in response to realism's privileging of national interest over human agency.[29] The emphasis for their framework was on decision makers:

> It is one of our basic methodological choices to define the state as its official decision makers—those whose authoritative acts are, to all intents and purposes, the acts of the state. State action is the action taken by those acting in the name of the state.[30]

Snyder, Bruck, and Sapin rejected the realist notion that national leaders, regardless of individual differences, would make the same national interest–based foreign policy choices. Instead, they suggested that foreign policy choice derives from multiple sources, including the "biographies" of the individual decision makers as well as the organizational framework in which decisions are made. Snyder, Bruck, and Sapin pointed the way to studying foreign policy using multiple levels of analysis, a key theme of this book. Their work was taken up in James Rosenau's field-establishing work that appeared in the mid-1960s.

Charles Hermann and Gregory Peacock write, "If Snyder's framework invited scientific inquiry, Rosenau insisted upon it."[31] In his famous and foundational article, "Pre-theories and Theories of Foreign Policy," James Rosenau sounded a clarion call to make the study of foreign policy into a science.[32] This is how Rosenau established the cause and scope of his call:

> To probe the "internal influences on external behavior" is to be active on one of the frontiers where the fields of international and comparative politics meet. Initial thoughts about the subject, however, are bound to be ambivalent; it would seem to have been both exhausted and neglected as a focus of inquiry. Even as it seems clear that everything worth saying about the subject has already been said, so does it also seem obvious that the heart of the matter has yet to be explored and that American political science is on the verge of major breakthroughs which will make exploration possible.[33]

Rosenau was frustrated because foreign policy study had remained behind the times and without significant recasting would fail to benefit from the "major breakthroughs" on the horizon.

The nontheoretical state of foreign policy research is all the more perplexing when it is contrasted with developments elsewhere in American political science. In recent years the discipline has been transformed from an intuitive to a scientific enterprise, and consequently the inclination to develop models and test theories has become second nature to most political scientists. [34]

Foreign policy suffered, according to Rosenau, from the lack of a central theoretical framework and the lack of a common methodology. He suggested that the common methodology be a commitment to comparative analysis, and that the central theory could be established through the efforts of scholars working within an agreed-upon framework. Rosenau offered his "pre-theory" framework—one in which he combined national attribute indicators to formulate "ideal nation-types." He hypothesized that factors at different levels of analysis might account for foreign policy differences that could be observed between these ideal nation-types. Using this "pre-theory," scholars could launch a systematic research program aimed at building a general body of theory that would, in time, define the scientific field of foreign policy. In response to Rosenau's call, a "self-conscious" field of foreign policy was begun by a more-or-less cohesive group of scholars whose collective efforts come under the heading of "comparative foreign policy,"[35] or what Neack, Hey, and Haney call the "first generation" of foreign policy study. [36]

Real-world events in the late 1960s and into the 1970s again influenced the direction of international relations, comparative politics, and foreign policy study. By the mid-1960s, most of the world's colonies had become independent states, entering the United Nations as an emblem of their sovereign statehood. The countries of the "Third World" brought different issues to the United Nations and to discussions of world politics. They shifted the debate within the United Nations to issues of economic development, and in world politics, oil exporters demonstrated a new kind of power when they withheld oil from the world market, causing the oil shocks of the 1970s. International relations scholars needed to develop frameworks for analyzing nonmilitary bases and definitions of power, as well as find a place for discussions of less than great power states. Further, the problems of Third World countries were not primarily strategic or military but involved issues of economic development and dependency, as well as issues of state and nation building. International relations scholars had to develop more diverse theoretical and conceptual tools to study this altered reality.

Western and non-Western international relations scholars began exploring alternative theoretical frameworks to realism. Some scholars in the West resuscitated the old idealist school under a newer, more interests-based rubric of "complex interdependence," or "transnationalism."[37] Today, the umbrella category of liberalism, or neoliberalism, is applied to various works in this tradition. Other scholars—in the West and especially from developing countries—proposed that the world should be understood in terms of the historical development of political and economic relations among states that has resulted in a world of "haves" and "have-nots." These scholars drew on Marxist understandings of politics. As these contending paradigms emerged in international relations to challenge the dominance of realism, so too was realism's insistence on positivist-behavioralist methodology challenged. By the end of the 1970s, more complex qualitative as well as quantitative research efforts were under way.

Similarly, the emphasis in comparative politics on modernization theory or developmental economics came under significant challenge. There were some early critics of modernization theory such as Raul Prebisch, head of the UN Economic Commission on Latin America (ECLA). Prebisch and ECLA proposed in the 1950s that economic development in the developing world—or the periphery of the world economic system—would always be impeded by ever-declining terms of trade. That is, non-oil primary product exporters would keep falling behind because what they sold on the world market (coffee, peanuts, cotton, and so on) would remain the same in price while what they bought on the world market (manufactured goods, petroleum products) would increase in price each year. Prebisch's view represented a Marxist variation called dependency theory, a theory with strong foundations in Latin America particularly and the broader developing world more generally. Although the dependency challenge to modernization theory was sounded in the 1950s, modernization theory remained dominant in comparative politics until the late 1960s and early 1970s. By this time, mainstream comparative politics had to make room for new voices and issues such as dependency theory.

Neack, Hey, and Haney describe the change in comparative politics at this time:

> Scholars from developing countries and Western "area specialists" who had rejected modernization theory were able to exploit the cracks in the crumbling modernization theory paradigm and assert the importance of studying complex domestic processes in comparative politics. . . . The study of domestic processes took a variety of forms in the 1970s, including the study of domestic class-based divisions caused by colonialism and perpetuated in post-independence dependent relations, political economy, state corporatism, and state-society relations. . . . The unifying feature of comparative politics from the 1970s onward was not a central theoretical core, but a central methodological agreement on the comparative method. [38]

Just as before, real-world political changes affecting international relations and comparative politics also affected the new field of comparative foreign policy. One result of the disequilibrium being felt in the fields of international relations and comparative politics was that divisions between the two were becoming less and less distinct. This was especially true in the case of political economy approaches to international and comparative politics. This blurring of divisions occurred precisely at the junction of these fields that foreign policy was supposed to bridge.

By the start of the 1980s, a variety of theoretical and methodological accountings from both international and comparative politics were adopted by foreign policy scholars. The impact of these accountings was evident in the growing number of contextualized, multilevel foreign policy analyses undertaken in the 1980s and into the early 1990s. This wave of scholarship has been called the "second generation" of foreign policy analysis by Neack, Hey, and Haney. A critical aspect of this second generation was the conscious choice by scholars to link their work to the major substantive concerns in foreign policy.

Second-generation foreign policy study reflected the complex issues of the times—the impact of the latest wave of **democratization**, the importance of the relative decline in US economic power in the early to mid-1980s, the collapse of the Soviet empire and Soviet-style communism, the unprecedented international collaboration in the Persian Gulf War of 1991, and the December 1991 dissolution of the Soviet Union.

## A NEW MILLENNIUM

The new millennium ushered in a period that some have called the age of intervention, while others call this a time of unprecedented peace between countries.[39] Two major, protracted wars in Iraq and Afghanistan fought by the United States in this period, the wider global war on terror, the ongoing carnage of the interstate and intrastate wars in the Great Lakes region of Africa, ongoing violence between Israel and other actors (Palestinian Hamas particularly), US and European intervention in support of rebels in Libya, French intervention in Côte d'Ivoire and Mali, Ethiopian and African Union interventions in Somalia, AU actions in Sudan, and a nuclear-armed belligerent North Korea make the new millennium appear more bellicose than pacific. Popular revolutions in the Arab world brought in heightened expectations about democracy and sometimes violent retaliation by old guard regimes. The new millennium seems fraught with tensions and possibilities, some of which will be discussed in these pages.

The two metalevel features of the new millennium—globalization and unipolarity—carried over from the last period but consolidated in this new period. These are forces that bring good and bad, and we will consider the implications of globalization and unipolarity for foreign policy making and behavior throughout this book. Chapters 8, 9, and 10 particularly put into consideration the cumulative effects of these forces on the international system.

Has foreign policy analysis moved into its third generation? The study, like so much else in the world today, seems to be hard to categorize. This could be a transition period for foreign policy analysis, much as it is a time of transition for foreign policy actors.

## BACK TO THE TANGLED TALE OF TIBET

Before this chapter closes, we should go back to the Tangled Tale of Tibet. In 2010, China's Panchen Lama, Gyaltsen Norbu, was the youngest person ever appointed to the Chinese People's Political Consultative Conference at the age of nineteen. The Chinese government paraded him throughout the country as the proper Panchen Lama and the person who would—in consultation with a divining committee—designate the next Dalai Lama when the fourteenth Dalai Lama died. The boy picked by the fourteenth Dalai Lama as the eleventh Panchen Lama was still in protective custody with his family as of 2013. Many Tibetans living in Tibet refused to acknowledge that Gyaltsen Norbu was the Panchen Lama and continued to protest Chinese rule. Some Tibetans used the strongest and most dramatic form of protest—self-immolations. In 2010, 2011, and 2012, nearly one hundred Tibetans set themselves on fire. Anti-Chinese protests and unrest in Tibet reached such high levels in the summer of 2012 that the Chinese government closed Tibet to foreign tourists and scrutiny.

Meanwhile, the Dalai Lama continued his mission to help his people. The Chinese government would correct this statement and say that the Dalai Lama continued his dangerous efforts to split the country. The Dalai Lama's long-standing view, however, was that Tibet should have autonomy in China much like that exercised by Hong Kong in China. He called his policy for Tibet a "middle way." Representatives of the Dalai Lama and the Chinese government met off and on for decades to find a resolution, even as the Chinese government pushed its claim that the Dalai Lama's goal was to seek an independent Tibet.

The Dalai Lama was not leaving the fate of Tibetan Buddhism in the hands of the Chinese government, however. Recall that the Dalai Lama was both the spiritual and the political leader of Tibet, or the government of Tibet in exile in India. In a move designed to bring the Tibetan political structure into the twenty-first century and democratize it, the Dalai Lama and his government advisors created a system that would make the prime minister, or Kalon Tripa, the head of government. In early 2011, an election was held in which Tibetans from around the world cast votes. In August 2011, Lobsang Sangay, a Tibetan born in India and a former researcher at Harvard, was installed as the elected head of the government in exile. Sangay's father was a former Buddhist monk and resistance fighter before he fled Tibet in 1959. Uncertain of his exact birthday, Sangay's parents listed his birthday as March 10, the Tibetan National Uprising Day marking the 1959 armed rebellion against the Chinese.

The Dalai Lama thus took care of one of his roles, and so he turned to the other. Rather than allow the Chinese to have their Panchen Lama pick his spiritual successor, the Dalai Lama suggested that when he was older he would consult the high lamas and "re-evaluate whether the institution of the Dalai Lama should continue or not."[40] Reincarnation was something that lamas do by choice to assist others seeking to live an ethical life. The Dalai Lama could choose not to be reincarnated. Alternatively, he suggested that he could name a successor who was already living, another option not without its controversy but within Buddhist teachings. In other words, the Dalai Lama made it clear that the matter of his spiritual successor would not be in the hands of the Chinese State Administration for Religious Affairs, which claimed the right to manage reincarnations.

Our venture into the Tangled Tale of Tibet discussed the position of candidate and then President Bill Clinton. The official American policy is that Tibet is part of China, but American presidents continue to meet with the Dalai Lama—and always with official Chinese outrage. President Barack Obama met several times with the Dalai Lama, in closed sessions, perhaps sharing their views on both being Nobel Peace Prize laureates.

But the matter of Tibet still entangles the foreign policies of states. India and China have argued over the borders of India and Tibet (therefore, the borders of India and China) since the time when India was still a British colony. India welcomed the Dalai Lama when he was a refugee, allowed him to begin his government in exile, and spent government funds to help Tibetan refugees get settled in exile. China was never happy with India's sheltering of the Dalai Lama and his followers, but the two countries maintained continuous diplomatic ties regardless. The two countries also fought a war in 1962 related to their border dispute (more on this in chapter 9). What angered the Chinese government more recently was that in 2011 India became the headquarters of a new international Buddhist organization, the Global Buddhist Congregation. The Chinese demanded that the Indian government prevent the Dalai Lama from speaking to the group, but the Indian government did not comply. India, it seems, sought a central role in the continuing Tangled Tale of Tibet.

## CHAPTER REVIEW

- The Tangled Tale of Tibet demonstrates how no policy issue is exclusively foreign or exclusively domestic in nature.
- The Tangled Tale of Tibet demonstrates, too, how state and nonstate actors try to build coalitions in support of their policy preferences, linking their issues with those of others.
- National leaders are said to play a two-level, dual, or nested game between the demands of the international system and those of domestic politics.
- The study of foreign policy is the study of both the statements or policies of decision makers as well as the behaviors or actions of states *and* the study of the processes that result in statements and behaviors.
- The levels of analysis used in the study of foreign policy are the individual, state, and system levels. These are heuristic devices or tools that help us manage our subject matter. The levels of analysis also ask different questions of and provide different answers to foreign policy puzzles.
- The study of foreign policy is primarily situated in the field of international relations. International relations is dominated by three worldviews: realism, liberalism, and Marxism.
- Foreign policy is also a bridging discipline, taking lessons from both the study of international relations and the study of comparative politics.

*Chapter Two*

# Rational Actors and National Interests

## IN THIS CHAPTER

- The Definition of "Leaders," Part 1
- The Rational Decision-Making Model
- Variations within Realism
- Rationality, Deterrence, and "Irrationality"
- Poliheuristic Theory: A Bridge to the Next Chapter?
- Chapter Review

## CASES FEATURED IN THIS CHAPTER

- Egyptian president Gamal Abdel Nasser's strategic calculations that led to the epoch-making 1967 Arab-Israeli Six Days' War.
- The rational calculations of Yasir Arafat and Saddam Hussein that short-term conflict would lead to long-term gains.
- The rational calculations by Israel that war with Hamas in 2012 would serve Israeli national interests by sending a message to Iran.
- The importance to neoclassical realists of considering domestic political limitations and capabilities when calculating the strategic choices made by Neville Chamberlain.
- The prisoners' dilemma and nuclear decision making by the United States and the Soviet Union during the Cold War.

## THE DEFINITION OF "LEADERS," PART 1

Consider this headline from the BBC Worldwide Monitoring service from mid-January 2013: "Japan PM Dismisses Beijing's Claim to Islands in South China Sea."[1] This kind of headline is fairly typical, although a literal reading of it would make a person wonder whether the city of Beijing had annexed islands in the South China Sea. Beijing is a city, and cities and municipalities in some countries do annex territory to increase their size and tax base. But Beijing the city did not lay claim to—annex—the islands in the headline. The confusion over a literal reading of the headline might get compounded by a literal reading of a sentence in the article that says, "Abe said ties with China are very important for Japan and vowed to improve communications between Tokyo and Beijing."[2] Shinzo Abe was the Japanese prime minister referenced in the headline, so no confusion there. But does the statement suggest that Tokyo and Beijing—the cities—were having communication issues that could complicate relations between Japan and China? Fortunately, most readers of the news story know that "Beijing" is a stand-in for "China" as "Tokyo" stands in for "Japan." And Abe making pronouncements in the role of prime minister is understood to be the same as if Japan were speaking for itself.

It is common in popular media, in academic writings, and in the announcements of governments to use the names of countries for the names of capitals and even for the names of current leaders or officeholders. Thus, what Abe had to say would be taken to be the same as what "Tokyo" or "Japan" would say, if the capital city or the country could speak. This common usage implies that states speak with one voice in international affairs and depicts states—or the capital cities of states—as individuals making decisions to which other states-as-individuals will respond. By the model we'll explore in this chapter, it does not matter that Shinzo Abe was the eighth Japanese prime minister since 2000, since all Japanese prime ministers should pursue the same long-term Japanese national interests.

## THE RATIONAL DECISION-MAKING MODEL

Our model in this chapter is the **rational decision-making** model. This model derives directly from the realist worldview that conceptualizes a state as a unitary actor pursuing long-term national interests. In international politics, by this view, states are only distinguishable by the relative power they hold, not by their internal characteristics. Government type, history, economics, and the qualities of the individuals holding political **leadership** positions hold no importance in and of themselves to the analyst. The decisions taken by the leaders of the state are seen as the decisions of the state. This conflating of leader and state is possible because of a key assumption that realists make about leaders: any and all leaders act in ways consistent with the long-term and persistent national interests of the country. Since the national interests do not change, changes in leadership have little consequence.

The clearest statement regarding leaders and national interest in the study of foreign policy comes from Hans Morgenthau, one of the most significant post–World War II international scholars in the realist tradition. In the statement below, note how the assumption binding leaders and national interests creates a simple model for the analyst to employ:

> We assume that statesmen think and act in terms of interest defined as power, and the evidence of history bears that assumption out. That assumption allows us to retrace and anticipate, as it were, the steps a statesman—past, present or future—has taken or will take on the political scene. We look over his shoulder when he writes his dispatches; we listen in on his conversation with other statesmen; we read and anticipate his very thoughts. Thinking in terms of interest defined as power, we think as he does, and as disinterested observers, we understand his thoughts and actions perhaps better than he, the actor on the political scene, does himself.
>
> The concept of national interest defined as power imposes intellectual discipline upon the observer, infuses rational order into the subject matter of politics, and thus makes the theoretical understanding of politics possible. On the side of the actor, it provides for rational discipline in action and creates that astounding continuity in foreign policy which makes American, British, or Russian foreign policy appear as an intelligible, rational continuum, by and large consistent with itself, regardless of the different motives, preferences, and intellectual and moral qualities of successive statesmen. A realist theory of international politics, then, will guard against two popular fallacies: the concern with motives and the concern with ideological preferences. [3]

The "concern with motives" or "ideological preferences" entails examining the characteristics of individuals or groups of individuals, or even examining the political dynamics within a country, pursuits that have no merit in the realist, rational choice view. Morgenthau does allow that, in rare cases, psychological disorders in an individual leader or the emotions of mass democratic politics may cause national decisions that are out of line with national interests. Morgenthau might tell us that when we study most foreign policy decisions we should follow the old advice given to fledgling doctors in medical school: when you hear hoof beats, think horses, not zebras. When you see a foreign policy decision, think rational decision making and national interests, not idiosyncrasy, not individual leadership differences, not domestic political calculations. The standard expectation is the one upon which to base your diagnosis or explanation.

How can rational choice theorists make the assumption that individual differences are insignificant when studying foreign policy decision making?

Michael McGinnis is a rational choice adherent who eschews the use of the word "individual" in favor of "regime" precisely because "regime" takes our focus away from personalities. McGinnis explains,

> Any individual who attains a position of major foreign policy responsibility will have been socialized through education and processes of political selection to pursue some set of common goals. Individuals differ in their perception of the national interest but role expectations reinforce a sense of common interests.[4]

For McGinnis, political culture and socialization matter, but not in a way that requires the study of such. Instead, culture and socialization produce regularities among the individuals who rise to national office, eliminating individual differences and any need to study those differences. Further, McGinnis's working assumption is that

> changes in foreign policy goals attributed to changes in individual leaders or ruling coalitions can be interpreted as random (but not necessarily insignificant) fluctuations around a common "regime interest," which is based on domestic support structures and geopolitical concerns which act as the primary sources of continuity in foreign policy interests.[5]

"Regime interest" can be read here as "national interests" (although at the end of this chapter, this claim will be revisited). The term "national interests" can be and has been used expansively by leaders seeking to justify various policies, but in the realist framework national interests refer to persistent, long-term values associated with the entire country and identifiable over the course of the country's history. These interests do not change, although the means for pursuing them may. George Kennan, the former US diplomat who famously warned about Soviet expansionism, explains that long-term national interests include ensuring the "military security" of the country, the "integrity of its political life, and the well-being of its people."[6]

In promoting and protecting the national interests, the regime or leadership operates as a rational actor. The rational actor model has its roots in basic decision-making theory. Decision making is defined as the "act of choosing among available alternatives about which uncertainty exists."[7] One of the first systematic discussions of the decision-making model was offered by Richard Snyder, H. W. Bruck, and Burton Sapin in 1954.[8] In their "general decision-making model," they set out the following details: Since states are unitary actors, the decisions and actions of the ultimate decision makers can be considered the same as the decisions and actions of the state. Since all states are said to pursue national interests, all states make decisions in the same way. State decision making can be portrayed as a process in which the ultimate decision makers examine the internal and external environments, define the situation at hand, consider alternate courses of action, and then select the course of action that is best suited to the pursuit of national interests. The actions are considered "planful"—that is, the result of strategic problem solving—and are embedded in an action-reaction interaction.

This decision-making model has often been imagined as a "black box." We cannot see inside the box and have no need to, since all black boxes (countries/regimes/leaders) work the same way. "In modern decision theory, the rational decision problem is reduced to a simple matter of selecting among a set of given alternatives, each of which has a given set of consequences: the agent selects the alternative whose consequences are preferred in terms of the agent's utility function which ranks each set of consequences in order of preference."[9] In other words, information about the problem at hand, possible courses of action, possible reactions, and estimates of success for the different courses of action are fed into the box. Inside the box, a basic economic utility calculation is made: which choice of action best maximizes national goals and minimizes costs? A decision then results or comes out of the box. The environment reacts to the decision/action, and the reaction becomes part of a new set of factors that are fed into the box again.

Of course, decision makers do not live in a perfect world and so do not have before them all the relevant information upon which to make the best decision. Given the imperfect nature of the available information, leaders make the best possible choice or even select the first option that satisfies the minimal requirements of a good choice. The rational actor model does not require perfect information, but recognizes instead that "rationality refers to consistent, value-maximizing choice within specific constraints."[10] Herbert Simon called this "bounded rationality," or rational decision making within limits.[11]

In terms of the daily affairs of state, "bounded rationality" may not be a major detriment to solid decision making since leaders have a chance to reconsider their choices in light of the steady flow of feedback. This feedback qualifies the next choices to be made, and the reaction of other actors can be anticipated and possible counterreactions planned in advance of actual feedback. The interactive nature of decision making (where country A's choices are dependent on country B's choices and vice versa) is explored in **game theory**, a topic we'll take up shortly.

Rationality is not just bounded by the limitations of humans as decision makers but by the environment in which multiple other actors are present and acting. How does the decision maker anticipate what other actors might do? This realist foundation of the rational actor model contains assumptions about the environment and other actors that help decision makers keep their focus. As already noted, realists assume that all states are unitary actors who make cost-benefit calculations about alternative courses of action. *All* states make such calculations and *all* states are motivated to promote and secure their interests through the acquisition and use of power. Furthermore, states act in an international environment characterized by anarchy, or the lack of an overarching legal authority. Although some realists conceptualize states as power driven and aggressive, others explain that it is the anarchic nature of international politics that requires states to make choices that are power driven. Graham Allison and Philip Zelikow say that this is the basic difference between classical realists (states are naturally aggressive) and neorealists (states are aggressive because of the dictates of anarchy).[12]

Whether one starts with the view that all states are motivated to arm themselves and acquire more power (classical realism) or that states must arm themselves because the international environment requires it (neorealism), all realists see states locked in an unavoidable situation called a security dilemma. Glenn Snyder explains the **security dilemma** in this way:

> The term is generally used to denote the self-defeating aspect of the quest for security in an anarchic system. The theory says that even when no state has any desire to attack others, none can be sure that others' intentions are peaceful, or will remain so; hence each must accumulate power for defense. Since no state can know that the power accumulation of others is defensively motivated only, each must assume that it might be intended for attack. Consequently, each party's power increments are matched by the others, and all wind up with no more security than when the vicious cycle began, along with the costs incurred in having acquired and having to maintain their power.[13]

Because of anarchy, states are motivated to amass power and rely upon only themselves for protection. Because all states are so motivated and thus are locked into action-reaction cycles, conflict is the distinguishing characteristic of international politics. The rational actor constantly seeks to increase its power in reaction to these "realities." Because the rational actor is engaged in a game of many iterations (or steps), the rational actor may seek short-term gains through risky foreign policy behavior in order to secure long-term goals and power. For many realists, no state should be content with the status quo given the dynamics of international politics. But discontent with the status quo drives states into unending security dilemmas that can only be "won" through short-term gains. Decision making in such circumstances can be understood as choosing between less-than-optimal alternatives and settling for the best of the worst, rather than the best of the best as envisioned by the rational actor model. This will be taken up again when we discuss **nuclear deterrence** and the prisoners' dilemma.

An example is in order here to demonstrate the kind of analysis conducted using the rational actor model. Ben Mor set out to understand the strategic calculations made by Egyptian president Gamal Abdel Nasser that resulted in the critical 1967 war with Israel—a war that Nasser had wanted to avoid.[14]

To establish Nasser's strategic rationality, Mor needs to connect Nasser's actions with long-term Egyptian national interests. According to Mor, Nasser had two primary goals: establish Egypt as the clear leader of the Arab states, and restore the displaced Palestinians to lands taken over by Israel. Earlier, in 1956, the Egyptian leader sought to nationalize the Suez Canal. The canal, opened in 1865, had been built by the British and operated by the British and French. It became the principal maritime route between the Mediterranean Sea and Indian Ocean, via the Red Sea. Nasser did succeed in nationalizing the Suez Canal, but only after a war with Israel in which Israel—with the collusion of the British and French—managed to quickly capture the Sinai Peninsula. The end of the 1956 war saw the placement of the first official United Nations **peacekeeping** operation, the United Nations Emergency Force (UNEF). The purpose of UNEF was to keep peace in the Sinai by maintaining a cease-fire between Egypt and Israel while maintaining the prewar borders of each state. Despite the recovery of the Suez Canal, the quick Egyptian losses and the agreement to allow foreign (UN) troops to be stationed on Egyptian soil were great humiliations to Nasser/Egypt.

According to Mor, Nasser wanted to undo the humiliations of 1956 and regain Egyptian leadership in the Arab world especially vis-à-vis the Israeli problem without having to engage Israel in a war. Toward these goals, Nasser undertook a series of steps in May 1967—steps that could be interpreted as provocative. First, Nasser ordered the Egyptian army into the Sinai Peninsula. Second, he ordered UNEF to withdraw from the Sinai.[15] Third, he ordered the blockading of the Straits of Tiran. The Straits of Tiran sit at the end of the Sinai Peninsula where the Gulf of Aqaba meets the Red Sea, roughly parallel to the Gulf of Suez. Blocking the Straits of Tiran effectively cut Israel off from direct access to the Red Sea via the Gulf of Aqaba. Israeli leaders—famous for their use of "red lines" establishing permissible ranges of action by their enemies—already had stated that any closing or attempted closing of the straits would be considered an act of war. When Nasser ordered the blockade, Israel did nothing in immediate response. Nasser then signed a defense pact with Jordan on May 30. Having seen enough and with its own security and power on the line, Israel launched a preemptive attack on Egypt on June 6, beginning the Six Days' War.

Mor's interest, as stated above, is to establish Nasser's strategic rationality even though Nasser appeared to take steps that led to the one thing that he wanted to avoid the most—war with Israel. According to Mor, Nasser assumed that Israel was content with the status quo and would not initiate war with Egypt. He then calculated that he had considerable room for movement vis-à-vis Israel. Nasser employed an escalation–de-escalation strategy involving a series of moves; Nasser would make a move and then await the Israelis' reaction. As long as the Israelis made no negative countermove such as issuing a warning, initiating diplomatic discussions, or mobilizing troops,

Nasser was free to continue with the next step. As soon as the Israelis signaled that Egypt had approached a "red line," Nasser would order a deescalation. This escalation–de-escalation strategy was supremely rational: Egypt could make relative improvements in its status while avoiding war.

Mor concludes that Nasser's decision making was rational given the limits of information available to him. This follows Simon's idea of bounded rationality. Nasser did not avoid war with Israel, but this was because Israel failed to provide Nasser with the feedback necessary for rational recalculation. Nasser approached and crossed a "red line" when Egypt blocked the Straits of Tiran but did not know this until Egypt was under military attack a step later.[16]

Of course, one could argue that Nasser failed as a rational actor to account for the possibility that it was not in Israel's interests to provide feedback in the expected form. More, the rational actor analysis employed in this study takes into account a two-player game, but other players were in this game. When Egypt blocked the Straits of Tiran, the Israeli policy makers wanted to give an immediate response, but US president Lyndon Johnson asked them to wait forty-eight hours while Johnson explored an international response to Nasser's activities.

Although Mor tells us that Nasser's provocations were calculated moves that were not intended to lead Egypt to war with Israel, war is not necessarily seen as a negative point along the calculated path of the rational actor. Remember that this model is based on realism, and war is an acceptable tool of foreign policy for realists. Media analyses of international events tend to privilege accounts in which conflict is seen as an acceptable short-term position on the road to larger relative gains. For example, in a *New York Times* report over failing peace talks between the Israelis and Palestinians in September 2000, Deborah Sontag asks why Palestinian leader Yasir Arafat would take an unyielding negotiating stance on the disposition of Haram al-Sharif (the Temple Mount to Israelis). Such an unrelenting stance gave Israeli prime minister Ehud Barak little room to maneuver, virtually guaranteeing continued conflict between the two sides. Arafat was willing to take this risk, suggests Sontag, because it served longer-term Palestinian interests. "Some Palestinian experts say Mr. Arafat thinks it less risky to protract the conflict than to seal a deal that would be perceived as selling out not just Palestinian, but also Arab and Muslim rights."[17] By this account, protracted conflict between Israelis and Palestinians was an acceptable cost on the way to obtaining a goal more important to Arafat than peace with Israel. This foreign policy case will be explored in more detail in chapter 6.

Similarly, in a news report with the curious title, "Attack on Iraq May Be Outcome Hussein Wants," Robin Wright considers the calculations of Iraqi leader Saddam Hussein in January 1998. According to Wright,

After seven years of diplomatic battles with the United States, Iraqi President Saddam Hussein may actually welcome a major military assault, say analysts in the US and diplomats from allied countries.

The Iraqi leader, they say, apparently sees a military showdown as a catalyst for settling a critical question: whether international sanctions, which have cost Baghdad $100 billion in lost oil revenues since 1990, will be lifted as long as he remains in power. [18]

Wright reports that the Iraqi leader might have been willing to incur military strikes in the short term on the assumption that such strikes by the United States would lead to international condemnation of America and international sympathy for Iraq. Ultimately, the United States would look like a bully and the sanctions on Iraq would be lifted, while Hussein stayed in power. Although the wisdom of such a calculation can be (and has been) debated, what is important for us is the clear presence of the rational choice model in these reports. Conflict and deaths and property damage are costs worth tolerating in pursuit of a longer-term national goal. Whenever you read that conflict "serves" a purpose, try to discern the calculations that surround the steps in pursuit of national interest. Also, pay attention to the costs that rational leaders seem willing to pay when pursuing national interests.

Strategic calculations about the long-term national interest usually involve more than the immediate events at play, and the immediate targets may not be the longer-term targets. In November 2012, Israel launched an airstrike that killed a Hamas leader inside of Gaza. This resulted in Hamas launching rockets at Israel in retaliation, which then resulted in a massive air campaign by Israel against Gaza. Israelis suffered very little from Hamas's retaliatory strikes because of a new Israeli missile defense system. After the missile defense proved effective, Israeli citizens would bring picnic lunches to missile defense sites to watch the system in action. While some Israeli spokespersons claimed that the Israeli military actions against the Hamas leader and Gaza were in self-defense after months of rocket attacks by Hamas, other commentators suggested that the whole episode had little to do with Hamas and Gaza. Instead, Israel had provoked Hamas into launching rockets in order to test the new missile defense system in anticipation of a not-too-distant war with Iran. That is, strategic thinking about a future war led Israeli decision makers to provoke a small war with Hamas in order to test Israel military capabilities. Further, the demonstration of the new missile shield should cause a rational Iran to think twice about provoking Israel or continuing with nuclear weapons activities. [19] The November 2012 war caused massive damage in Gaza, but by this calculation it had little to do with Gaza or the people living there.

Returning briefly to the Tangled Tale of Tibet discussed in chapter 1, note that both the Bush 1 and Clinton administrations drew criticism for not linking issues of human rights to issues of trade in their China policies.

Ultimately, the defense each administration gave for its China policy was one that suggested many calculated moves on the way to a long-term goal. Engagement with China would not only promote the short-term interests of American business and farm groups but would also integrate China into the world community. As this integration occurred, and as American business interests penetrated China, China would move toward greater opening, both in terms of its relations with foreign partners and at home. Ultimately, down the road several years, the human rights situation in China would improve as China started to conform to the behavioral expectations of the United States and the international community.

Ultimately, the United States could gain power over China in the long run as American products penetrated the Chinese market and American political ideas penetrated the Chinese polity. China would be bound by its economic interdependence with the world economy, and it would have to curb its internal and external negative behaviors or risk considerable economic loss. These calculations by two American presidents of different political parties demonstrate the realist proposition that particular leadership does not matter; what matters is the long-term, persistent, rational pursuit of national interests.

## VARIATIONS WITHIN REALISM

All international relations theories have within them variants. Variants within theoretical traditions emerge when scholars agree with the starting assumptions but disagree about critical details. Classical realists believe that states are self-interested, power seeking, and predatory *by nature*, but neorealists believe that the anarchic structure of the international system requires states to act in self-interested, sometimes predatory ways. Offensive neorealists believe that states are always inclined to be looking for advantage over other states and that major states are always driven to become the **hegemon** even in times of relative safety and security. Defensive neorealists believe that states may sometimes be satisfied with the status quo and are inclined to act only when a threat begins to materialize. Classical realists and neorealists of various sorts all agree on how unimportant it is to look within states to understand what motivates them.

Neoclassical realism is another variant on realism. Like realists of any sort, neoclassical realists are mostly concerned with major powers. We'll discuss this in more detail when we discuss major powers and analysis at the system level in chapter 8. Neoclassical realism departs from other variants of realism when the analyst turns inward to the dynamics within a state to explain major power behavior. Christopher Layne explains that,

> like neorealists, neoclassical realists believe that great powers' grand strategies
> are shaped fundamentally by the distribution of power in the international

system and by each great power's capabilities relative to those of its (actual or potential) rivals. There are questions neorealism cannot explain, however. Why do specific great powers choose one grand strategic alternative over another? What motives underlie the grand strategic behavior of a specific great power?[20]

Despite the use of the word "motives," Layne isn't rejecting Morgenthau and the realist tradition of eschewing the search for "motives, preferences, and intellectual and moral qualities of successive statesmen."[21] What Layne does is "open the black box"[22] —look into the state—and look at the internal factors that influence choices. That is, if rational decision making involves a study of all possible factors associated with a decision, Layne proposes that internal factors are nearly as important as external factors in shaping the decisions made. Layne isn't opening the black box to understand the motives and beliefs of individual leaders, but to understand material factors—like budget constraints set by a legislature—that would limit a great power's response to other great powers.

Layne uses British **grand strategy** during the 1930s to demonstrate how neoclassical realists examine domestic and external factors. Rejecting standard realists' views that Chamberlain failed to make the appropriate adjustment to the changing strategic environment, Layne says that Chamberlain (he uses Chamberlain interchangeably with senior British decision makers) "was playing a weak hand and did the best he could with the cards he was dealt."[23] Specifically, "Britain's strategic predicament in the 1930s was simple. It had too many enemies, too few allies, and insufficient resources to cope with the myriad of strategic threats it faced."[24]

With limited resources due to budget constraints, Britain had to prioritize the threats it faced. Chamberlain decided that Germany was the primary threat and that the Royal Air Force (RAF) was the primary way to meet that threat and that Germany could be deterred through a significant buildup of the RAF.

Unfortunately for the strategic-thinking British decision makers, Hitler was the one person in Europe who did not understand the message of deterrence.[25] In other words, Chamberlain did not avoid war—much the same as Nasser did not avoid war—not because of miscalculations or the failure to think rationally but because the target failed to understand and do the appropriate, rational thing. Layne, like Mor, returns to Morgenthau's exception to explain what appears to be a failure in rational thinking: the decision maker was rational, the opponent was not.

# RATIONALITY, DETERRENCE, AND "IRRATIONALITY"

Realism, with its emphasis on rational choice, was the dominant grand theory of international relations throughout much of the twentieth century. Its dominance was at its peak at the close of World War II and the start of the Cold War. Realism dictated that the United States needed to pursue greater military might than the Soviet Union—indeed, the United States needed to pursue global domination—lest the world be dominated by the Soviet Union.

As the Cold War deepened and both the Americans and Soviets developed massive nuclear weapons capabilities, the Americans and Soviets achieved a balance of nuclear power that former British prime minister Winston Churchill called a "balance of terror." This particular balance was struck on the assumption that the nuclear arsenals of both sides were sufficient to ensure that an attack by either would be met with an unacceptable nuclear response. Thus, policy makers and some realist scholars began to reassess the role nuclear weapons played in the pursuit of power and security in international anarchy. The rational choice of any leader confronting a nuclear foe of similar strength was to avoid any action that might be punishable with a nuclear reaction/retaliation.

In situations where both parties to a conflict possess nuclear arsenals of more or less similar size and destructive power, both are said to understand that aggression by either would likely result in unacceptable costs for both. Each side, then, is deterred and the situation is one of mutual, "mature," or stable nuclear deterrence. Taken further, when both sides hold sufficient nuclear weapons that a nuclear attack initiated by either side could be absorbed by the target and then matched with an equally punishing counterattack (that is, both sides possess what is called second-strike capability), the awareness of the likelihood of **mutual assured destruction (MAD)** should deter both from provocative, directly confrontational acts toward the other.

Given the understood costs of a nuclear war (in terms of immediate destruction and the long-term aftermath), *rational* leaders would not entertain the idea of using nuclear weapons in a conflict. Realists proposed that nuclear weapons were not for fighting a war but for deterring a war. Indeed, Kenneth Waltz declares that a world of nuclear-armed states would be a more stable and peaceful one because of mutual nuclear deterrence.[26] However, recent history provides us with at least one example of a leader who was willing to think the unthinkable—think about using nuclear weapons—in the name of protecting national interests (a realist pursuit). Former US president Ronald Reagan was a committed realist in his approach to foreign affairs, yet Reagan was also committed to the development of a strategy and capability for fighting and winning a nuclear war. He was not convinced that a nuclear "holocaust" was inevitable if either side in the Cold War initiated war with the other. Instead, Reagan urged his military strategists to think about what the United States needed in order to engage the Soviet Union in nuclear war and win. The Strategic Defense Initiative was seen as one tool to use for potentially winning a nuclear war. There is no way to understand the Reagan desire for a winnable nuclear war fighting strategy outside a realist framework.

For Reagan, "winning" the ultimate game between the United States and the Soviet Union meant considering how to use nuclear weapons not as threats but as weapons. This is but one contradiction in the realist/rational choice framework. There are other paths by which we can encounter problems inherent to the rational actor model and nuclear deterrence, paths that also derive from realism. We will examine two of these. The first involves the use of game theory to demonstrate that "rational decisions" are made by humans who may choose very destructive courses of action. The second takes us back to an old realist assumption: states will seek to dominate if at all possible.

The assumption that actors are rational decision makers is critical to a line of realist-based research called game theory. Game theory borrows from mathematical reasoning and the formal study of logic in order to develop mathematical models of the strategies adopted in the "games" of foreign policy, such as **crisis** and noncrisis **negotiations**, alliance formation, and arms racing. In the following explanation of game theory from James Dougherty and Robert Pfaltzgraff, we can see the rational actor model inserted into an interactive relationship:

> Game theorists say . . . : If people in a certain situation wish to win—that is, to accomplish an objective that the other party seeks to deny them—we can sort out the intellectual processes by which they calculate or reach decisions concerning what kind of action is most likely to be advantageous to them, assuming they believe their opponents also to be rational calculators like themselves, equally interested in second-guessing and trying to outwit the opponent.[27]

All games contain common features: every player seeks to "win," certain rules govern the behavior of players in the game (with the primary rules privileging cost-benefit analyses and self-interest), players perceive that different moves are associated with different rewards or payoffs, and all the choices made in the game are interactive. Some games are said to be zero-sum in that when one player wins, the other loses. Zero-sum games reflect the most distilled version of realism: when your country increases its power, it is only because my country has lost power. In other games, the results are non-zero-sum, or mixed, in that players can register relative wins or gains over other players, reflecting the more sophisticated recent discussions of realism.

One of the most frequently discussed mixed-motive games is that of the prisoners' dilemma. In this game, players attempt to "win," but the interactive choices they make leave each in a position of achieving only the best of the worst situation, rather than the best possible situation. It is important to note here that all the basic realist assumptions are in place: actors are self-interested or selfish, actors have no reason to trust other actors because there is no ultimate authority to enforce justice, and actors are presented choices that involve limited information on different alternatives and their conse-quences. Karen Mingst describes the standard setup of this game:

> The prisoners' dilemma is the story of two prisoners, each being interrogated separately for an alleged crime. The interrogator tells each prisoner that if one of them confesses and the other does not, the one who confessed will go free and the one who kept silent will get a long prison term. If both confess, both will get somewhat reduced prison terms. If neither confesses, both will receive short prison terms based on lack of evidence. [28]

Faced with this dilemma, and working on realist assumptions, both pris-oners confess. Or, to put it another way, both confess because each assumes that the other—acting in self-interest only—will confess. Although neither "wins" by being set completely free, neither "loses" to the other by drawing the harsher penalty. The prisoners don't achieve the best solution—no jail time—but they achieve the best of the worst—a shorter sentence and parity. Parity—ending up in the same bad situation with one's opponent, even in terms of mutual punishment—is preferred over sacrifice in a realist, self-help system.

The prisoners' dilemma illustrates the most fundamental realist problem: because no action is made in a vacuum but instead is part of a series of interactions with other actors, actors rarely can obtain ultimate security or freedom or superiority or whatever they seek to achieve over other actors. Instead, actors can only hope to obtain relative security or relative freedom or relative superiority, and so forth. In the realist model, actors acknowledge this reality but still make choices that would, only under ideal circumstances, earn them the best possible result.

This dilemma can be taken further with far worse results. Akin to the prisoners' dilemma is the realist security dilemma. As we've seen, the secur-ity dilemma is the result of choices a state makes to secure itself against sometimes unspecified but predictable outside threats. Although the initial step is only taken in self-defense, other states perceive it with suspicion and fear, and due to the logic of anarchy where no one will come to their assis-tance, they must react to it. Ultimately, the states caught in this cycle find their environment to be more dangerous and more threatening than ever. To return to the first actor, the initial moves it made to increase its security have served only to lessen its overall security—and the security of others as well—and thus the state is trapped in a dilemma. Realists acknowledge that this dilemma is real and unfortunate but also as inevitable as conflict in the international system.

We can use the prisoners' dilemma framework to consider the use of nuclear weapons. Nuclear deterrence tells us that each side recognizes that it is more rational not to initiate an attack with nuclear weapons because of the expected result—a counter nuclear attack. But in competitive relationships (as always exist in the realist world), "winning" (dominating the opponent) is the best possible result and "losing" is the worst. In between is "breaking even" with one's competitor. Using the basic prisoners' dilemma setup, the rational choice of either side is to attack the other side first. If you attack first and your opponent does nothing, you win. But since your opponent is also a rational actor (as all states are assumed to be, or at least *most* states), it also has decided to pursue a "win," and it attacks. Both sides attack and both sides suffer nuclear war, but they both break even with the other. The best possible solution is not possible; the best of the worst—mutual war, even mutual nuclear war—is both possible and rational.

Robert Jervis, one of the leading early scholars in the cognitive school to which we turn in chapter 3, proposes that **deterrence** theory is dangerous because decision makers and scholars misperceive the "rationality" of others. Jervis authored a number of articles and books in which he elaborates on important misperceptions made by decision makers. For example, Jervis hypothesizes that "actors tend to overlook the fact that evidence consistent with their theories may also be consistent with other views."[29] One "partner" in a relationship premised on stable nuclear deterrence might accept the "fact" of mutual assured destruction and may assume that the other "partner" also accepts this rational "fact." But what if the second partner believes, as Ronald Reagan did, that MAD was not inevitable and that a nuclear war could possibly be won? The actor who believes that MAD is incontrovertible and who bases decisions on this could be confused and alarmed by the "inconsistent" behaviors of the other partner—or, at the very worst, this actor could be destroyed by the opponent who was looking at the "facts" and drawing very different conclusions all along.

As another example, Jervis hypothesizes that it may be very difficult for an actor to understand that the other actor is "playing an entirely different game."[30] During the Cold War, the Soviet Union and the United States seemed at times to be "playing" the nuclear "game" with very different rules. The Soviets had a policy of "no first use" of nuclear weapons. Soviet leaders announced that they would not be the first to introduce nuclear weapons into any conflict, but once such weapons were introduced by others, the Soviets would use them to the fullest and maximum extent. American leaders refused to make a pledge of no first use. Instead, American leaders retained the right to use nuclear weapons as needed, but they pledged to use those weapons in a limited, rational manner, deescalating to conventional weapons as the situation allowed. Both sides assumed that the other would appreciate and conform to the other's expectations and rules—but what guarantees were there that this would happen? Who would yield to the other's rules? When? There was within the view of each side a rationality, yet on a battlefield the failure to understand that two different rationalities were at play could have resulted in nuclear holocaust.

To blend in a lesson learned from the Chamberlain discussion above, what if the opponent in a nuclear confrontation isn't "rational" at all? What if the leaders of one side come to a determination that the other side isn't rational and so won't play by the "right" rules? The "rational" choice of the rational side facing an irrational enemy might involve leaving behind "rational" ideas in order to deal with the irrational foe. As many military planners say, no battle plan survives first contact with the enemy!

## POLIHEURISTIC THEORY: A BRIDGE TO THE NEXT CHAPTER?

The systematic study of perceptions and misperceptions is part of the cognitive approach to understanding why individuals decide what they decide. This approach is the topic of the next chapter. Typically, foreign policy scholars explain that the rational actor model and the cognitive model are incompatible approaches. This is the position taken in this book. Some scholars have argued that the approaches are not necessarily incompatible but only focus on different subjects. As Jerel Rosati explains, "Those who emphasize rationality tend to focus on 'preferences' and 'outcomes,' while cognitive perspectives tend to focus on 'beliefs' and 'process,' as well as where 'preferences come from' and 'how preferences are established' among policymakers."[31] Of course, the reason why rational actor scholars focus on "preferences" and "outcomes" is because they believe they understand the "process" in decision making: inputs, cost-benefit calculation, outputs, feedback, and so on. To return to the ideas of Morgenthau presented at the start of this chapter, when you see a foreign policy decision, think rational choice. The decision to focus on outcomes versus process results from a bias that says process is not important.

A relatively new approach to studying foreign policy at the individual level also contends that the rational actor and cognitive approaches are not incompatible and takes the position that process is important. This approach, one that is firmly at home in the rational actor school, is called "poliheuristic theory" (PH). A "heuristic" is a guide or a method or a problem-solving technique. Another way to think about a heuristic is to consider it an approach to understanding a subject matter. Thus, rational choice is an approach or heuristic; **cognition** is an approach or a heuristic. PH theory proposes that a better way to understand decision making is to use both rational choice and cognition (thus the "poli" and the "heuristic").

Scholars who use PH theory explain that all decisions involve a two-step decision process. In the first step, leaders "simplify the decision problem by the use of cognitive short-cuts." These shortcuts involve discarding some alternatives outright.[32] What helps decision makers discard some alternatives in this first step? Alex Mintz, David Brulé, and others in this research program explain that domestic political survival is always the guiding principle. Thus, faced with a foreign policy problem, leaders rule out any course of action that might have bad consequences for them in domestic politics.[33] Then, the remaining alternatives are evaluated in the second step of the decision process by using the "analytical calculations" of rational choice.[34] PH scholars contend that this process describes the decision making of leaders "regardless of their nationality or ideological position" and regardless of the type of government they lead.[35]

As we will see in the next chapter, this use of the term "cognitive short-cuts" is not in line with standard usage. Indeed, rather than combine rational choice and cognition in a two-step process, PH scholars just change our focus from national interests to regime interests and borrow the idea of "shortcuts" from cognitive scholars (the next chapter explains the idea of cognitive short-cuts). That is, PH theory says that instead of selecting among alternative foreign policy actions that serve the national interests, decision makers first select among foreign policy actions that serve their own domestic political needs, or that help them survive. The promotion and protection of interests is still what drives decision makers in this theory whether in the first step or the second. Rational calculations about domestic political survival drive the first step (the discarding of unacceptable courses of action), and then rational calculations are made in the second step.

PH theory does not bridge the gap between theories of the rational actor and individual cognition, but it does provide an example of how scholarship works to continually refine our understandings of our subject matter.

## CHAPTER REVIEW

- The rational decision-making model is derived from the realist worldview.
- The rational decision-making model assumes that all leaders are motivated to preserve the long-term national interests, and thus individual differences between leaders are insignificant.
- Culture and socialization produce regularities among individuals who rise to national office, eliminating the need to study individual differences.
- Rational decision making involves a simple model in which inputs are considered, cost-benefit calculations about different courses of action are

made, and the best course of action is selected. The decision causes changes in the environment which then return as new inputs to the decision-making "black box."

- Rational decision making is understood to be bounded by limited information and time.
- The security dilemma is the unavoidable result of rational actors making self-interested choices in a competitive international environment.
- Because of the security dilemma, rational decision making is the act of choosing between less-than-optimal choices and settling for the best of the worst rather than the best of the best.
- The strategic calculations made by an actor in a "game" may actually be directed at targets in a different "game."
- Rational choices made by the head of a state may result in short-term harm to the people and property of that state, but short-term losses are often acceptable on the way to long-term gains.
- Rational choice assumptions underscore the notion of stable nuclear deterrence.
- The poliheuristic theory posits that decision making is a two-step process involving "cognitive shortcuts" and rational choice.

*Chapter Three*

# Cognition and Personality

## IN THIS CHAPTER

- The Definition of "Leaders," Part 2
- Cognition: A Different View of Rationality
- Belief Sets and Cognitive Structure
- Operational Code
- Personality
- Analyzing Angela Merkel
- Chapter Review

## CASES FEATURED IN THIS CHAPTER

- The worldviews of British prime ministers Neville Chamberlain and Tony Blair and how these contributed to each man's view of alliances and wars.
- Mikhail Gorbachev's decision to view the breakup of the Soviet bloc as a nonthreatening event.
- The inability of Bush administration officials to accept warnings about al Qaeda planning to attack inside the United States because these warnings did not fit their established belief set.
- The ill-structured "security" belief set of Mikhail Gorbachev that permitted him to learn "new thinking" about Soviet security.
- The way that rigid beliefs about America's support for democracy and freedom distort Americans' recall of news to the contrary.
- Israeli prime minister Ariel Sharon's use of the Munich analogy after September 11, 2001, in order to preempt Bush administration plans to push for a new Palestinian-Israeli peace plan.

- Egyptian president Anwar Sadat's operational code and its implications for the 1973 Arab-Israeli War and the 1979 peace treaty between Egypt and Israel.
- The aggressive leader personality profiles of British prime minister Tony Blair and US president George W. Bush.
- A preliminary attempt to construct the operational code of German chancellor Angela Merkel as she confronted the Eurozone debt crisis.

## THE DEFINITION OF "LEADERS," PART 2

Former British prime minister Tony Blair was a committed partner to US president George W. Bush in the lead-up to the invasion of Iraq in March 2003. Although the United Kingdom and the United States had what is called a "special relationship" or partnership, Blair's ardent support for the Iraq war was not seen as an outcome of this relationship but instead a product of Blair's personality. "Reflecting upon the decision to attack Iraq, a senior British cabinet minister commented that 'had anyone else been leader, we would not have fought alongside Bush.'"[1] Stephen Dyson recounts that Blair had opportunities to step away from Bush's war plans, especially in the face of growing public opposition to the war in Britain and serious dissent within his own party, but Blair remained steadfast. Dyson concludes that Britain's participation in the Iraq war can be understood by assessing Blair's personality traits, traits that predisposed him to take Britain firmly and resolutely into the war.[2]

An earlier, much-maligned British prime minister—Neville Chamberlain—has become synonymous with the word "appeaser." In the months before the United Kingdom went to war with Germany, British, French, and Soviet officials had been involved in negotiations about forming a military alliance or some kind of mutual defense arrangement in case of military aggression by Germany. Government officials and politicians from across the British political spectrum, including opposition leader Winston Churchill and the military chiefs of staff, put aside their own distrust of and hostility toward the Soviet Union to urge Chamberlain to make an arrangement with the Soviets for the sake of British national security interests.[3] Yet Chamberlain was never willing to put aside his ideological animosity toward and political suspicion of the Soviet Union. Indeed, he deliberately withheld important military assessments and undermined negotiations with the Soviets to ensure that Britain would not be committed to assist the Soviet Union in the event of war. Some of the British elite thought that an agreement with the Soviet Union would deter Germany from taking *any* military action, and so by refusing to reach such an agreement, Chamberlain signaled that war with Germany was *better* for Britain than working with the Soviets.[4]

Both of these examples—Tony Blair predisposed and committed to go to war alongside a key ally and Neville Chamberlain willing to go to war without a key ally—suggest that "rational" cost-benefit calculations (as discussed in chapter 2) were not involved in these premiers' decision making. Political survival also did not figure into the calculations of either prime minister—each acted against the strong tide of political opinion. According to one insider in the Bush 2 administration, no cost-benefit calculation about the 2003 Iraq invasion and war occurred there either. Richard Haas, the former director of planning in the State Department, said that the decision to go to war "was an accretion, a tipping point. . . . A decision was not made—a decision happened, and you can't say when or how."[5] To understand why these leaders made the choices they did, we need to examine these decision makers as individuals with particular worldviews, personality traits, and behavioral dispositions. In this chapter, we explore two approaches to understanding individual decision makers: the cognitive approach and the personality approach. All through this chapter the working assumption is that leaders or individuals matter.

Consider another example: As the last leader of the Soviet Union, Mikhail S. Gorbachev made active, determined policy choices that led to the relatively peaceful dissolution of communist single-party states throughout Central and Eastern Europe. When the people of the countries of the former Soviet bloc took hold of their national destinies in order to construct new political systems, Gorbachev could have reacted with pleas, promises, threats, coercion, and even military force to hold the Soviet bloc together. The leader of the weakening superpower might not have been able to hold the bloc together for long, but he could have *tried*—with great loss of treasure and blood. Instead, Mikhail Gorbachev decided to let the Eastern bloc go. The decision credited to this single leader no doubt saved many lives and prevented much pain and destruction.

Gorbachev saw the Soviet Union and the world in which it operated as changing in fundamental ways. Had Gorbachev been an older man with different life-shaping experiences, he might have decided to hold on to the Eastern bloc and the former Soviet republics at all costs. Margaret Hermann and Joe Hagan explain Gorbachev's role and the importance of all leaders in this way:

> Leaders define states' international and domestic constraints. Based on their perceptions and interpretations, they build expectations, plan strategies, and urge actions on their governments that conform with their judgments about what is possible and likely to maintain them in their positions. Such perceptions help frame governments' orientations to international affairs. Leaders' interpretations arise out of their experiences, goals, beliefs about the world, and sensitivity to the political context.[6]

Leaders—even single, supreme leaders—do not work alone, cannot just consider their own judgments and concerns, and cannot afford to pay attention to just one context (domestic or foreign). As noted in chapter 1, leaders are engaged in a **two-level game** between domestic and foreign interests. This two-level game is interpreted by and filtered through the orientation of leaders. In this way of thinking, leaders can be considered the nexus of the domestic and international political systems.[7]

Hermann and Hagan take this a step further. After surveying the research on leadership, they conclude that

> the lesson learned so far is that international constraints only have policy implications when they are perceived as such by the leaders whose positions count in dealing with a particular problem. Whether and how such leaders judge themselves constrained depends on the nature of the domestic challenges to their leadership, how the leaders are organized, and what they are like as people.[8]

Gorbachev scanned the international environment and concluded that the old security threats which previously made controlling the Eastern bloc so critical to the Soviet Union had changed in fundamental ways. Further, he believed that Soviet restraint in the face of the self-opening of Eastern and Central Europe might earn the Soviet Union more international credibility and friendship (**soft power**), thereby allowing the Soviet leaders to turn inward to the serious crises proliferating in their domestic realm. Thus Gorbachev decided to view the tide of anticommunism rising in the Eastern bloc as a nonthreatening phenomenon.

How leaders define situations before them has much to do with their personal characteristics, including their social and educational backgrounds, previous experiences, ambitions, and worldviews. In September 1970, air reconnaissance photos of southern Cuba convinced US national security advisor Henry Kissinger that the Soviet Union was building a naval facility at Cienfuegos.[9] Kissinger's worldview and personal experience convinced him that the only way to protect national interests was to stand up to totalitarianism and confront the threat directly, promptly, and with force. Further, Kissinger felt deceived by previous commitments made by the Soviet leadership to stay out of Cuba. Kissinger's boss, President Richard Nixon, had a much different interpretation of the nature of the situation and a different interpretation of national interests. To Nixon, the situation was less a crisis than an example of "adventurism" that should be handled quietly through diplomatic circles.[10] Nixon believed that the Cuban Missile Crisis of 1962 had been mishandled by President John F. Kennedy, and he was determined to demonstrate better leadership.

Whose interpretation of the problem in Cienfuegos won? Kissinger was able to orchestrate a campaign of information "leaks" to the media in order to frame the situation as a crisis in the minds of American political elites and the public. By doing this, Kissinger forced Nixon into taking a strong and public stance against the Soviet action—rather than the quieter diplomatic approach Nixon preferred—in order to avoid appearing soft on US national security. This example demonstrates both the importance of how leaders define and interpret the international (and domestic) environment, and the ways key individuals within a single administration (or regime) can and do differ in their interpretations.

## COGNITION: A DIFFERENT VIEW OF RATIONALITY

Not every foreign policy analyst has been satisfied with conceptualizing leaders as decision-making "boxes," utility maximizers, or rational actors (based on a single notion of rationality). Scholars have long studied great leaders and notorious leaders in order to understand their motivations, thoughts, and actions. In the post–World War II era, political biographies of leaders were regarded by mainstream political scientists as too unscientific for the nascent field of foreign policy analysis. The study of individuals needed to take on the same scientific rigor as the competing study of rational decision making.

The move toward incorporating a more thorough, scientific investigation of individuals into the study of foreign policy took off in the 1950s. In the aftermath of World War II, behavioral scientists and psychologists had begun to examine issues such as whether aggression was inherent to humans or a learned (socialized) behavior that could be unlearned. Kenneth Waltz and Jerel Rosati—writing in different time periods and with very different orientations—credit the peace researchers of the 1950s with bringing the insights of psychology into the study of foreign policy.[11] The motivation of peace researchers was simple: if humans learn to make war, then they can learn to make peace. If, instead, aggression is part of human nature, perhaps aggression could be channeled into nonviolent pursuits. Behavioral scientists and psychologists were studying cognition, defined by the *American Heritage Dictionary* as "the mental process or faculty of knowing, including aspects such as awareness, perception, reasoning, and judgment." Peace researchers believed that the insights from the study of cognition could be used to shape peaceful leaders and peaceful countries.

A key starting assumption for the study of cognition is that "rationality" is context driven. Even while acknowledging that individual differences can have a huge impact on foreign policy decision making, cognitive scholars propose that it is possible to systematize our understanding of basic human thinking in order to develop insights that can be used for analyzing many different individuals in a variety of settings.

In his important early work on misperception, Robert Jervis offers this starting point for understanding the focus of cognitive foreign policy study:

> In determining how he will behave, an actor must try to predict how others will act and how their actions will affect his values. The actor must therefore develop an image of others and of their intentions. This image, may, however, turn out to be an inaccurate one; the actor may for a number of reasons misperceive both others' actions and their intentions. [12]

Why might actors misperceive? What are the processes that cause this to happen?

> The evidence from both psychology and history overwhelmingly supports the view . . . that decision makers tend to fit incoming information into their existing theories and images. Indeed, their theories and images play a large part in determining what they notice. In other words, actors tend to perceive what they expect. [13]

Is the process that Jervis proposes an example of irrational thinking? Jervis says that it is not, or rather that we need to rethink "rationality" in terms of the logic of the actor's existing beliefs and images. Borrowing from others, Jervis asserts that there is a "psycho-logic" that structures each individual's cognitive processes. To paraphrase Jervis, we might say that I have a logical structure to my beliefs that makes it difficult for me to understand why you look at the same world I do and draw very different conclusions than I do. Indeed, I may not even be able to comprehend that you draw different conclusions, I might assume that you see a problem in the same way I do, and—worse—I might proceed to make decisions based on that mistaken assumption. Miscommunications and antagonistic foreign policy behaviors can easily result from the clash of different, often unknowable, yet internally consistent or "rational" belief sets.

Another important early contributor to the study of cognition is Irving Janis. Janis proposes that in every situation there is a "decisional conflict" that distorts decision making. [14] A decisional conflict refers to the situation in which opposing tendencies within an individual interfere with what realists would call "rational" decision making.

A quick example is in order. Imagine a group of top foreign policy advisors meeting in a cabinet session. Present at the meeting is a new appointee, a young "rising star." This new member might have several personal and professional goals wrapped up in the situation. She might want to be well liked and well respected by all the others in the cabinet, and to have an impact on the group's process and final decisions. During the meeting, another cabinet member—older and very influential—begins to make an argument in favor of one particular course of action. As the newest member listens to the older member explain his reasoning, the newest member begins to feel rising alarm. She believes the speaker is fundamentally wrong and potentially could take the group and the country down the wrong path. But as she looks around the room and notices other key cabinet members nodding in agreement, she begins to doubt her own view about what is right. Wanting to be part of the group and wanting to be respected and accepted, the newest member feels conflicted about speaking out—it would be correct to speak out, but it would jeopardize her standing in the group if so many others agree with the older speaker.

During the Lyndon Johnson administration, a similar sort of self-censorship was exercised by some conflicted members of the president's Vietnam War decision-making circle. This self-censorship was encouraged by the fairly ruthless exclusionary practice exercised by President Johnson in his so-called Tuesday lunch group. People who spoke out against the direction favored by the group were told pointedly not to return for the next group meeting. Those who wanted to stay in the group thus silenced their own concerns. From the many books written by former insiders of the Bush 2 administration, it appears that similar self-policing and self-censoring took place in the aftermath of 9/11 and in the lead-up to and early days of the Iraq war that began in 2003.[15]

Adopting a realist view, we might conceptualize these opposing tendencies as distortions in rational decision making. These distortions might be imagined as screens or filters that keep altering the direction in which information or thoughts are processed. Still assuming a realist view, we might conclude that the presence of these filters has a limiting effect on the range, creativity, and responsiveness of the decision maker. As Jerel Rosati suggests,

> Where the rational actor perspective assumes individual open-mindedness and adaptability to changes in the environment, a cognitive approach posits that individuals tend to be much more closed-minded due to their beliefs and the way they process information—thus, they tend to resist adapting to changes in the environment.[16]

Leaving realism, we encounter a different view, again as explained by Rosati:

> A cognitive approach assumes a complex, and realistic, psychology about human reasoning and decisionmaking. It does not assume individual awareness, open-mindedness, and adaptability relative to an "objective" environment, but assumes individuals are likely to view their environment differently and operate within their own "psychological environment."[17]

## BELIEF SETS AND COGNITIVE STRUCTURE

Cognitive scholars have tried to elucidate the various kinds of screens or filters that produce what realists may call "nonrational" or irrational decisions. A number of concepts are foundational to this work, starting with the rather simple notion of a belief set. A belief set is a more or less integrated set of images held by an individual about a particular universe. This set of images acts as a screen, letting in information that fits the belief set and keeping out information that does not.

One illustration of a belief set is the **enemy image**. Images of other international actors can be categorized according to stereotyped views of the motivations of the subject and the behaviors that result from such.[18] The "enemy" is imagined as evil by nature, with unlimited potential for committing evil acts. The enemy is also imagined as a strategic thinker and consummate chess master—establishing and carrying out a plan bent on destroying its enemies and their way of life. When a foreign policy maker holds a fairly strong enemy image of an opponent, only those images that confirm the inherently evil and cunning nature of the opponent are stored and remembered. Images that suggest a more complicated nature in the opponent, or that suggest less capability by the opponent, are screened out. Arguably, the inability of the US leadership and intelligence community to predict the sudden and terminal collapse of the Eastern bloc and the Soviet Union can be attributed to a firmly entrenched enemy image that failed to take note of signs of a rapidly deteriorating Soviet empire and a differently oriented Soviet leadership under Gorbachev. Former US president George W. Bush's active use of the idea that the terrorist enemy was always plotting and planning to attack innocent people derived from this same basic assumption that the evil enemy may be more organized and proactive than the good guys. Enemy images may do more than cause an actor to miss signs of change or weakness in the enemy—the presence of strong enemy images may sustain international conflict over time. This was a prophetic conclusion drawn by Ole Holsti in the 1960s regarding American decision makers' images of Soviet leaders.[19]

A related concept is **cognitive consistency**. This is the idea that the images contained in a belief set must be logically connected and consistent. Cognitive theorists propose that when an individual holds conflicting beliefs, the individual experiences an anxiety known as cognitive dissonance. Individuals strive to avoid this dissonance and the anxiety it produces by actively managing the information they encounter and store in their belief sets. This active management is not as energetic or as conscious as it sounds. Individuals are assumed to be *limited* information managers—or **cognitive misers**—who rely on cognitive shortcuts to understand new information. Individuals use existing beliefs not only to screen out dissonant information but to interpret new information. The new information is "recognized" as similar to an existing belief and so is stored as the same. Great distortion can occur in this act of interpreting and storing, but the distortion is quicker and easier than actually working through new situations, and this unconscious categorizing prevents individuals from having to confront new and potentially dissonant information.

Accepting information that is consistent with one's beliefs and rejecting or discounting information that is inconsistent can contribute to major disasters, such as the failure to read the warning signs before the 9/11 terrorist attacks on the United States. On August 6, 2001, President George W. Bush received a daily intelligence briefing entitled "Bin Laden Determined to Strike in US." When this was revealed in a 2004 congressional investigation into 9/11, the administration claimed that there was nothing in the August 6 briefing that could be acted upon. Administration officials claimed that the August 6 report contained background information that constituted part of the everyday "noise" generated by the intelligence community.

However, reporter Kurt Eichenwald contends that this August 6 briefing was one in a series of intelligence warnings about al Qaeda starting around May 1, 2001—warnings that the administration refused to acknowledge as credible.[20] Rather than take the warnings of the intelligence community seriously, **neoconservatives** in the White House believed that the CIA had been fooled by a disinformation campaign conducted in concert by al Qaeda and Saddam Hussein to distract the administration from the *real* threat posed by Saddam Hussein. Administration officials refused to believe analysts who presented evidence that al Qaeda and Saddam Hussein were not working together and looked with disdain on those who thought al Qaeda posed any real threat. They were looking for anything the Iraqi leader might do—or anything they might be able to attribute to the Iraqi leader—to confirm their beliefs. After the 9/11 terrorist attacks, administration officials began to plan for a major war, not against al Qaeda, but against Saddam Hussein and Iraq. The administration also set up a special intelligence operation within the Pentagon—because it was believed that the CIA *would not look for* the right information—to find proof of the links between Saddam Hussein and 9/11 which the administration believed must exist.

It is important to note here that although cognitive scholars propose that individuals tend to avoid or distort dissonant information, these scholars do agree that sometimes individuals may accommodate dissonant information by adding a new dimension to their belief set. That is, although beliefs tend to be rigid and unchanging, there are times when individuals can change what they believe and learn something new. Scholars who study how beliefs may change engage in the study of learning. Learning involves the "development of new beliefs, skills, or procedures as a result of the observation and interpretation of experience."[21] Learning is possible and belief sets can change, but only under limited circumstances.

Janice Gross Stein's study of Mikhail Gorbachev provides an interesting example of how cognitive scholars explain the conditions under which beliefs can change. Stein argues that learning—a change in held beliefs— occurs easiest with problems that are "ill-structured" in the mind of the individual. An ill-structured problem is akin to an incomplete belief set. Gorbachev's primary interests within the Central Committee and, after 1980, within the Politburo centered on the domestic economy of the Soviet Union. On topics of external security including issues related to the United States, Stein proposes, Gorbachev held few preexisting beliefs. Stein explains that "learning is the construction of new representations of the problem"[22]; new representations of a problem occur most easily when there is an underdeveloped existing representation of the problem in the mind of the individual. Gorbachev was unconstrained by well-structured existing beliefs about Soviet external security, and so he was "free" to learn. Stein argues that Gorbachev was prompted to learn new ideas about Soviet security and about the United States because of the failure of Soviet policy in Afghanistan. Learning, then, requires two elements: the lack of strongly established beliefs and some "unanticipated failures that challenge old ways of representing problems."[23] Learning requires a prompt and a need.

However, beliefs that are firmly held and supported by one's society and culture are more rigid and unlikely to change. Matthew Hirshberg's research provides a demonstration of the rigidity of preexisting beliefs and the reconstruction of information to make it resemble preexisting beliefs. Hirshberg presented fictional news stories to three groups of college students (a standard subject pool for this kind of research) to test two hypotheses. His first hypothesis was that "the stereotype of a prodemocratic America serves to maintain its own cultural dominance by filtering out information that does not fit it, making it difficult for Americans to test the validity of their preconceptions."[24] The fictional news accounts portrayed the United States intervening in three different ways: (1) on the side of a democratic government besieged by rebels, (2) on the side of an unspecified type of government besieged by communist rebels, and (3) on the side of an unspecified type of government besieged by democratic rebels. When asked to recall the events depicted in the particular story read, most students recalled that the United States had intervened in support of democracy.[25] The students' strongly held belief that the United States always supported democracy and freedom caused them to re-create the information in the news account to fit what they believed.

Hirshberg tested a second hypothesis on what is called **attribution bias**. An attribution bias or error is triggered by information that is inconsistent with preexisting beliefs and cannot be re-created to fit those beliefs. The attribution bias involves both the enemy image discussed above and a related concept called the mirror image. The starting belief in an attribution error is that we are a people who are inherently good and well intentioned. Our opponent, on the other hand, is evil and has malevolent intentions—the opposite or mirror image of us. In an attribution error, the individual goes a step further in order to explain behavior, especially behavior that does not fit one's beliefs about one's own country as good and well intentioned. When our evil opponent does bad things—such as using military force or coercing another country into a one-sided trade arrangement—it is because such bad behavior is in our opponent's nature. Conversely, we are by nature good and so only do good things. When we do bad things, it is because we have been forced to do so by external events. When an individual must explain a behavior that is inconsistent with preexisting foundational beliefs, cognitive scholars say the individual will attribute the inconsistent behavior to outside circumstances.

Hirshberg's second hypothesis was tested with fictional news accounts that either depicted the United States dropping "tons of incendiary bombs," causing "panic" and "horror" among villagers, or depicted the United States dropping "tons of relief supplies," causing "joy" and "glee" among villagers. [26] After having his subjects read one version of the fictional accounts, he had them answer questionnaires on the "nature of the United States" and why it acted as reported. Hirshberg found that 70 percent of those reading about the dropping of relief supplies agreed that it was American nature to do so (an internal attribution bias). However, he did not find significant statistical support for the external attribution bias—that the United States dropped bombs because it was forced to do so by external events.

Although Hirshberg's subjects didn't exhibit an external attribution bias, it is not uncommon to hear national leaders make use of such. Consider the Bush 2 administration explanations for why the United States went to war in Iraq. In May 2004, the president said,

> We did not seek this war on terror, but this is the world as we find it. We must keep our focus. We must do our duty. History is moving, and it will tend toward hope, or tend toward tragedy. Our terrorist enemies have a vision that guides and explains all their varied acts of murder. [27]

Note in this quote the use of an image of the enemy as determined and cunning (the enemy has a vision that guides its actions). In a similar address in November 2005, the president explained, "We didn't ask for this global struggle, but we're answering history's call with confidence, and with a comprehensive strategy." [28] And in January 2006, the president said, "You know, no President ever wants to be President during war. But this war came to us, not as a result of actions we took, it came to us as a result of actions an enemy took on September the 11th, 2001."[29]

Consider another example from outside the US context. During the Bosnian war of 1992–1995, United Nations peacekeeping personnel were scattered around parts of Bosnia and neighboring Croatia to try to limit the violence and thereby stem the outflow of refugees. The peacekeepers were not an effective deterrent or buffer, and they often found themselves under fire. In one episode of this war, the Croatian military sought to retake a sector that was under the watch of UN peacekeepers. A demand was issued for the peacekeepers to give up their position and move. The peacekeepers refused, prompting a warning from the Croatian military about what might happen if the peacekeepers continued to refuse to move. When the peacekeepers held their position, the Croatian military bombed the peacekeepers. The official explanation—a clear demonstration of an attribution bias—was that the peacekeepers had given Croatia no other choice but to bomb them! The Croatian government intoned, "Croatia deeply regrets and is very sorry for what happened. We were doing our very best to avoid such incidents before commencing military activities."[30]

When preexisting beliefs are used to interpret, re-create, or explain away behavior, cognitive scholars say that the individual is acting as a cognitive miser, using shortcuts to deal with the new information. The name given by some scholars to these cognitive shortcuts is a schema. A schema is a shortcut like a menu that is more or less particular to a situation. When scholars study schemas, they are interested in identifying the nature or internal structure of schemas and the policy decisions that might result from different schemas.

For example, it is well known that individuals use analogies to understand a new situation and to determine a course of action. An analogy is a comparison made to similar events or phenomena. For instance, if a leader uses the "Munich analogy" to determine a course of action, he or she has decided that events at hand resemble the events of 1938 when the British prime minister Neville Chamberlain "appeased" Adolf Hitler. In the Munich Treaty—which effectively amounted to a green light for Germany to move east into Czechoslovakia, thereby sparing countries to the west—Chamberlain proclaimed that he had bought "peace in our time." But the Munich Treaty did not satisfy Hitler's aggression; he ultimately brought war to countries in all directions. When a leader says that a new situation brings to mind the "Munich analogy," he or she is saying that it does no good to try to appease an aggressive leader; instead, the aggressor must be met with immediate and decisive force. Keith Shimko writes that when individuals use a schema to understand a new problem, they "fill in the blanks of current events with knowledge accumulated from past experiences."[31] Once a leader decides that a new situation resembles the effort to appease Hitler, the leader need not seek out detailed information about the new situation in order to know what policy is necessary.

Policy makers can cause problems for themselves in their use of analogies. We can see this in a diplomatic tussle that resulted from remarks made by the Israeli prime minister in the immediate aftermath of the September 11, 2001, terrorist attacks on the United States. In pursuit of Arab support for its campaign against international **terrorism**, the Bush 2 administration announced in early October that it was in favor of a long-standing demand of the Arab world—Palestinian statehood. This announcement prompted a speech by Israeli prime minister Ariel Sharon in which he made use of the famous analogy discussed above. Sharon intoned,

> I call on the Western democracies and primarily the leader of the free world, the United States: Do not repeat the dreadful mistake of 1938 when enlightened European democracies decided to sacrifice Czechoslovakia for a convenient temporary solution. Do not try to appease the Arabs at our expense. This is unacceptable to us. Israel will not be Czechoslovakia. Israel will fight terrorism. [32]

The Israeli prime minister's use of the Munich analogy provoked an unusual public rebuke from the White House press secretary: "The president believes that these remarks are unacceptable. Israel can have no better or stronger friend than the United States."[33] Opposition party members from within Israel also condemned Sharon's remark. Sharon subsequently retracted the remark—in part—agreeing that the United States was a good friend of Israel's.

Besides prompting an angry US retort, Sharon's use of the Munich analogy telegraphed a new course of action—an abandonment of the most recent cease-fire between Israel and the Palestinian National Authority (this conflict is explained in more detail in chapter 6). Within a few hours of his use of the Munich analogy, Sharon ordered Israeli tanks, infantry, helicopter gunships, and armored bulldozers into parts of Palestinian-controlled Hebron. Analogies can signal leaders' intentions to embark on certain courses of action. Rather than allow Israel to be sacrificed by the United States in order to curry Arab favor, Sharon demonstrated that he was prepared to take Israeli security into his own hands, setting his own policy direction. Abandoning the cease-fire was a clear statement to this effect, especially in the face of US pressure on Israel to be more accommodating with the Palestinians in order to help the Bush 2 administration's new war on terrorism.

Finally, some scholars have been interested in mapping out the cognitive complexity or simplicity of decision makers' demonstrated beliefs. Allison Astorino-Courtois explains that the "cognitive complexity-simplicity construct reflects the degree to which individuals both differentiate and integrate various sources of information in considering a decision problem."[34] Peter

Suedfeld and colleagues elaborate: "**Integrative complexity** is an attribute of information processing that generally indicates the extent to which decision makers search for and monitor information, try to predict outcomes and reactions, flexibly weigh their own and other parties' options, and consider multiple potential strategies."[35]

The study of integrative complexity involves an examination of the public utterances of leaders. The utterances, or statements, are scored as to whether they demonstrate simple information processing, more complicated contingency-based reasoning, or highly complex, multicausal information processing. Scholars have found that leaders demonstrating higher levels of complexity tend to be more cooperative in their international initiatives than those demonstrating lower levels.[36] However, in situations of prolonged stress, such as the 1962 Cuban Missile Crisis or the months leading up to the 1991 Persian Gulf War, the measured integrative complexity decreases for all decision makers as they begin to feel that time and options are running out.

In many respects, these scholars equate cognitive complexity with more rational decision making, and cognitive simplicity with decision making through the use of preexisting beliefs:

> At the lower end of the complexity scale, the amount of information used in cognitive processing is limited . . . decision makers often rely on analogs or stereotyped images, and discrepant information is either ignored or discounted. . . . Complex thinking, on the other hand, involves a broader search and use of varied information sources concerning the decision problem. Discrepant information is integrated most thoroughly at higher levels of cognitive complexity, and more flexible consideration is given to the complete set of options and outcomes relevant to a decision situation.[37]

By equating high levels of complexity with the tasks typically associated with rational decision making, this line of research attempts to bridge the differences between rational choice and cognitive studies. It should be noted as well that scholars in this tradition link more "rational," high levels of complexity with liberalism and good behavior like cooperation, while lower cognitive complexity is associated with the less desirable use of cognitive shortcuts, conservatism, and belligerency.

## OPERATIONAL CODE

When a leader makes use of an analogy, it is possible to make a safe guess about the kind of behaviors that follow. Once a leader identifies an opponent as another Hitler and therefore the lessons of Munich must apply, we can safely predict that the leader thinks that some kind of forceful reply to the new Hitler is in order. Once a leader declares that his or her country will not be abandoned in the same way that Czechoslovakia was abandoned, we can safely predict that the leader will demonstrate the willingness and capability to go it alone. If we as analysts can map out the operating beliefs of a leader we are studying, looking for the analogies and other pronouncements that demonstrate the leader's worldview, we can use this "map" to explain why certain policies were made and certain actions taken. A cognitive map that details both the normative beliefs held by an individual and his or her behavioral beliefs is called an **operational code**. "Operational code analysis provides a means of testing a leader's fundamental predispositions toward political action."[38]

Alexander George is the scholar who brought the discussion of operational codes to the forefront in foreign policy study in the late 1960s. George defines the operational code as a "political leader's beliefs about the nature of politics and political conflict, his views regarding the extent to which historical developments can be shaped, and his notions of correct strategy and tactics."[39] Delineating a leader's operational code involves a two-step process, as described by Stephen Walker and colleagues:

> First, what are the leader's philosophical beliefs about the dynamics of world politics? Is the leader's image of the political universe a diagnosis marked by cooperation or conflict? What are the prospects for the realization of fundamental political values? What is the predictability of others, the degree of control over historical development and the role of chance? Second, what are the leader's instrumental beliefs that indicate choice and shift propensities in the management of conflict? What is the leader's general approach to strategy and tactics and the utility of different means? How does the leader calculate, control, and manage the risks and timing of political action?[40]

Operational code studies typically depend on an examination of the writings and statements of a leader from which philosophical beliefs can be extracted. Scott Crichlow explains that,

> although it may be altered (e.g., by learning) or modified in specific situational environments, the operational code of a leader rests on a core set of predispositions, such that the taking of actions that contradict it is by definition out of the norm. Therefore, it is expected that such patterns of preferences in a leader's political statements are indeed largely accurate illustrations of his or her basic predispositions regarding the nature and conduct of politics.[41]

By way of example, consider Ibrahim Karawan's efforts to elaborate the operational code of Egyptian president Anwar Sadat in order to explain Sadat's decision to sign a peace treaty with Israel in 1979.[42] Anwar Sadat became the president of Egypt in 1970 upon the death of Gamal Abdel Nasser. Recall that in the last chapter we explored the rational choices made by Nasser in the events leading up to the 1967 war between Egypt and Israel. The losses incurred by Egypt and the Arab states collectively in the 1967 war—the Old City of Jerusalem, the Sinai Peninsula, the Gaza Strip, the West Bank, and the Golan Heights—caused Nasser to lose his leadership position in the Arab world. Although Nasser attempted to resign from the presidency after the 1967 defeat, his popularity among Egyptians remained high, and he remained as president until he had a heart attack and died in 1970. The political ramifications of the Six Days' War continue to reverberate to this day in the Middle East.

According to Karawan, Sadat took over the Egyptian presidency committed to setting Egypt on a different foreign policy course than that pursued by Nasser. Rather than follow Nasser's pan-Arab policy, Sadat embarked on an "Egypt first" course. Karawan contends that Sadat's writings and speeches indicate that "Egypt first" was the driving philosophical belief of Sadat's operational code.[43] The instrumental belief that followed was that Sadat would negotiate Egypt's future without regard for the opinions and interests of the other Arab states. To illustrate Sadat's "Egypt first" operational code, Karawan points to Sadat's speeches and actions at several key junctures in the 1970s.

In 1973, Egypt and Syria launched a concerted two-prong attack on Israel. Egyptian forces managed to reclaim a small part of the Sinai Peninsula in this attack, a victory Sadat attributed to the power of Egyptian **nationalism**. This was the first time an Arab leader made battlefield gains against Israel. Following his "Egypt first" philosophy and despite the fact that he had engaged in the war alongside ally Syria, Sadat declared a unilateral cease-fire and negotiated a subsequent disengagement without consulting or even informing Syria. Similarly, Sadat pursued peace with Israel in the 1978 Camp David talks, which led to the 1979 peace treaty between Egypt and Israel, in order to pursue Egypt's national interests. Sadat's decision to engage in peace talks with Israel occurred in the absence of any consultation with or consideration of the other Arab states. Sadat's pursuit of Egyptian national interests constituted the behavioral manifestation of his driving philosophical belief.

Sadat's pursuit of his "Egypt first" philosophy caused the other Arab states to turn their backs on Egypt. His decision to negotiate peace and normal relations with Israel ultimately gave incentive to some Egyptian Islamic fundamentalists to assassinate him in 1981. But his actions in the 1970s flowed directly from his primary beliefs. The elaboration of Sadat's operational code explains the foreign policy he followed; that is, the elaboration of Sadat's cognitive map points out the direction of the course he set for Egypt.

# PERSONALITY

When operational code scholars propose that a leader's core set of philosophical beliefs make it unlikely that the leader will act in ways inconsistent with this norm, these scholars link operational code to cognitive studies. When operational code scholars explain that they ultimately are establishing a leader's fundamental behavioral predisposition, they link operational code to the study of personality.

Margaret Hermann is the pioneering scholar in this study. Hermann's research reveals that six personality traits are related to specific foreign policy behaviors. These traits are the need for power, the need for affiliation, the level of cognitive complexity, the degree of trust in others, nationalism, and the belief that one has some control over events.[44] Other studies have added an additional trait: task orientation.[45] Two basic leadership types and expected foreign policy behaviors arise out of certain configurations of these traits:

> If we examine the dynamics of the traits associated with the **aggressive leader**, we find a need to manipulate and control others, little ability to consider a range of alternatives, suspiciousness of others' motives, a high interest in maintaining national identity and sovereignty, and a distinct willingness to initiate action. . . . [Such leaders] urge their governments to be suspicious of the motives of leaders of other nations. When interaction is necessary, they expect it to be on their nation's terms.[46]

> The personal characteristics of the **conciliatory leader** indicate a need to establish and maintain friendly relationships with others, an ability to consider a wide range of alternatives, little suspiciousness of others' motives, no overriding concern with the maintenance of national identity and sovereignty, and little interest in initiating action. These dynamics suggest a more participatory foreign policy. . . . [Conciliatory leaders] will probably keep attuned to what is going on in international relations, being sensitive and responsive to this environment.[47]

Based on her research and that of her colleagues, Hermann developed a Leadership Trait Analysis (LTA) system. One illustration of the use of the LTA system comes from a study by Vaughn Shannon and Jonathan Keller on the inner circle of the Bush 2 administration. Shannon and Keller's specific concern is whether the personality traits evidenced in the Bush 2 inner circle made the administration more or less likely to invade Iraq, thereby violating the international norm against the use of force except for self-defense. With some slight exceptions, they found that Bush administration officials did demonstrate traits that made them more likely to engage in aggressive behavior. Their conclusion was that a "belief in ability to control events, need for power, ingroup bias, and especially distrust may be particularly important predictors of one's willingness to violate international norms."[48] In 1999 Hermann drew conclusions from her own LTA work that aptly described the Bush administration's foreign policy more than a decade later. For leaders who are high in distrust and in-group bias, Hermann writes, "international politics is centered around a set of adversaries that are viewed as 'evil' and intent on spreading their ideology or extending their power at the expense of others; leaders perceive that they have a moral imperative to confront these adversaries; as a result, they are likely to take risks and to engage in highly aggressive and assertive behavior."[49]

Another recent study of the Iraq war makes use of Hermann's LTA system. Stephen Dyson used LTA to compare Tony Blair to fifty-one other world leaders and twelve previous British prime ministers.[50] Using Blair's answers to parliamentary questions from 1997 to the day that the Iraq invasion began, Dyson concludes that Blair scored far above the average on his belief in his ability to control events, well below the average on cognitive complexity, and far above the average on the need for power.[51] That is, Dyson finds that Blair fits Hermann's depiction of an aggressive leader. Putting these two studies together, we might conclude that there was a "perfect storm" forming for war with Iraq because the leaders of both the United States and the United Kingdom were predisposed to see other actors in the world as suspicious (particularly the regime of Saddam Hussein) and to see themselves as having a high ability to control world events, and they were generally insensitive to international norms, views, or information that would have moderated their actions. This also helps to explain the puzzle of Tony Blair set out in the introduction to this chapter. The issues of a leader's orientations to the world—how the leader views his or her state in the world—and the sensitivity of leaders to advice and information must be understood in terms of the context in which the leader makes decisions.

## ANALYZING ANGELA MERKEL

Throughout the long and politically contentious year of 2012, one person generated more fear and anger and more hopes and frustrations than any other: German chancellor Angela Merkel. This statement is true beyond the European Union because of the implications of the **Eurozone** crisis for the economies of so many non-European states. Was Merkel a rigid conservative who wanted to punish the Greeks and others for their reckless accumulation of debt or a German nationalist who had little affection for Europe and so was loath to intervene in the debt crisis? Or are there alternative ways to characterize the chancellor's views and actions? Here, a brief and *very* preliminary exploration of Angela Merkel's personality and operational code will be offered, with the caveat that a full scholarly study requires so much more use of evidence than that examined here.

Angela Merkel became the first woman elected chancellor of Germany in 2005. She was born in the former German Democratic Republic (East Germany) in 1954 and earned a doctorate in theoretical physics. Merkel entered politics at the end of the communist era in East Germany and served briefly in the democratically elected government there. Upon unification she was elected to the Bundestag (lower house) of the German national legislature as a member of the Christian Democratic Union (CDU). She served in two cabinets of CDU chancellor Helmet Kohl but broke publicly with Kohl over a financial corruption scandal. This break with CDU leadership left her in the strong political position to take control of the party when Kohl and his successor were forced out of politics. Merkel led two cabinets as chancellor, from 2005 to 2009 and from 2009 to this writing at the start of 2013. Merkel faced elections in mid-2013.

The aim in this section is to try to use the tools of cognitive scholars to understand Merkel's actions regarding the Eurozone debt crisis from 2009 through the end of 2012. A full analysis would require, at the very least, a much more thorough study of Merkel's public utterances (speeches, press conferences, interviews) and writings. We would also need to analyze her foreign policy statements and policy decisions regarding the debt crisis in exhaustive detail. But here we can make an initial, exploratory assessment using some secondary analyses of Merkel's first government along with a speech she gave in 2009. This initial analysis based on sources up until about the time the Eurozone debt crisis hit in 2009 might help us understand Merkel's decision making in 2009 through the end of 2012. Perhaps a reader of this book will go on to conduct a thorough and rigorous scholarly study using this initial exploration.

In an early analysis of Merkel from the winter of 2005–2006 entitled "Who's Afraid of Angela Merkel?" Werner Reutter offers an assessment of the person he (like others) calls the "least likely of all to become the first female chancellor of Germany."[52] Merkel's rise to power in the CDU was unlikely because she was a Protestant woman from the former East Germany while the CDU was a socially conservative, predominantly Catholic party with traditional views about women and firm roots in Southern Germany.[53]

Reutter notes that Merkel has a strong "will to power and is a most adept political strategist. She learns quickly, never repeats a mistake, and is able to adjust easily to new circumstances."[54] Further, he claims that Merkel is not a person "driven by ideology," that she shows no emotion in public, and that she learned "to keep private things to herself and not to tell openly what she really thinks." And she thinks about and approaches politics rationally as her physicist background would suggest.[55]

In 2008, Sarah Elise Wiliarty published an analysis of "Angela Merkel's Path to Power" which attributes Merkel's rise both to CDU party dynamics and Merkel's own leadership style.[56] Wiliarty tells us that the CDU is a "catch-all" party that attempts to catch all voters by "using bland appeals to notions like democracy or prosperity." But, the CDU is also a "corporatist catch-all party" in which "important societal interest groups are organized and represented within the party."[57] Thus, as "a female Protestant from the former East Germany, Merkel by herself fulfilled three important internal party quotas. This fact made her a particularly desirable choice whenever internal decision-making bodies were being constituted."[58]

Merkel learned politics in a corporatist structure in which "internal party losers may be more willing to support party policies they disagree with if they feel that they had a chance to air their concerns."[59] And Merkel came to her posts in the CDU with a leadership style that complemented the party structure that rewarded her. Wiliarty proposes that Merkel is "a master of the party manager approach." This approach "involves balancing these internal groups so that no group becomes too strong and no group is eliminated." This balance creates a situation in which "all internal groups believe the party manager represents their interests."[60] Wiliarty adds that Merkel "is known for her tendency to avoid commitment to a particular policy direction until the last possible moment,"[61] a tendency that keeps losers and winners aboard when a decision is made.

A few last observations from Wiliarty should be included in our analysis. Wiliarty notes that as a government minister, Merkel demonstrated an ability to learn her portfolio quickly and then to pursue its interests and her own advancement with great competence.[62] This was true whether she had interests aligned with that ministry previous to her appointment or not. Finally, Merkel learns from her mistakes, including the lesson that came when she deviated from her leadership style in a failed bid for chancellorship candidacy in 2002.[63]

We'll add to this discussion by turning to Ruth Wittlinger's 2008 study of Merkel.[64] Wittlinger notes that she personally had some doubts about Merkel's sensitivity to the German collective memory when Merkel lectured George W. Bush and Vladimir Putin on human rights issues (German collective memory is discussed in more detail in chapter 5).[65] Wittlinger and Martin Larose explain that postwar German foreign policy has always been in tune with three themes: respect for the lessons of the Holocaust, wariness about the dangers of aggressive nationalism and going it alone, and gratefulness for the steadfast solidarity of the United States and NATO with Germany during the Cold War.[66] Wittlinger explains that her worry was that Merkel might emphasize the memory of German suffering "possibly at the expense of the memory of the Holocaust."[67] This would strike a more nationalistic, defensive tone than that typically taken by post–World War II German governments. Instead, Wittlinger concludes that Merkel's close relations with Israel demonstrate that the chancellor's foreign policy is quite sensitive to the collective memory.[68] Merkel successfully links a "special" German responsibility toward Israel because of the Holocaust to an internally supported appreciation of German suffering during and immediately after the world war; this linkage brings different and sometimes contentious views together in a common foreign policy.

The last bits of evidence from the pre–debt crisis period that we'll assemble here come from a speech given by Merkel at the American Academy of Berlin in 2009 when she was awarded an honorary degree from the New School. The chancellor began her remarks by noting that Germany was celebrating sixty years of the constitution, the Basic Law. Merkel noted, "I have not been spared some disappointments as regards the subject of rational explanations for everything that happens in this Federal Republic. But the political rules that are most widely accepted—of this I am still convinced today—are those that can be explained by reference to common sense."[69] Governing by common sense is a good rule for national as well as international society. And the problems of globalization—such as the 2008 world financial crisis—demonstrate the need for international society to give "globalization a political dimension."[70] Further, rational people fix problems when they arise, and the community of states should do the same, acknowledging that "We all agree that it is no longer possible for any country in the world to solve the problems on its own. For this reason international rules will follow."[71] The global financial crisis resulted from "market excesses combined with insufficient regulation. We therefore have to draw the right lessons from this. In other words, freedom always requires action by the state to provide a framework within which all may live in freedom."[72] And individual freedom "must be exercised responsibly," which "entails a mutual give and take. This can ultimately only really happen on the basis of dialogue and tolerance, be it in society in general or politics in particular, be it at [the] national or international level."[73]

So far, we've assembled some evidence about Angela Merkel that fits Margaret Hermann's description of a conciliatory leader. Merkel's leadership style as of 2009 involved withholding her opinion in order to hear from all the stakeholders and bring them together behind a common policy decision. To do this she needed to maintain friendly relations, consider a wide range of alternatives, and be trusting and not suspicious of others. Also, as Hermann's description says, Merkel seemed to show "little interest in initiating action"[74] lest she be identified with a particular position and alienate those with different views. This leadership profile is complemented by the description of Merkel as nonideological and pragmatic, as these attributes might suggest that she would be less concerned with maintaining national identity than an aggressive leader would be.

We might even be able to offer a preliminary set of Merkel's philosophical and operational beliefs that form part of her operational code. Because this is a preliminary investigation, these will be presented in unified form rather than disaggregated into two different sets with the operational beliefs roughly stated after the philosophical beliefs.

1. The best societies (national and international) are inclusive and diverse. Governments (and all social organizations such as political parties) should encourage and facilitate inclusion and diversity.
2. Rules of governance and public policy are best when they result from a process in which all stakeholders are heard. Leaders should take into account the opinions of as many stakeholders as practical when formulating policy.
3. Government leaders should not follow ideological principles too rigidly. The best policies and rules are those based on common sense, incrementalism, and tried and proven methods.
4. Individuals in national societies and states in international society should be free to pursue their own interests, but they also must be responsible actors who are held accountable for their actions. Governments exist, in part, to establish frameworks to facilitate freedom and responsibility.

Now we'll see whether this preliminary understanding of Angela Merkel's operational code might be useful for understanding her reaction to the Eurozone debt crisis that began in 2009. In 1999, a majority of European Union countries formed a monetary union which adopted a single currency, the euro; thus the Eurozone came into being. In time, seventeen countries would become members. Part of the criteria for joining the Eurozone involved agreements to keep government deficits and debt within certain parameters. When the global financial crisis hit in August 2008, the resulting global economic downturn exposed the dangerously large deficits and government debt of several Eurozone members. In 2009, the Eurozone crisis began when the Greek government admitted that its debts doubled the Eurozone limits of 60 percent of gross domestic product, causing immediate speculation and fear that Greece would default on its debts.

By the spring of 2010, Greece was no longer able to borrow on the open market, resulting in a bailout organized by the European Union (EU), International Monetary Fund (IMF), and the European Central Bank (ECB). By the end of the year, Ireland was in a banking crisis after its housing bubble popped; Ireland received a bailout in November. At the end of 2010, Merkel declared continued German support for the Eurozone idea and her belief that the euro would survive the crisis, but she was adamantly opposed to collectivizing the risks of the growing crisis. Merkel stood opposed to eurobonds and the sharing of the responsibility for the debts of individual countries and national banks by the whole Eurozone. [75]

In May 2011, Portugal became the third country to need a bailout. As new bailout funds were being discussed for Greece at the start of the summer, Merkel insisted that private banks pay part of the costs of the debt crisis by taking losses on Greek bonds. In an open conflict with Merkel, ECB officials stood opposed to this, saying that such a move would appear to be a default, something everyone was trying to avoid. In July new funds were approved for Greece, as news came that Italy and Spain were on the verge of crisis.

In August 2011, Merkel met with French president Nicolas Sarkozy. Together they announced their plan for closer political and economic union for the countries of the Eurozone and that each member should make changes to its constitution requiring balanced budgets and debt reduction. Greater fiscal responsibility was the theme of their plan, with more strictly delineated national responsibilities. Merkel and Sarkozy stated that they remained opposed to eurobonds and declared that there should be no further increase in the size of the bailout fund. Merkel said "there was 'no magic wand' to solve all the problems of the euro, arguing that they must be met over time with improved fiscal discipline, competitiveness and economic growth among weaker states." [76] Trying to rally her party in support of the Eurozone, Merkel said Europe was in its toughest hour since World War II. [77] But growth in the Eurozone continued to decline, and Germany's growth flatlined. By the end of the year, investors were pulling their money out of Spanish and Italian banks and moving it to German banks.

Europe went into a second recession in 2012, with Greece and Spain facing record unemployment and budget deficits. Against Merkel's wishes, the EU-IMF-ECB established a framework for a safe default on Greek private banking debt. Meanwhile, Merkel attempted to inject herself into the French presidential election by rebuking Sarkozy's opponent on his announced plan to renegotiate the EU pact in order to focus less on **austerity** and more on growth. [78] That opponent, François Hollande, won the French presidency in a voters' rebuke of Sarkozy's austerity policies. Greeks, too, elected a left-leaning government in disgust over crippling austerity measures. In June, ECB head, Mario Draghi, called for Eurozone-wide deposit insurance and bank regulation. Merkel responded not by denouncing Draghi et al., but by announcing that Germany would support pooling the growing Eurozone debt and was starting to favor a move toward creating a eurobond market, an idea she had flatly dismissed the year before. That same summer, Spain received a bailout. Finally, in December 2012, Eurozone heads met and agreed to form a banking union that would have a common banking supervisor located in the ECB, a sharing of bailout costs and a common bailout resolution framework, and common deposit insurance for individual investors. In response, a BBC commentator concluded that Germany had used the crisis as a way to relaunch the European project.[79]

Let's try fitting Merkel's views on and actions during the crisis into the operational code constructed above. Early in the crisis in 2009, Merkel stayed rather quiet on the crisis and didn't assert a German "answer" or opinion on the problems. As the crisis moved into 2010 and 2011, Merkel proposed that austerity measures and public and private responsibility were the appropriate responses to the crisis—a view that would have summed up the prominent German voices she was hearing on the crisis with the addition of French president Sarkozy.

Outside of Germany, Merkel became the public face of how the powers that be refused to acknowledge the human costs of the crisis and the austerity solutions. By 2012, the crowds in the streets of Greece and Spain, along with other important voices like the ECB's Draghi and US president Barack Obama, began calling for less austerity and more growth-based solutions to the debt problem. Further, views were coalescing around collectivizing the debt problem as the best common approach. It was, after all, a problem that no single country in the Eurozone could solve on its own, to paraphrase Merkel's thoughts from years earlier.

Meanwhile, as voters in France and Greece demonstrated their views, Draghi's opinions and actions—which Merkel had opposed—worked to stabilize markets at critical times. As Merkel heard from a larger number of stakeholders, as public sentiment began demanding a change in policy and greater German commitment to the collective, *and as Draghi's interventionist policies seemed to work where austerity policies had not*, Merkel changed her position and moved to stabilize the Eurozone with an agreement on a banking union. Throughout the crisis she was gathering up the different views and working to put in place a commonsense, rational solution that would keep as many stakeholders happy as possible. And Merkel's actions throughout the crisis can be explained as driven by the goal of making the European Union a stronger organization. That is, Merkel's views maintained the importance of solidarity, one of the critical strands in the German collective memory as discussed earlier.

Despite the dismay over Merkel's slow response, she did what we would expect her to do given the operational code we assembled (albeit on thin evidence). Merkel was not rigidly wedded to austerity policies, but they reflected the prevailing wisdom in her primary community. As the community seeking action from her grew, she gathered in many more views and looked for methods that would work, without worrying about grand ideological visions or previously held stands. She even prepared her own party in November 2011 for the coming change in policy, an inclusive move that we would expect her to make. As of the end of 2012, it appeared that Merkel's leadership style and the operational code we've drawn from it made her fairly well suited to find a commonsense, incrementalist solution that accommodated the voices of most stakeholders and attempted to keep everyone invested in the common European solution. The readers of this book can judge whether this held true beyond the start of 2013.

We can add one final observation here. Earlier in this chapter, we discussed what cognitive scholars call learning. Changes in belief sets can occur regarding problems that are "ill-structured" in the mind of the decision maker and when there is some failure that creates the need for new thinking. The situation faced by the Eurozone was unique: the crisis and the context were new ground for all the Eurozone leaders. We might conclude that Merkel (like all the leaders) held an ill-structured set of beliefs about a debt crisis among sovereign states involved in a monetary union. The policy initially applied to the crisis—limited bailouts with strict austerity conditions—did not work to calm investors and did nothing to address the unique situations of the countries involved. A new policy was needed. Merkel, new to the problem and a person who learns by trial and error, demonstrated what scholars would call learning in the years 2009 to 2012.

## CHAPTER REVIEW

- Individual differences matter—individual leaders perceive international and domestic constraints differently based on their worldviews and beliefs.
- Leaders are engaged in a two-level game, and the nature of that game is interpreted by and filtered through the orientation of those leaders.
- The study of cognition is the study of how individuals perceive, reason, and judge issues before them.
- Cognitive scholars propose that it is possible to systematize our understanding of human cognition in order to develop insights that can be used for studying many different individuals in a variety of settings.
- A cognitive approach assumes that individuals are closed-minded and insensitive to new information.
- A belief set is a more-or-less integrated set of images held by an individual about a particular universe.
- Belief sets act as rigid screens, letting in information that fits established views and re-creating or keeping out information that is contradictory.
- Individuals are assumed to be cognitive misers who rely on shortcuts to understand new information.
- Learning is possible when individuals hold "ill-structured" beliefs on an issue and they are prompted to learn new information in response to a failure.

- Beliefs that are strongly supported by one's society and culture are rigid and unlikely to change.
- An attribution error is when an individual explains his or her own bad behavior (or that of his or her country) by blaming outside circumstances and events.
- Integrative complexity is the degree to which utterances are determined to involve more complicated contingency-based reasoning or less complicated absolutist reasoning.
- Operational codes describe individuals' philosophical and operational beliefs.
- Leadership trait analysis examines how leaders' emotional traits predispose them to certain kinds of action. Studies have demonstrated "aggressive" and "conciliatory" leadership personality types.

*Chapter Four*

# Decision Units, Small Groups, and Autonomous Groups

## IN THIS CHAPTER

- The Decision Units Framework
- Predominant Leader
- Decision Making within Single Groups
- Multiple Autonomous Actors and Bureaucratic Politics
- Chapter Review

## CASES FEATURED IN THIS CHAPTER

- The decision rules in and key members of Iran's top decision unit involved in formulating Iran's position on nuclear negotiations with the International Atomic Energy Agency and the West in 2007 and in 2012.
- The decision rules and decision units involved in Turkey's 1974 decision to intervene militarily in Cyprus.
- How the use of US military force is a decision constitutionally mandated to involve both the president and Congress, although in practice the president acts without restrictions or under broad congressional authorizations that after the 9/11 terrorist attacks have included the targeted killings of individuals who may not be "known" terrorists.

## THE DECISION UNITS FRAMEWORK

Who speaks for Iran? Who makes the decisions that put Iran on a course of confrontation with other states over its possible acquisition of nuclear weapons? Which voice coming from Iran counts the most when leaders and analysts in other countries try to predict what Iranian motivations and intentions are on the nuclear issue? Realists would answer that there are persistent Iranian national interests—say, to become a great power—and that individual persons sitting in particular positions in the Iranian government are all committed to those national interests. Cognitive scholars might want to use the speeches and actions of Iranian supreme leader, the Grand Ayatollah Ali Khamenei, to construct an operational code that would help outsiders understand Iran's pursuit of nuclear technology. These same scholars might want to take into account the beliefs of others in the government as well. Khamenei and other top political figures in Iran might have the same basic objective to make Iran a great power, but they might hold different opinions about how best to achieve that objective. Can the analyst safely conclude that the supreme leader's opinion is the one that matters? What if Khamenei stayed silent on certain foreign policy issues, deferring to publicly known as well as behind-the-scenes advisors to make policies?

If the foreign policy analyst hears different voices and opinions coming from Iran, the rational decision-making model cannot explain those differences. Similarly, the cognitive approach cannot tell the analyst whose worldview among many different worldviews controls Iranian foreign policy. Instead, the analyst needs to identify the ultimate decision maker in Iran and elaborate on how that ultimate decision maker operates. As Margaret Hermann and Charles Hermann explain,

> [recognizing] that numerous domestic and international factors can and do influence foreign policy behavior, these influences must be channeled through the political structure of a government that identifies, decides, and implements foreign policy. Within this structure is a set of authorities with the ability to commit the resources of the society and, with respect to a particular problem, the authority to make a decision that cannot be readily reversed. We call this set of authorities the "ultimate decision unit," even though in reality the unit may consist of multiple separate bodies rather than a single entity. It is our contention that the configuration and dynamics of such an ultimate decision unit help shape the substance of foreign policy behavior.[1]

Who speaks for Iran? Who is the **ultimate decision unit**? Power in Iran is split between different leadership roles and different elected and nonelected groups. Understanding who speaks for Iran means understanding the configuration of the ultimate decision unit and the decision-making rules governing conflict within that unit. In trying to do this, we need to avoid the mistake of assuming that foreign policy decision making in other countries occurs in the same institutional frame as our own. In Robert Jervis's "Hypotheses on Misperception," he cautions that the decision maker can make this fundamental and easy error because "experience with his own system will partly determine what the actor is familiar with and what he is apt to perceive in others."[2] As foreign policy analysts, we need to avoid this mistake and not assume that since our government works in a certain way, other governments work in the same way.

There are three basic decision units, according to Hermann and Hermann and others who have elaborated upon the approach: the single, predominant leader; the single group; and the group that is comprised of multiple autonomous units.

## PREDOMINANT LEADER

The predominant leader is a "single individual [who] has the power to make the choice and to stifle opposition."[3] Not all single, predominant leaders are the same, however, and so it is important to know whether "a leader's orientation to foreign affairs leads him [or her] to be relatively sensitive or insensitive to information from the political environment."[4] A sensitive predominant leader is likely to use diplomacy and cooperation, taking an incremental approach to action in order to stay tuned to feedback from the environment. An insensitive leader is not open to external influence, and so knowledge of his or her personality or operational code is important. Drawing upon cognitive studies, Hermann and Hermann explain that "if a leader's orientation suggests that he has a strongly held view of the world and uses his view as a lens through which to select and interpret incoming information, the leader is likely to be looking only for cues that confirm his beliefs when making foreign policy decisions. As a result, he will be relatively insensitive to discrepant advice and data."[5] This topic was discussed in the previous chapter.

## DECISION MAKING WITHIN SINGLE GROUPS

The single group is a "set of individuals, all of whom are members of a single body, [that] collectively select a course of action in face-to-face interaction."[6] This group may be as small as two people or "as large as a parliament of hundreds, so long as there is a collective, interactive decision process in which all the members who are needed to make authoritative commitments participate." The individuals in this single group must be able to "form or change their positions on a problem without outside consultation"; that is, the members of the single group are not bound by decisions made elsewhere and do not need to defend those decisions made elsewhere.[7] For instance, the group may be assembled from heads of departments, but for the particular problem at hand the group members do not represent their departments and do not need to answer to their departments for the decision made.

Although members do not represent departments, members of the single group may be open to external influences, especially information that is relevant to the group's decision. But the single group may also be self-contained (not open to outside information) and quick to reach consensus. Crucial to understanding decision making in the single group is understanding the "techniques used for managing conflict in the group" and the degree to which group loyalty is required.[8] Closed single groups that privilege group loyalty and suppress dissent are associated with the notion of **groupthink**.

Groupthink is a process described by Irving Janis.[9] Generally speaking, we associate groupthink with a distorted and failed policy process. It is important to note that this process develops out of certain group dynamics and is not a conscious process. However, people who study groupthink do think there are ways for groups to consciously avoid falling into groupthink. The small group that falls into groupthink puts the maintenance of the group and the loyalty of its members at the center of its purpose as a group, rather than focusing on the problem to be solved. The group self-monitors or self-polices to suppress nonconforming views from within and discounts information from outside sources that might challenge the group's judgment and inherent morality. Janis offers a list of ten antecedents that suggest when a situation of groupthink might arise, but of these, one antecedent is most important. As Janis explains, "only when a group of policymakers is moderately or highly cohesive can we expect the groupthink syndrome to emerge."[10] Groupthink typically is associated with policy failure because the decision-making group fails to critically assess all the relevant information on the problem at hand, settling on the perceived policy preference of the dominant leader in the group. The classic case of groupthink in American foreign policy study is the failed decision making around the Bay of Pigs fiasco.

Mark Schafer and Scott Crichlow agree that group cohesiveness is a critical antecedent to groupthink, but they find that leadership style and group procedures that privilege group cohesiveness are the most damaging preconditions for failed group decision making. The key to better decision making is to focus on eliminating the adverse antecedents *prior* to the time the group meets, they advise, because "by the time the group engages in information processing, it is generally too late to avoid faulty decision making."[11]

Charles Hermann, Janice Gross Stein, Bengt Sundelius, and Stephen Walker propose that groupthink is less a "syndrome" (with its negative implications) than a "premature closure around an initially advocated course of action."[12] "A group experiences premature closure when it accepts the option prominently presented, usually by an authoritative member, early in its deliberations without engaging in a serious evaluation of its potential limitations or understanding a careful comparison of it with any other possible alternatives."[13]

Hermann, Stein, Sundelius, and Walker see groupthink as one dynamic that produces a tendency to avoid group conflict and moves the group to quick concurrence. Some small-group processes, however, do not lead to concurrence but instead lead to unanimity (full resolution of group conflict), or to plurality (acceptance of group conflict). Group identity, rather than group cohesiveness, is the crucial variable for this research team in their study of small groups. A primary consideration for the analyst is whether group members have their primary identities in the small group or in their "home" departments or agencies. Hermann, Stein, Sundelius, and Walker create a decision tree that takes the researcher through different branches or permutations exploring the role of leaders, group members, and group decision-making norms. These branches lead to four possible decision types: the adoption of the dominant solution, a deadlocked solution, an integrative solution, and a subset solution. This decision tree is presented in figure 4.1. The reader will find it handy to consult figure 4.1 frequently in the following discussion.

The first point in this decision tree is to ask whether the members' primary identity lies with the group. If yes, then the second question is whether the leader suppresses dissent. If the answer is yes, the next question is whether the group norms reinforce the leader's suppression of dissent. If the answer is yes, then it is very likely that the dominant solution advocated by the leader will be selected. Alternatively, the answer to the second question—does the leader suppress dissent?—could be no. Then the researcher asks whether group norms discourage dissent. If the answer is no, then the question is does the group evaluate multiple options regarding the problem at hand? If no, then the dominant solution advocated by the leader is very likely to be chosen. If the group does evaluate multiple options, then it is likely that the group will choose an integrative solution.

If the answer to the first question is no—the members' primary identities are not with the group—then we take different branches in the tree. Following figure 4.1, the next question to ask is, do all members have the same initial preferences? If no, then do the decision rules require that all members agree? If no, is the group expected to meet again on other issues and continue as a group? If the answer is no, then is there a respected minority within the group that expresses intense preferences? If no, then it is likely that the solution will be one that reflects a subset of the group members' preferences.

This tree has a lot of branches, and perhaps some leaves (that is, real-world information) might help us evaluate its usefulness for case study. Let's continue with the problem posed at the start of this chapter: Who speaks for Iran? We'll rephrase this inquiry to ask who makes foreign policy decisions for Iran and how. The specific problem will be how to understand Iranian

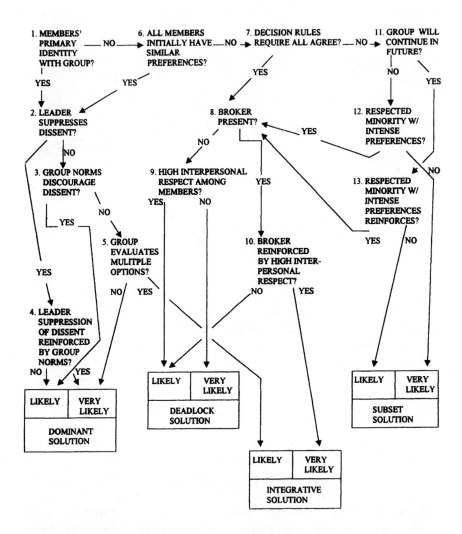

Figure 4.1. Decision Tree *Source:* This figure originally appeared as figure 2 in Charles F. Hermann et al., "Resolve, Accept, or Avoid: Effects of Group Conflict on Foreign Policy Decisions," *International Studies Review* 3, no. 2 (Summer 2001): 146. Used with permission of Wiley-Blackwell Publishers.

negotiations with the West or Iran's failure to negotiate with the West on matters of nuclear technology specifically related to nuclear weapons.

The International Atomic Energy Agency (IAEA) is the UN agency responsible for ensuring countries' compliance with the Treaty on the Non-Proliferation of Nuclear Weapons (NPT). The NPT essentially says that countries with nuclear weapons technology agree not to transfer that technology and countries without nuclear weapons technology agree not to acquire it. Iran is a signatory to the NPT and so has obligations under it. In 1983, the IAEA acknowledged that Iran had a right to acquire nuclear technology for civilian energy use, and Iran agreed to suspend its enrichment of uranium and allow IAEA verification inspections.

Jumping ahead two decades, the George W. Bush administration was convinced for various reasons that Iran was pursuing nuclear weapons technology; in the international commotion over the issue, Iran removed IAEA seals from its research plants. In 2006, Iranian leaders claimed Iran had succeeded in enriching uranium, and the Iranian president stated that Iran had a sovereign right to produce nuclear weapons. In response, the UN Security Council passed two resolutions calling on Iran to stop its enrichment activities and return to compliance with IAEA agreements. Limited sanctions were imposed to back the resolutions.

Iranian negotiators continued to talk with European Union (EU) negotiators during these tense years, but mutually acceptable agreements proved elusive. Despite the sanctions, Iranian leaders appeared prepared to compromise with the IAEA and the West until the summer of 2006. By the end of 2006, the Iranian position seemed to harden, making compromise unlikely.

Although it took longer than the Bush administration might have wanted, the Security Council passed another resolution in March 2007 (Resolution 1747) condemning Iran for its noncompliance with earlier resolutions and placing economic and other sanctions on Iran. By fall 2007, an apparent shake-up occurred in the top Iranian leadership, including the resignation of the lead nuclear negotiator. Meanwhile, the Bush administration kept beating the drums of war against Iran for its nuclear weapons ambitions and for its alleged support for insurgents in Iraq.

Did the hardening of the Iranian negotiating position signal changes in leadership? Can we even begin to understand what might be happening at the highest decision-making levels with only news accounts and a couple of expert analyses? We can try! Let's begin with a quick primer on the structure of and the personalities in the Iranian government circa 2007.

According to the Iranian constitution, there are elected and nonelected institutions in the government. The most powerful post is the unelected position of supreme leader. The supreme leader is chosen by the Assembly of Experts, an elected body composed of eighty-six religious officials. The Assembly of Experts has the power to monitor the supreme leader's performance, but generally the position is held for life (there have only been two supreme leaders since the Islamic Republic of Iran was founded in 1979). In the fall of 2007, the supreme leader was Ayatollah Ali Khamenei. The supreme leader controls the armed forces and all decision making on security, defense, and major foreign policy issues. The supreme leader also appoints half of the unelected Guardian Council, a body that must approve all legislation and must approve all candidates for the presidency and parliament.

Khamenei was a hard-line conservative who completely supported President Mahmoud Ahmadinejad in 2007, but Khamenei had also appointed opponents of Ahmadinejad to critical posts (more on this later). The International Crisis Group, a nongovernmental organization that monitors conflict in the world, calls Khamenei a balancer among different factions in the leadership.[14] Ray Takeyh, writing in *Foreign Affairs*, takes a different view that Khamenei was indecisive, with weak religious credentials that made him dependent on reactionaries like Ahmadinejad for support.[15] Both of these views will be accommodated in the discussion below.

The second most important position in Iran is the elected presidency. In 2007, the president was Mahmoud Ahmadinejad, a former mayor of Tehran, noncleric and hard-line conservative, who was elected to the presidency in 2005. Ahmadinejad was known for his threatening rhetoric, especially against Israel. Inside Iran, Ahmadinejad appeared to be close to Khamenei and the ultraconservative chair of the Guardian Council, Ayatollah Ahmad Janati. Additionally, Ahmadinejad had the support of the Islamic Revolutionary Guard Corps and awarded lucrative government contracts and positions to its officers to maintain that support. In terms of the nuclear issue, Ahmadinejad had never supported compromise with the IAEA or the EU negotiators. In December 2006, elections for municipal councils and the Assembly of Experts went against Ahmadinejad's faction in favor of the faction headed by the man who ran against Ahmadinejad for president in 2005 (more on this man soon).

The unelected institutions—the supreme leader, armed forces, judiciary, Expediency Council, and Guardian Council—would seem to have more power than the elected institutions—the presidency, cabinet, and parliament. The exception is the elected body of the Assembly of Experts. In September 2007, the Assembly of Experts elected as its chair former Iranian president Ali Akhbar Hashemi Rafsanjani, the man who lost the 2005 presidential elections to Ahmadinejad. Right after the 2005 elections, Khamenei had appointed Rafsanjani as the chair of the Expediency Council to check Ahmadinejad's power. When Rafsanjani was president of Iran (1989–1997), he had favored more cooperative negotiations with the West on the nuclear issue. He and his chief negotiator, Hassan Rowhani, were vocal critics of Ahmadinejad's uncompromising position regarding the West.[16] The position of chair of the Assembly of Experts is an extremely influential post, since the assembly chooses the supreme leader. A key ally of Rafsanjani and a protégé of Khamenei was Ali Larijani, the head of the Supreme National Security Council and outspoken opponent of Ahmadinejad. Until October 2007, Larijani was the chief nuclear negotiator for Iran but resigned and was replaced with a hard-line, relatively unknown supporter of Ahmadinejad's.

In this discussion so far, some of the key members of Khamenei's inner circle (presumably the decision-making circle) have been named: Ahmadinejad, Janati, Rafsanjani, and Larijani. Using open-source news reports, we might also include Ali Akbar Velayati, Khamenei's advisor on foreign affairs, who had made it clear that Ahmadinejad's rhetoric did not always represent the official government view. We might also include in the inner circle former nuclear negotiator Rowhani; General Mohammed Ali Jafari, the newly named head of the Revolutionary Guard (in September 2007); and Kamal Kharrazi, the foreign minister under the previous reformist president who served as chair of the relatively new Strategic Committee for Foreign Policy in late 2007.

For the most part, this list merely reflects news reports that mention key officeholders and advisors rather than any authoritative list. The top Iranian leadership is an opaque body. However, analysts agree that the most important leaders are in strong agreement on critical Iranian national interests and that they differ on how best to pursue these interests. Takeyh says that Iranian politics is dominated by the "new right."[17] The new right is split between two primary factions, the hard-line conservatives represented by Ahmadinejad, and the pragmatic conservatives represented by Rafsanjani and Larijani. The new right is in agreement that Iran is destined to be a great power while the United States is a declining great power. The new right is split over how best to facilitate Iran's rise—through taking a hard-line approach to the failing United States and West or through compromise and coexistence.[18] These two factions of the new right were inside Khamenei's inner decision-making circle.

Where did that inner decision-making circle stand on the issue of nuclear negotiations with the IAEA and West? If all we had to base our guess on was the October 2007 resignation of Larijani from the role as chief negotiator, we might conclude that the pragmatists had fallen out of favor and the hardliners controlled the policy. But the election of Rafsanjani to the chair of the Assembly of Experts suggests that the pragmatists were in an excellent power position, especially with Khamenei reported to be in such poor health. Perhaps the resignation of the pragmatist negotiator Larijani was Khamenei's way to give Ahmadinejad enough rope to hang himself (as the expression goes) since Ahmadinejad blamed Larijani for failed negotiations. Thus perhaps the hard-liners were out of favor. Alternatively, the situation might have been in a kind of stalemate. Takeyh concludes about that time period that the "supreme leader, who is generally prone to indecision, now seems disinclined to settle the internal debates in Tehran in a conclusive manner."[19] The West might have perceived a hard-line Iranian regime that refused to negotiate, but it might have been more accurate to see the regime as deadlocked. Hermann, Stein, Sundelius, and Walker's decision tree can be a very useful tool for examining this situation as of late 2007.

Using the decision tree in figure 4.1, we start our analysis with question 1: Do all the members of the small inner circle have their primary identity with the group? Although they all are conservatives, they are conservatives with very different views about how best to pursue Iranian national interests. Thus, the answer is "no."

This takes us to question 6: Do all members initially have similar preferences on how to conduct nuclear negotiations? The answer is emphatically "no." Question 7 then asks, do the decision rules of the group require that they all agree? From the speculations above, we would be safe to conclude that there are not rules that require unanimity. Indeed, if Khamenei imagined himself to be a balancer among different factions (and he did act as such with his appointments), then this suggests the absence of unanimity rules. The answer to question 7 is "no." This takes us to question 11: Will the group continue into the future? There appear to have been significant power shifts in the top leadership and with some important reshuffling at the next highest level of leadership in different institutions. It seems likely that this particular group would not continue into the future.

This takes us to question 12: Is there a respected minority with intense preferences in the group? Although close to Khamenei, Ahmadinejad's position is closer to a minority in the changing inner group. Smyth notes that in 2006 when the inner circle was willing to make greater compromises on the nuclear negotiations, Ahmadinejad already was in a minority position among the top leaders.[20] The municipal losses and the rise of Rafsanjani also point to Ahmadinejad's minority position. Yet his preferences regarding negotiating with the West are well known, and he still has the "respect" that comes with powerful allies elsewhere in the government (such as the Revolutionary Guard). The answer to question 12 would be "yes," taking us to question 8.

Is there a broker present who can mediate between views? On this question, a "yes" is just as plausible as a "no" answer, and either answer will eventually take us to the same place. Following the "yes" branch, we can say that Khamenei serves as a broker. This takes us to question 10: Is the broker reinforced by high interpersonal respect? The answer here is "no," since key members of the top decision-making circle have publicly criticized each other's stances. A "no" here means that a deadlock solution is likely.

Going back to question 8, which could be answered "yes" or "no," let's follow the "no" branch—"no," there is no broker because Khamenei was unable to balance the interests of the main factions. This takes us to question 9, which asks again whether there is high interpersonal respect among members of the group, and the answer here remains "no." This leads to the conclusion that deadlock is very likely.

Using what we have learned about Iran's highest decision-making group, the facts surrounding Iran's negotiations with the West on its nuclear program, and the small-group decision tree in figure 4.1, we arrive at the conclusion that many analysts have made: the top Iranian decision makers were deadlocked on how to proceed with the nuclear negotiations. From the outside, this may have looked like defiance and for some a cause for war. But a more judicious reading of this situation might be to understand the deadlock that Khamenei had set in place. If this assessment were correct, the United States might have attempted to strengthen the position of the pragmatists by offering some relief from the sanctions in order to reward the view that compromise and coexistence were the best foreign policy paths to follow. [21]

There was no compromise struck between the West and Iran during the Bush administration, nor during the first administration of Barack Obama. In his first inaugural address, Obama sent a message to countries like Iran about his administration's willingness to talk when he said, "We will extend a hand if you are willing to unclench your fist." But the Iranian government appeared to take a harder turn in the summer of 2009 when irregularities surrounding the Iranian national election brought protestors to the streets as part of the Green Movement. No talks resumed, and the United States and the European Union intensified their crippling sanctions on Iran. By October 2012, Iranian oil production was reduced to a thirty-two-year low and the value of the currency had dropped more than 50 percent. [22] In this same time period, Israeli prime minister Benjamin Netanyahu was pressuring the Obama administration to issue a red line to the Iranian government. Republicans in the United States reinforced this demand by invoking the image of hardliner Ahmadinejad and the unnamed "mullahs" in Iran. What these observers couldn't explain were the contemporaneous reports of Iranian offers to begin one-on-one talks with the United States on nuclear matters. [23]

What changes may have occurred within the top Iranian decision-making circle surrounding Khamenei? According to a Congressional Research Service report by Kenneth Katzman, the inner circle appeared to have changed dramatically after the 2009 uprisings. Khamenei himself assumed a more direct role over key decisions. [24] The changes culminated when Ahmadinejad's political faction suffered enormous electoral losses in the March 2012 Majles legislative elections. "Following the Majles elections, many experts concluded that the Supreme Leader had consolidated his authority and rendered Ahmadinejad virtually irrelevant in his final year in office." [25] The pragmatists appeared to be fully in charge. Two of the these pragmatists, Ali Larijani, the speaker of the strongly pro-Khamenei Majles, and Ali Akbar Velayati, Khamenei's foreign policy advisor, were particularly elevated in the inner circle, and in the fall of 2012 both were seen as likely 2013 presidential candidates. The readers of *The New Foreign Policy* will be able to assess whether Katzman was prescient when he says, "Some speculate that Velayati would be able to garner Khamenei's backing for a nuclear compromise with the international community were he to become president." [26]

Returning to the decision tree and figure 4.1, we can begin to understand why media reporting in the fall of 2012 about proposed Iranian-American talks were not too surprising at all. The first question in the tree asks if the people in the single group identify with the group. The answer would be "yes" because Khamenei had driven out the hard-liners in favor of conservative pragmatists who were his strongest supporters. Question 2 asks, does the leader suppress dissent? A safe answer (and one in line with the 2007 assessment) would be "no," so the next question is, do group norms discourage dissent, to which we could again answer "no." (Again, this is in line with the assessment regarding the 2007 inner circle.) This takes us to question 5: Does the group evaluate multiple options? Khamenei was still opposed to talking to the West and suspicious of all things Western, but he surrounded himself with pragmatists who saw no harm in talking with the West and who might convince Khamenei to agree to a nuclear compromise in time. This suggests that the group must have been open to a discussion of different options or no one would be able to convince Khamenei of anything. Thus, the answer to 5 is "yes." This answer takes us to the end point in which an integrative solution is likely. And so we might expect the inner circle as of late 2012 to be open to talking to the United States and the international community about nuclear matters. Such talks commenced in Kazakhstan in late February 2013.

## MULTIPLE AUTONOMOUS ACTORS AND BUREAUCRATIC POLITICS

The third decision unit in the framework proposed by Hermann and Hermann is a collection of multiple autonomous actors. In this unit, the "necessary actors are separate individuals, groups, or coalitions which, if some or all concur, can act for the government, but no one of which has the ability to decide and force compliance on the others; moreover, *no overarching authoritative body* exists in which all the necessary parties are members."[27] Within this unit,

> one actor can block another's initiatives by (1) using a formal, sometimes constitutionally defined, veto power; (2) threatening to terminate a ruling coalition by withdrawing from it or overthrowing it with force; (3) withholding part of the resources necessary for action or the approval needed for their use; or (4) initiating countermeasures that can seriously harm the other actors or their objectives.[28]

Complicating interactions within this decision unit is the problem that members of the coalition are "representatives of multiple autonomous actors [and thus] have no authority except as agents of their respective entities."[29] To understand this decision unit, we need to understand that the members are motivated to protect the interests of the groups they represent. To understand how this impacts the motivations of members of this unit, we need to turn briefly to the bureaucratic politics model, sometimes known as the organizational politics model. The basics of the model are explained in this way:

> Because most players participate in policymaking by virtue of their role, for example as secretary of the Treasury or the ambassador to the United Nations, it is quite natural that each feels special responsibility to call attention to the ramifications of an issue for his or her domain. . . . Because their preferences and beliefs are related to the different organizations they represent, their analyses yield conflicting recommendations.[30]

In such a system dominated by parochial interests, "government decisions and actions result from a political process."[31] The political process is dominated, as always, by a competition for resources. The competition for resources is "won" by the actor or group that dominates the discussion of policy choices in favor of its parochial interests. Winning this competition can become more important than solving the problem at hand; that is, "the domestic objectives of bureaucrats may be more significant than the international objectives of governments."[32] For the chief executive who awaits policy recommendations percolating up from different bureaucracies, he or she may find that the recommendations are limited and skewed because they are the result of political compromises that were reached among competing agencies to suit their own bureaucratic needs or ambitions.

In the multiple autonomous actors decision-making unit, the chief executive is one of many actors involved in the bargaining process that eventually results in a decision. Drawing from the single-group discussion above, we know that chief executives and others may play the role of broker among different interests in order to try to put together an integrative or subset solution. But, of course, at times the process may also tend to stalemate and deadlock. "Deadlocks result because (by definition) no entity has the capacity to act alone on behalf of the regime."[33]

An example of how this works would be useful here. Esra Çuhadar-Gürkaynak and Binnur Özkeçeci-Taner have used the decision unit framework to analyze Turkish foreign policy decision making during the Cyprus crisis of 1974.[34] Cyprus is a country that contains people of Turkish and Greek origin. When Cyprus became an independent country in 1960, a Treaty of Guarantee was signed between the interested parties of Great Britain, Turkey, and Greece, giving one or all the right to intervene should the independence of Cyprus be threatened by anyone. Upon independence, former Greek nationalists who had fought Great Britain for Cypriot independence turned their attention to Turkish Cypriots. Intercommunal violence broke out, and eventually a UN peacekeeping force was deployed to Cyprus in late 1964 to establish a buffer zone between the communities. Nationalist Greek Cypriots, encouraged by Greece, continued to push for Cypriot unification (enosis) with Greece. In 1974, those committed to enosis conducted a coup against the Cypriot power-sharing government and then announced that they would proceed to unification. Turkish authorities were faced with the problem of the Greek Cypriot coup, the threat to unite Cyprus with Turkey's enemy Greece, and the fate of the Turkish Cypriots if this unification occurred.

Çuhadar-Gürkaynak and Özkeçeci-Taner explain that three choices were considered by the Turkish leadership: (1) unilateral military intervention to stop the coup under the authority of the Treaty of Guarantee, (2) bilateral military intervention with the British under the Treaty of Guarantee, or (3) no military action out of concern for Greek or American reaction.[35] What was the nature of the decision unit grappling with this problem? Çuhadar-Gürkaynak and Özkeçeci-Taner rule out the single predominant leader. Prime Minister Bülent Ecevit "had neither the sole authority to commit the resources of the government during any occasion for decision, except at the implementation stage, nor were his decisions irreversible by another entity within the Turkish political system."[36] Further, no single group qualified as the authoritative decision unit since any decision to use the military had to be formally approved by the Turkish senate and agreed to by the National Security Council representing the military. Thus, the decision unit was a coalition of multiple autonomous actors.[37]

Having identified the decision unit, the analyst must determine the decision rules within the unit. By the Turkish constitution in place in 1974 and by established rules and practice, a majority decision was permitted.[38] Members of the coalition held different views about the proper response to the Cypriot coup. Prime Minister Ecevit had a strong preference for bilateral military intervention working with Great Britain. If Britain would not act, then Ecevit preferred unilateral intervention. Çuhadar-Gürkaynak and Özkeçeci-Taner conclude that Ecevit convinced the military and other members of the coalition that a military response could be successful, thereby brokering a majority of actors in favor of intervention. In the coalition, there may be several actors engaging in the broker role; in this case the foreign minister also worked to create a majority in favor of Ecevit's preferences. Ultimately Britain refused to intervene, and so Turkey intervened unilaterally. This caused the Cypriot coup to fail. Turkish forces remained in Cyprus, in time assisting in the creation of a Turkish Republic that no state recognized except Turkey.

Under the constitutional arrangement in Turkey at the time, the National Security Council did not act as an equal member of the multiple autonomous groups decision unit. The National Security Council, a council then dominated by the military chiefs, held virtual veto power over all other political actors. Constitutional reforms made in 2003 modified this power by making the National Security Council a largely consultative body whose membership was altered to include more civilian and fewer military voices. The reason for this change was in part driven by the European Union, a body that would not begin membership discussions with Turkey while the military held virtual veto power over the civilian government.

We can see another example of the multiple autonomous actors decision unit in the war powers authorized by the US Constitution. The power to declare war, to raise and support an army and naval forces, and to tax to fund a war are held by Congress, while the president is given the power of commander in chief of the armed forces, and the military services are organized under the executive branch. This division of powers over the use of force was intended to make such use a shared responsibility that could not be entered into easily and without proper consultation between Congress and the president. However, despite the constitutional arrangement, the use of force generally has not been a shared activity of Congress and the president. As the *New York Times* reports, "presidents have dispatched forces abroad between 120 and 200 times, but Congress has only formally declared war on five occasions: the War of 1812, the Spanish-American War, the Mexican-American war and the two World Wars."[39]

Should we, then, understand that the US president acts unconstitutionally when using force abroad? There are plenty of observers who would say yes, but Congress can still exercise its power within the ultimate decision unit by "withholding part of the resources necessary for action"[40] should Congress decide that the president has overstepped his or her authority.

Sometimes Congress offers the president the authority to conduct what is for all practical purposes a war without a declaration of war, but in doing this there is the implicit acknowledgement that Congress may change its mind and reassert its authority. In August 1964, Congress passed the Gulf of Tonkin Resolution, which gave the president the authority to take all necessary measures to defend US forces and to assist state members of the Southeast Asia Collective Defense Treaty. This resolution was used as the basis for full-scale US military action in Vietnam. The war in Vietnam was always controversial, and Congress began trying to repeal the Gulf of Tonkin resolution within a few years of its passage. In 1971, Congress repealed the resolution, but then-president Richard Nixon determined that he was the ultimate decision maker acting as commander in chief to protect US troops in Southeast Asia. Congress responded with the War Powers Act of 1973, an act that was sustained even in the face of a presidential veto.

The War Powers Act was designed to limit the presidential use of forces abroad by putting a time limit on such use without congressional approval. The president can deploy US forces abroad into combat for sixty days, but then Congress must authorize the continued use of those forces. If Congress doesn't authorize the continued use of force, the president may use the troops for thirty more days, but then presumably the troops must be withdrawn from the combat area. Nixon and every president since argued that the War Powers

Act was an unconstitutional restriction on presidential authority as commander in chief. Whether one agrees with this or not, Congress may still provide the president with nearly unlimited authority for the use of force abroad if it so chooses. Members of the multiple autonomous groups decision unit need *not* exercise their separate decision authority within the group, while still retaining that authority for a later time.

How far might a US president go in the use of force abroad without a formal congressional war declaration? This is a question that was asked of the George W. Bush presidency in the wake of the 9/11 terrorist attacks and then of the Barack Obama presidency in the ongoing US war against terrorist groups. On September 14, 2001, the US Congress authorized the president to take all necessary measures against those nations, organizations, and persons determined to have been behind the terrorist attacks *and to prevent all future attacks*. Congress noted that the authorization was fully consistent with the War Powers Act. The Bush administration read this authorization liberally, and some of the national reaction/backlash to Bush's activities created the momentum that contributed to the 2008 election of Barack Obama. But Congress did not act to limit Bush's expansive reading of the September 14, 2001, authorization.

Despite the political differences between Bush and Obama, many Bush administration policies regarding the war on terror continued under the Obama administration. One Bush administration practice that was intensified under Obama was the use of unmanned aerial vehicles or drones for the purposes of targeted killings of persons associated with terrorism. Initially, the Obama administration targeted known al Qaeda leaders using drone attacks and sometimes using special forces, but then the administration started expanding the use of drones to attack militants or suspected militants who were engaged in conflicts against the government forces of Pakistan or Yemen. As Scott Shane reports in the *New York Times*, the administration had gone beyond so-called personality strikes against named terrorists to "signature strikes" against unknown persons, especially males of sufficient age as to be potential militants in areas "controlled by extremist groups."[41] The Obama administration contended that these killings were permissible under the September 14, 2001, authorization and did not constitute a violation of a presidential ban on assassinations. More than a decade after the 9/11 attacks, the US presidency was using unrestricted force in the form of targeted killings against people abroad—including American citizens—whether those people were known terrorists or not without incurring congressional restrictions or threats of restrictions.

The US Congress has not been silent on the use of all armed force by the Obama administration. In March 2011, a coalition of forces including the United States began an air campaign in support of rebels against the Libyan government of Muammar Qaddafi. The president did not request authorization for American participation in this intervention. In a highly contentious partisan atmosphere, the Republican-controlled House of Representatives passed a resolution in June declaring that the president had missed the sixty-day request for authorization as per the War Powers Act and defeated a resolution that would have approved US military involvement in the Libyan campaign for a year. Obama's view was that the US air campaign did not rise to the level of hostilities covered by the act, and so the president did not need congressional approval. A Republican measure to cut funding for American participation in the Libyan air campaign was also defeated. The episode shows how within the American constitutional structure the decision to use military force must be authorized by multiple autonomous groups, but that one of those groups might pick and choose when to exercise its constitutional authority.

## CHAPTER REVIEW

- The ultimate decision unit is the authority or set of authorities with the ability to commit the resources of the state.
- The ultimate decision unit may be composed of a single predominant leader, a single group, or multiple autonomous groups.
- Groupthink is a dynamic in which members of a single group attempt to avoid group conflict before all else.
- In decision unit analysis, a key issue is whether the group's norms discourage dissent or open discussion.
- In decision unit analysis, individuals may play the role of broker to forge a compromise solution.
- Despite constitutional requirements that certain foreign policy decisions be the joint product of multiple autonomous groups, some of those groups may decide to ignore the authority of the others in the group or give expansive authority to others in the group.

*Chapter Five*

# National Self-Image, Culture, and Domestic Institutions

## IN THIS CHAPTER

- Similar Countries but Different Foreign Policies?
- Rosenau's Ideal Nation-Types
- National Self-Image
- Culture and Institutions of Governance
- Culture, Institutions, and the Democratic Peace
- Chapter Review

## CASES FEATURED IN THIS CHAPTER

- The similar characteristics but different foreign policies of Denmark and the Netherlands.
- Serbian and Soviet siege mentality and how this national characteristic leads to expectations about relations with other countries.
- The disagreement in Israel over who should serve in the military and how the most hawkish Israeli Jews have been exempted from defending the country.
- Swiss neutrality policy that is a manifestation of distrust of the outside world and how this contributes to a nonprovocative defense posture.
- Japan's antimilitaristic political culture and Peace Constitution and the nationalist challenges to these.
- Germany's antimilitaristic political culture and how contemporary interpretations of German collective memory have allowed German leaders to make selective use of military force abroad.

SIMILAR COUNTRIES BUT DIFFERENT FOREIGN POLICIES?

Denmark and the Netherlands are two small European countries situated on the northwestern coast of the continent. Both have approximately the same amount of territory, although the Netherlands has three times the population of Denmark. Both are founding members of the United Nations and the North Atlantic Treaty Organization (NATO), and both are members of the European Union (EU). Finally, both are parliamentary democracies.

Despite their similarities, there is a difference between the two countries that some scholars have attributed to a difference in **national self-image**. For example, in a cross-national study that included Denmark, Ulf Hedetoft depicts the Danes as being "peaceful nationalists"[1] who are somewhat disdainful of countries whose nationalism is bolstered by war. Instead,

> political defeats in war(like) situations have regularly been used to boost the country's cultural nationalism and the reputed "homogeneity" between state and people. This anomaly is based on three distinctive criteria: Denmark is small; Denmark is not the aggressor; Denmark has survived.[2]

Hedetoft writes that, in sport as in war, the Danes hold a different view of themselves when compared to others: "The UK has its violent, racist 'hooligans'; [Germany] has its often intimidating 'Schlachtenbummler' (soccer rowdies); but Denmark takes pride in its 'roligans,' i.e., 'peaceful supporters,' and laps up the international praise it can collect on that account."[3]

Internationally, the Danes contribute substantially to UN peacekeeping in line with the notion of "peaceful supporters," but as a people they tend to be reluctant to cooperate too quickly with others. The Danes are famous for the "no" vote they cast on the Maastricht Treaty on the European Union in June 1992. The Maastricht Treaty was the plan for the broadening of the European Community into the European Union—a monetary and economic union that gives citizens of each member state European citizenship and ushered in the single European currency, the euro, among other things. In order for the European Union to go forward, voters in each of the member states needed to approve it. When the Danes took a vote on union, they initially voted "no," demonstrating their reluctance to jump onto any bandwagon, no matter how carefully planned. In May 1993, the Danes took another vote and this time agreed to the union on the promise that Denmark would be exempted from certain expectations in the new European Union.

The Dutch could also be considered "peaceful supporters" of the international system, but there is no reluctance on their part to participate. The Netherlands is a country that takes the lead in the writing and promotion of international law. The Hague has been the long-standing home of the International Court of Justice and, since 1993, has been the site of the International

Criminal Tribunal for the Former Yugoslavia (ICTY). What is especially remarkable is that the Dutch people have paid most of the costs of the ICTY since its inception. The Hague is also home to the International Criminal Court (ICC), established formally in July 2002.

Peter Baehr asserts that the Netherlands is a country unusually committed to the rule of law internationally, and to human rights law particularly, because of the combination of system-level factors and national self-image. On the system level, the Netherlands always has been dependent on international trade, and the development of international law was crucial to protecting the interests of a trading state. In terms of national self-image, the Dutch as a people believe they must "do some good" in the world, a belief that derives from their religious heritage.[4] This combination of national interest and national self-image creates an interesting domestic political arena where all the major political parties stand committed to an activist human rights policy. Because of this widespread agreement, the details of such policy are left to the Foreign Ministry. By law and practice, Foreign Ministry officials work side by side with human rights nongovernmental organizations (NGOs) to plan and execute Dutch human rights foreign policy.

To understand how the Netherlands came to be called the international legal capital of the world or to understand why Denmark voted "no" initially on Maastricht, we need to go "inside" each country to explore the dynamics at play within each. A more complete understanding of these phenomena would require us also to examine where each country "sits" in the world (in terms of the power hierarchy of states) and its relations with other countries (i.e., system-level factors explored in later chapters), but an examination of the inner workings of each country can yield interesting insights into how and why these countries follow the distinct foreign policies that they do.

Foreign policy study that proceeds from the state level of analysis involves examining different features of a country to see which of those factors shape its foreign policy. At this level of analysis, we include leaders and leadership as important factors, but we add into the mix the country-specific context. This level of analysis is the one that most directly borrows from the insights of comparative politics and regional area specialists. The focus here is that what goes on within states has an impact on what goes on between states.

There are two broad categories of factors that we examine at the state level: governmental and societal. Governmental factors include the type of political system and its constitutional framework, the type of regime that sits atop the government, how decisions are made in different parts of government from the highest levels to the basic bureaucratic level, the division of powers and authority between government institutions, bureaucratic in-fighting among government agencies, and the size and institutionalization of bureaucracies. Societal factors include the type of economic system; the history of the people(s) in the country; the ethnic, racial, and religious mix of the people; the number and activities of interest groups and political parties; and the role of the media in setting the public agenda. These two categories are not exclusive; for instance, it would prove informative in some cases to study state–society relations, the lobbying of government officeholders by interest groups, and the mobilization of **public opinion** by national leaders.

## ROSENAU'S IDEAL NATION-TYPES

There have been some serious efforts to develop midrange theories of foreign policy at the state level of analysis, and some of these go back to the beginning of the field. In his foundational work (the "pre-theories" article discussed in chapter 1), James Rosenau hypothesized that three national attributes taken together influence foreign policy choice and behavior: size (large or small as measured by population), economic system (developed or underdeveloped as measured by gross national product), and political system (open or closed as measured by whether the country is democratic or not). Rosenau proposed that these factors could be grouped into eight configurations or "ideal nation-types."[5]

Rosenau's primary focus was to develop a typology for ranking variables from many levels of analysis according to what he proposed to be the relative importance of each in the foreign-policy-making process of the eight nation-types. Rosenau hypothesized that foreign policy making for each nation-type would be best studied at particular levels of analysis and not at others. For instance, a highly developed, closed society would have very little societal influence on foreign policy decision making because the "closed" nature of the society meant that **civil society** actors were not permitted to operate or be involved in the policy-making process. The following is a list of Rosenau's eight nation-types, his examples of each, and a ranked list of which level of analysis he hypothesized would be most important to study for each nation-type.

1. Large, developed, open; example: United States; key levels of analysis: role, societal, governmental, systemic, individual.
2. Large, developed, closed; example: Soviet Union; key levels of analysis: role, individual, governmental, systemic, societal.
3. Large, underdeveloped, open; example: India; key levels of analysis: individual, role, societal, systemic, governmental.
4. Large, underdeveloped, closed; example: China; key levels of analysis: individual, role, governmental, systemic, societal.
5. Small, developed, open; example: Netherlands; key levels of analysis: role, systemic, societal, governmental, individual.

6. Small, developed, closed; example: Czechoslovakia; key levels of analysis: role, systemic, individual, governmental, societal.
7. Small, underdeveloped, open; example: Kenya; key levels of analysis: individual, systemic, role, societal, governmental.
8. Small, underdeveloped, closed; example: Ghana; key levels of analysis: individual, systemic, role, governmental, societal.

Rosenau wrote his "pre-theories" article in the mid-1960s, and so some of his examples do not make sense in this new millennium. For instance, the Soviet Union and Czechoslovakia no longer exist, while India and China have large economies in 2013.

The purpose of the "pre-theories" article was to sound a call to action (really, a call to research) for foreign policy scholars. Rosenau didn't know whether these nation-types were accurate, nor did he know whether the ranked levels of analysis he listed for each were accurate. Hypotheses are guesses about reality based on the analyst's existing understanding of that reality. After the hypotheses are constructed, the analyst then explores the evidence to find proof that the hypotheses might be correct or might not be correct. Rosenau hypothesized or guessed that countries could be categorized usefully by size, economic system, and political system, but he didn't know this to be the case. Rosenau hypothesized or guessed that some levels of analysis were more important than others given a country's type, but he didn't know this to be the case either. He was sounding a call to other scholars about where they might begin to engage in a broad and collaborative research effort.

With Rosenau's hypotheses as launching pads, scholars could begin a systematic search for pieces of knowledge that could be used both for grounding future research as well as for building generalized theory around which the scientific study of comparative foreign policy could coalesce.

> The concept of nation-type [made] it unnecessary to examine individual nations in considering the certain types of foreign policy activity. To this extent, [scholars could] move away from analysis of discrete objects and concentrate on classes of objects and the different patterns of foreign policy associated with each.[6]

That is, ideal nation-types were conceived as tools for facilitating the development of general statements linking state type and foreign policy behavior. If we knew that a country was a certain type of state, then we would benefit from previous research that had connected certain kinds of foreign policy behavior with that type of state. The more evidence generated that a country of type A was most likely to engage in behavior B under certain conditions, the more certain we could be that we had discovered a "law" of foreign policy.

Upon Rosenau's call, other researchers started searching for statistical evidence to support the proposition that physical size, economic development, and political accountability were significant in explaining the variation in states' foreign policy behaviors. Maurice East and Charles Hermann were among a group of scholars directly inspired by Rosenau's "pre-theories." East and Hermann constructed and used the Comparative Research on the Events of Nations (CREON) data set to test twenty-seven bivariate hypotheses linking size, economic development, and political accountability with nine foreign policy behaviors. Of the single indicators, East and Hermann concluded that physical size best accounted for behavior. The next most important indicator was political accountability, especially when combined with economic development.[7] On the other hand, they were unable to find much support for Rosenau's ideal nation-types. That is, "large, developed, open" states did not engage in foreign policy behaviors that were distinctive from, say, the behaviors of "small, developed, open" or "small, underdeveloped, closed" states. Indeed, researchers found little evidence that Rosenau's ideal nation-types were useful categories.

Although Rosenau's ideal nation-types were not shown by research efforts to be linked to specific foreign policy behaviors, the idea that particular kinds of states engaged in particular foreign policies was not put to rest. Researchers have attempted to rank states on combinations of national indicators that suggest something about the degree to which states are penetrated by and successful at globalization,[8] are failing or have failed as states,[9] or create and sustain peace.[10]

It is worth taking a moment to look at one of these. The Global Peace Index (GPI) is produced by the Institute for Economics and Peace, an independent research organization, with the collaboration of the *Economist* Intelligence Unit. The first GPI was released in 2007. The 2012 index was presented as a measure of 158 states' peacefulness based on twenty-three indicators. The indicators were grouped into three categories: those that measured the state's involvement in domestic and international conflict (such as the numbers of deaths from internal and external conflict, and relations with neighboring countries), those that measured the state's societal safety and security (such as the perceived criminality in society, terrorist acts, and homicides), and those that indicated the degree of militarization in the state (such as military spending, number of armed services personnel, and transfer of major conventional weapons).[11] The use of twenty-three indicators makes this index much more sophisticated than Rosenau's nation-types, but Rosenau proposed his typology at a time when there was much less available and reliable data on a large number of states.

According to the GPI, 2012 was more peaceful than the years 2010 and 2011, reflecting some stabilization of states after the global financial crisis that hit in 2008.[12] The ten most peaceful states in 2012 were, from most peaceful to tenth most peaceful: Iceland, Denmark, New Zealand, Canada, Japan, Austria, Ireland, Slovenia, Finland, and Switzerland. The ten least peaceful states, listed from number 149 to 158 (least peaceful), were Pakistan, Israel, the Central African Republic, North Korea, Russia, the Democratic Republic of the Congo, Iraq, Sudan, Afghanistan, and Somalia. The countries most responsible for international peace and security—the permanent members of the Security Council—were a mixed bunch with Russia ranked 153, China ranked 89, the United States ranked 88, France ranked 40, and the United Kingdom ranked 29.[13]

Among the top twenty countries on the GPI for 2012 were seventeen Western democracies. This finding supports one of the more enduring research hypotheses linking state type and foreign policy behavior: the **democratic peace** theory. The democratic peace theory proposes that a democratic country's culture and the resulting political institutions make the country more likely than not to engage in peaceful foreign policy behaviors, especially toward other democratic countries. To get to this theory (discussed at the end of this chapter and the beginning of chapter 6), we first need to consider the impact of a country's self-image and culture on its foreign policy.

## NATIONAL SELF-IMAGE

National self-images "consist, at least in part, of idealized stereotypes of the 'in-nation' which are culturally shared and perpetuated."[14] The Dutch view that their country should "do some good" in the world is a manifestation of aspects of the Dutch self-image that comes out of a common sense of history, religious imperative, and social obligation. As suggested earlier, Baehr attributes the substantial strength and depth of Dutch commitment to an international legal system in part to this Dutch national self-image.

A national self-image is basically the story a people in a country tell about who they are as a people, who their country "is" in the world, and what their country does in the world. The national story—or dominant national narrative—can be found in the official history of the country (as spread by schools and religious institutions and supported by national holidays), is present in the national culture (as seen and reinforced by media of all sorts), and can be discerned in public opinion polling among other methods.

That a national self-image can be called a "dominant" cultural narrative indicates that alternative or subnational narratives may also exist in a country. Subnational narratives tell a different story about the subnational group's struggle against the dominant group and its narrative, just as the dominant group may "other-ize" subnational groups. Indeed, arguments over what the "nation" is, or who composes the nation, are linked to disagreements about the story of the nation and how other people might or might not fit into that story.

For example, consider what happened after the French national team didn't win a single match in the 2012 World Cup. Some critics of the team concluded that its terrible performance was because the individuals on the team weren't sufficiently nationalistic and so failed to play like a team.[15] The team was multiethnic, and the failure of the team was blamed on the failure of the ethnic minorities on the team—and in the country more generally—to assimilate as Frenchmen. The education minister complained on television about how the captain of the team didn't even sing the national anthem, "The Marseillaise." A French sports historian concluded that "France is confused about its identity and uncomfortable with the growing numbers and sometimes the attitudes of its immigrants and their children."[16]

Whether the in-group is comprised of the people within a country and the out-groups are the people in other countries, or there is an internal divide between the dominant and subordinate groups within a single country, the development of a positive in-group self-image depends upon this in-and-out dichotomy. A group is not a group unless it has boundaries that set it apart from other groups. Whether in domestic politics or in foreign affairs, this means that competition is intentionally built into the promotion of a group identity.[17] In the domestic political realm, my group must compete against yours for limited resources. In the international system, this competition pits my state against your state. Further, the in-group/out-group distinction is embedded with subjective claims about the goodness of the in-group and the bad nature of the out-group to distinguish why the in-group deserves the limited resources more than the out-group does.

A country without subnational competition over who gets to define the "nation" and in which a significant number of people share and support a positive national self-image should be a country with significant societal stability and tranquility. Positive national self-image, thus understood, can contribute to stable governance. As Matthew Hirshberg writes,

> The maintenance of a positive national self-image is crucial to continued public acquiescence and support for government, and thus to the smooth, on-going functioning of the state. . . . This allows government to go about its business, safe from significant internal dissension, and to expect a healthy level of public support in times of crisis.[18]

Positive national self-image also may impair the ability of the people to hold its government accountable. Recall from chapter 3 in the discussion of cognition that a belief set functions as a screen to keep out information that is incongruent with an individual's established beliefs. National self-image can be understood as a national belief set, and the national belief set also may screen out information that is incompatible with a positive national self-image. This was demonstrated by Matthew Hirshberg when he tested the hypothesis that a positive, patriotic self-image interferes with Americans' ability to keep watch over the government's foreign policy behaviors. Hirshberg's subjects were only able to recall details of fictional news stories that featured the United States doing stereotypically good things, and his subjects re-created the details of news stories that featured the United States doing bad things (such as supporting nondemocratic governments against prodemocracy dissenters) in order to select out the negative information about the United States. Hirshberg claims that his findings show that "Americans rarely interpret or remember things in . . . ways that threaten their patriotic self-image." As a result, he concludes,

> Even if American news consisted equally of information consistent and inconsistent with this [patriotic American] stereotype, Americans would, at least in the short term, tend to find its confirmation in the news. The stereotype interferes with information otherwise capable of cuing alternative perspectives. This increases popular support for military interventions that are or can be viewed as instances of a benevolent America protecting freedom and democracy from a perceived threat, such as communism. It also allows politicians and officials to elicit such support by promoting the application of the stereotype to specific conflicts.[19]

The danger in this, Hirshberg warns, is that "in the end, citizens' abilities to critically monitor and evaluate American foreign policy [are] impaired, and the ability of government to pursue unsavory policies with impunity is enhanced."[20]

National self-image contains a subjective message (implicit or explicit) about those outside the nation—our nation is good, therefore other nations are not (as) good. This mirror image is usually accompanied by what we call an attribution bias (as discussed in chapter 3): our country does good things because we are good people, but if we do bad things it is because we were forced to do so. Conversely, a bad country does bad things because it is in its nature to be bad. Given this understanding of us and them, we need to be constantly vigilant about outsiders and their intentions. Studies of siege mentality, such as Daniel Bar-Tal and Dikla Antebi's study of Israeli siege mentality, suggest that governments are given permission to conduct aggressive, preemptive foreign policies in order to protect the good nation from the actions of evil nations. Bar-Tal and Antebi define **siege mentality** as "a mental state in which members of a group hold a central belief that the rest of the world has highly negative *behavioral* intentions toward them." This culturally shared and perpetuated belief is complemented by the belief that the group is alone in the world, that it cannot expect help in times of crisis from anyone, and that therefore "all means are justified for group defense."[21] Siege mentality is not a group-shared paranoia; paranoia is an unfounded fear of others, whereas a historical, evidentiary basis exists for siege mentality.

Yugoslavia in the postcommunist era is an excellent example of a country manifesting strong elements of siege mentality. The former Yugoslavian president Slobodan Milosevic manipulated historical examples of Croatian and Turkish or Muslim attacks on the Serbian nation to foster a strong and particularly aggressive modern Serbian nationalism. Milosevic used this nationalism to wage war on Croatia and then Bosnia in the early 1990s toward the goal of creating a greater Serbia. When Milosevic turned Serbian nationalism on the ethnic Albanian people of the Yugoslavian province of Kosovo in early 1998, his Serbian forces managed to displace or kill a third of the total population in a matter of weeks. This prompted nearly two months of NATO air strikes against Serbia, which only reinforced Serbian siege mentality and nationalism. These air strikes came on the heels of nearly a decade of international economic sanctions against Yugoslavia. Ultimately Milosevic was forced from power through elections and a "people's revolution," but the new Serbian leaders demonstrated the same suspicion of the intentions of the outside world. Countries exhibiting high degrees of siege mentality require careful handling by the outside world in order not to cue automatic distrust and noncooperation. Bringing Yugoslavia back into the community of states will take time and patience given the intensity of Serbian nationalism and siege mentality during the 1990s.

The leaders of the former Soviet Union displayed siege mentality when they viewed their country as a "besieged fortress" in the 1950s. There was clear cause for suspicion about the intentions of other countries. By 1955, the United States had managed to form military alliances with a series of countries that, taken altogether, nearly encircled the Soviet Union and communist China. Present-day, post-Soviet Russia appears to have retained this suspicion about the outside world, even as it struggles with an age-old identity conflict over whether it is essentially a European country or a uniquely Slavic country. A conflicted national self-image results in a conflicted, sometimes contradictory foreign policy as competing tendencies vie for control over who and what defines the nation.

## CULTURE AND INSTITUTIONS OF GOVERNANCE

A culturally maintained national self-image sets the stage for the institutions of governance built by the in-group to promote the group's interests. It should be intuitive to say that a people's culture will influence the shape and type of its political structures when that people is self-governing. For example, once we have found that a country exhibits high degrees of siege mentality, it should come as no surprise to find mandatory, universal military conscription. The urgent need to protect the in-group results in the practical need for a strong and ready military. The need for a strong military necessitates conscription.

In Israel, Jews (and Druse) must serve in the military—men for thirty-six months and women for twenty-one months. The state of Israel was founded to protect and promote the Jewish nation, and the "people's army" with mandatory military service was seen as critical to this. However, not all Jews are required to serve in the military. Since its founding, Israel has exempted ultra-Orthodox Jews from the draft. Ultra-Orthodox political parties formed in order to promote and maintain this exemption, although these parties also tend to be hawkish about national security threats. (Bar-Tal and Antebi find that more religious Israeli Jews demonstrate more siege mentality than secular Israeli Jews.[22]) In 2012, the Israeli Supreme Court ruled this exemption illegal, but the negotiations over how to replace the conscription law—and require service of ultra-Orthodox Jews—threatened the continuation of the **coalition government** of Benjamin Netanyahu.[23] Thus, we might conclude that most Israelis share the belief that because of the urgent need to protect Israel, there must be a draft, but those with the strongest attitudes about the need to protect the Jewish nation wish to continue to exempt themselves from the burden of national defense. As many Israelis have noted, the issue of national military service had become a significant problem for Israeli national identity.[24]

Switzerland's well-known image as a neutral country contains similar elements of distrust of out-groups. **Neutrality** is the stance that the country will not take sides in international disputes or form military alliances of any sort. Switzerland's neutrality policy doesn't come out of a peaceful orientation to the world, just a clear preference not to take sides in an often war-torn and divided Europe. Indeed, we might argue that Switzerland is neutral because the Swiss hold a generalized lack of trust in outsiders, and this belief results in a shared and long-standing agreement among the Swiss about the need for maintaining defense preparations even in the absence of external threats. Thus, Swiss men between nineteen and twenty years of age must perform fifteen weeks of active military duty, followed by ten three-week reservist training periods over the subsequent twenty-two years.

Neutral Switzerland is a country with a **nonprovocative defense** posture. Geoffrey Wiseman describes Switzerland's policy as "deterrence by denial" by which Switzerland would "deter attack by setting a high price for invasion."[25] Wiseman explains,

> In the event of an external armed attack, the armed forces would assume the major role in defending the country. . . . Should large parts of Switzerland

become occupied, citizens would carry out activities ranging from guerilla warfare to sabotage and civil disobedience. No form of retaliation or punitive action against the adversary's population is planned. Switzerland would rely heavily on passive defenses, such as obstacles against tanks, anti-aircraft missiles, and early-warning radar systems.

Undoubtedly, these military preparations are manifestly defensive. Switzerland seeks only to defend its territory, it does not threaten others, and will not fight unless attacked. [26]

Japan and Germany are countries whose post–World War II national self-image was intentionally altered in order to create states that would no longer pose a military threat to others. In both cases, the national culture adopted an antimilitaristic orientation reinforced by constitutional arrangements. In both cases recently, elites wanting to expand the range of foreign policy options for their countries had to attempt to navigate both the cultural and constitutional prohibitions against the deployment of military personnel abroad.

As a result of losing World War II, Japan and Germany were forced into nonprovocative defense postures. [27] Military arsenals that are said to be for defense can often be easily transformed into offensive capabilities. Military arsenals and preparations that can only be used to protect national territory, or that can only be converted into offensive capabilities with much difficulty, are considered to be "defensive defense" or nonprovocative defense. The transparency of one's capabilities is critical to this posture for reassuring other countries. The idea is that if others know—can see and verify—that you cannot attack them, they won't attack you.

Japan and Germany assumed antimilitaristic national self-images and nonprovocative defense postures as the price of losing World War II. Of course, each country is different, and neither Japan nor Germany looks like Switzerland or each other on the matter of defensive postures or military capabilities. Indeed, both Japan and Germany have considerable military capabilities, and leaders in both countries have been attempting to move away from strict antimilitarism to more active, "normal" foreign policies that make use of all types of power, including military power.

Japanese defense is built on three pillars: its military alliance with the United States, its membership in the United Nations, and its Peace Constitution. Chapter II, Article 9 of the Japanese Peace Constitution reads,

> Aspiring sincerely to an international peace based on justice and order, the Japanese people forever renounce war as a sovereign right of the nation and the threat or use of force as means of settling international disputes.
>
> In order to accomplish the aim of the preceding paragraph, land, sea, and air forces, as well as other war potential, will never be maintained. The right of belligerency of the state will not be recognized.

Japanese nationalism since 1945 until the present has been channeled into the pursuit of economic security, especially the goal of reducing reliance on imported raw materials through the development of "technological autonomy."[28] Two dominant cultural norms—antimilitarism and economic nationalism—informed and reinforced the institutions of governance as well as defined what the Japanese perceived as appropriate foreign policy behavior. For instance, on the issue of human rights, the Japanese believed that they were in no position to preach to others given their militaristic past, opting instead to pursue straightforward, nonpolitical economic goals in bilateral relations, especially in Asia.[29]

As might be expected, the Japanese government agencies in charge of pursuing economic security were given more real power and authority than those tasked with military defense. What is surprising is the degree to which this was the case. The three most powerful state institutions—and the ones with essential control of national security policy—are the Ministries of Foreign Affairs, Finance, and International Trade and Industry.[30] Conversely, the Japanese Defense Agency (JDA) did not have cabinet-level status until 2006. The civilian staff of the JDA was "colonized" by civil servants from other ministries, and the JDA lacked a mobilization plan, an emergency civil defense system, and rules for engaging the enemy.[31] Military ambitions were kept in check by cultural norms that structured institutional constraints.

In the new millennium, American pressure on Japan to commit greater resources toward its defense along with international pressure on Japan to play a more significant role in global affairs (especially UN peacekeeping) and certain elite aspirations about restoring Japan's status in the world collided with Japanese cultural and institutional insistence on antimilitarism. Junichiro Koizumi served as Japanese prime minister from 2001 to 2006. Koizumi viewed the Iraq war that started in 2003 as "a major opportunity" to pursue Japanese interests. Specifically, Koizumi thought that Japanese participation in the war would help to reinforce the US-Japanese alliance, help Japan recover a stake in Iraqi oil lost in the 1991 Gulf War, earn Japan greater respect, and "reshape national norms in a way more favorable to Japan's remilitarization and hence mark a major step in redressing its lopsided strategic profile as an economic giant without commensurate military capabilities and hence global political clout."[32] Although Koizumi was able to get the Cabinet Legislation Bureau (CLB)—the government agency that serves as "the guardian of national norms in policy making"[33]—to approve the deployment of Japanese troops (the Self Defense Force or SDF) to Iraq, the CLB limited the troops to noncombat roles. And, although Koizumi enjoyed enormous popularity initially, his efforts to change the antimilitarist norm by extending the activities of the SDF in support of US-led wars led to a precipitous loss of support in public opinion polls.

Koizumi's successor as premier, Shinzo Abe (2006–2007), attempted to continue pushing against the antimilitarist national culture. Abe supported issuing revised history textbooks that would eliminate references to Japanese wartime human rights abuses abroad, such as those committed against so-called "comfort women." And in late 2006 Abe pushed two laws through the Japanese parliament that were intended to be the start of rewriting the Peace Constitution.[34] At the same time, on Abe's urging, the Japanese parliament "broke two postwar taboos" by passing legislation that upgraded the status of the JDF to ministry level and required schools to teach patriotism.[35] Schools are one of the most effective transmitters of patriotic and nationalistic values in any country, as every government knows. The new education requirements were supported by school boards but strongly opposed by Japanese teachers as too reminiscent of Japan's war-era education system that encouraged support for imperialism and the military.

The governing party's nationalist turn and its inability to overcome persistent economic problems led to the Liberal Democratic Party's (LDP's) electoral loss of the upper house of parliament in July 2007. The Democratic Party won the upper house by focusing on domestic issues, although its opposition to Abe's nationalist goals and the deployment of troops to Iraq were well known. The Democratic Party flexed its muscle by refusing to reauthorize the refueling of American and allied warships by Japanese tankers, contending that the refueling missions violated the pacifist constitution. With the lower house in the hands of the LDP and the upper house in the hands of the Democratic Party, parliamentary paralysis resulted. This paralysis ultimately contributed to the resignation of Abe, and haunted the new LDP prime minister, Yasuo Fukuda, as well. Fukuda met the US president at the White House in November 2007 against the backdrop of Japanese tankers heading toward home. Ultimately, the refueling mission was restarted, but the Democratic Party was able to unseat the LDP in parliamentary elections in 2009, taking over the premiership.

In the new millennium, while Japanese political parties argued over what the constitution and the culture would allow, the SDF increased its regional profile even while overall defense spending continued to fall. Japan participated in naval training drills with Australia in 2009 and then with the countries of Southeast Asia and India in 2012. Japan also extended military aid to Cambodia and East Timor for training in disaster relief and reconstruction. The Japanese cabinet approved a military alliance with South Korea in 2012, but opposition in South Korea put the alliance on hold. And the nationalists of the LDP managed to use anti-Chinese rhetoric in a successful parliamentary bid to return to ruling status. In December 2012, the LDP and the nationalistic Shinzo Abe regained control of the government in late-year elections.

The return of Abe and the LDP did not mean necessarily that the nationalists had won the debate over whether Japan's self-image and constitution should change so that Japan might acquire "normal" great power status. This issue has been argued over in the context of two decades of economic duress and failure of leadership. This leadership failure is reflected in the fact that from 2001 until the end of 2012, Japan had eight different prime ministers and ruling governments. Seven of those governments came in a span of six years.

In Germany, antimilitarism also was embedded in the national self-culture after World War II and was reinforced by the constitution, or Basic Law. Ruth Wittlinger and Martin Larose explain that "German foreign policy behavior as well as political culture traditionally has consisted of a set of policies and norms the roots of which were clearly a result of a particular view of the National Socialist experience and the Second World War."[36] Wittlinger and Larose write about these policies and norms as the "collective memory" of Germany, a notion that works well in our discussion of national self-image. The collective memory of Germany has three strands: a call to remember the lessons of the Holocaust, a reminder of the dangers of aggressive nationalism, and a solidarity with the United States and NATO for their support of Germany through the Cold War. German foreign policy has had to remain true to these strands. "No more war" was understood as the baseline for any foreign policy that lived by the parameters established by the collective memory.

After the end of the Cold War, German political leaders were dismayed by Germany's constitutional prohibitions against contributing to international military operations, particularly broad-based operations such as the 1991 Gulf War and the United Nations peacekeeping operations in Somalia. In 1994, the Federal Constitutional Court gave Germany more room to contribute to international peace and security by ruling that German military forces could participate in missions outside of Europe when conducted in a multilateral framework and approved by the legislature.[37] Because of this change, Germany was able to participate in the 1998 NATO air campaign against the Yugoslavian government in response to the ethnic cleansing in Kosovo. Wittlinger and Larose explain that elites successfully justified this use of force by telling the public that "because of its past, Germany has a particular moral responsibility to use military means to avoid dictatorships and/or genocide going on elsewhere."[38] "No more war" was altered to mean no more holocausts, and the use of force was necessary to stop genocide.

After the 9/11 terrorist attacks on the United States, the German elite called upon the collective memory to warn against the dangers of "going it alone." Since the United States and NATO had stood with Germany during the Cold War, Germany had an obligation to assist the United States in Afghanistan.[39] But, standing with one's ally was a limited obligation when the ally sought to go to war for self-interested purposes, and so the German government refused to follow the United States into Iraq in 2003. The lessons of the past warned against "warmongering" such as that evidenced in the US Bush administration by its war in Iraq. The "German Way" was to oppose preemptive wars, which hearkened back to the collective memory of the dangers of aggressive nationalism. [40]

Kosovo, Afghanistan, and Iraq allowed the German elite to offer an expanded use of the German military abroad in a way that fit the collective memory and maintained a national culture committed in general to antimilitarism. Where the Japanese push for **"normal power"** status was driven by the power ambitions of some elites, German elites focused on making the German military a tool for promoting moral internationalism with "the self-confidence of a grown-up nation." [41]

When the Arab Awakening of 2011 came to Libya, armed rebel groups formed to liberate the country from the regime of Muammar Qaddafi. The regime responded with expected ruthlessness and proclaimed that it would eliminate all armed opposition. In March 2011, the United Nations Security Council approved a **civilian protection** mandate for Libya that included establishing a no-fly zone to stop Qaddafi's forces from using air power to engage in the widespread killing of the rebels and their supporters. NATO member states then began the enforcement of the no-fly zone and subsequently started targeting the military assets of the regime in support of the rebels.

In the middle of what seemed to be international agreement on the need for collective action to stop the impending widespread killing of Libyans by their government, Germany surprised many observers by abstaining from the Security Council resolution and refusing to participate in the NATO-led air campaign. [42] A critic concluded that the German government of Chancellor Angela Merkel had "illusions" about the lessons of German collective memory. [43] Within a few weeks of the Security Council vote, Germany announced that it would allow its troops to help with the provision of humanitarian aid in Libya if the United Nations were to request such of the European Union. [44] This announcement came after friends of the chancellor let the media know that the foreign minister—a leader of a junior coalition partner in the government—had been responsible for the German abstention and would have voted against the Security Council resolution but for the intervention of the chancellor herself. [45] That is, friends of the chancellor wanted everyone to know that the episode demonstrated less about a change in German national culture than domestic political competition between members of the coalition government.

## CULTURE, INSTITUTIONS, AND THE DEMOCRATIC PEACE

The greatest concentration of scholarly activity on the impact of culture and institutions on foreign policy has been on the idea of the democratic peace. This research finds its intellectual roots in philosopher Immanuel Kant's proposition that democracies are peace-loving countries.[46] In the first modern variation on this idea, it was asserted that democracies are less likely to go to war than nondemocratic states. In a later version, the idea was refined to the proposition that democracies do not fight wars with other democracies. If true, a world of democracies would be a world freed from war. When national leaders, such as former US president Bill Clinton, speak about "enlarging the circle of market democracies," they suggest that the idea of the democratic peace is more than an idea; it is an operating reality.

There are two explanations for why democracies are or should be more peaceful than nondemocracies—the first explanation emphasizes the culture of democracies and the second emphasizes domestic institutional structures. The cultural explanation proposes that "liberal democracies are more peace loving than other states because of the norms regarding appropriate methods of conflict resolution that develop within society."[47] Further, "leaders choose to employ the standards and rules of conduct which have been successful and acceptable at home in their international interaction."[48] Leaders of democracies are not constrained by peaceful standards when dealing with nondemocracies, since nondemocracies cannot be expected to be similarly constrained. The second explanation stresses the constraining role of democratic institutions on foreign policy decision makers. The division of and checks on power within democratic governments and the ultimate restraint of officeholders having to face voters in regular elections prohibit violent (and costly) foreign policy behaviors.[49]

The idea of the democratic peace has generated much excitement and much criticism. Critics point out a number of weaknesses in the proposition: that interstate war is rare; that the number of democracies at any given point in history has been small; that, for the bulk of the second half of the twentieth century, most democracies were primarily Western states bound together in military alliances against the Soviet bloc; and that these same democracies were also the world's richest states bound together by class-based interests. The democratic peace idea also has been accused of being another justification for Western imperialism.[50] This criticism is that Western states claim moral cause to impose their political and economic structures on other peoples in the name of creating a more peaceful world. During the Cold War, these same states claimed the need to defend democracy against communism as their justification for **neoimperial** policies in the developing world. Other criticisms of the democratic peace literature focus on the methodology or the manner in which democratic peace research is conducted.

Despite the criticism, proponents declare that the proposition of the democratic peace is so robust that it amounts to the only "law" in the study of international relations.[51] The criticisms have not deterred research programs intent on fleshing out the nuances of the proposition. It may well be, however, that the democratic peace idea has had a setback with the more militaristic foreign policies of the US Bush administration and the British Blair government. For Bush and Blair, and people called "neoconservatives," democracies were duty bound to bring democracy to nondemocratic places like Iraq, and the use of force was a morally correct use of "might for right." In this interpretation, it was appropriate for democracies to use war to promote democracy and the democratic peace. Bruce Russett, one of the leading theorists on the democratic peace, criticized the Bush administration for its gross distortion of the theory in order to justify war against Iraq:

> Many advocates of the democratic peace may now feel rather like many atomic scientists did in 1945. They had created something intended to prevent conquest by Nazi Germany, but only after Germany was defeated was the bomb tested and then used—against Japanese civilians whose government was already near defeat. Our creation too has been perverted.[52]

In the next chapter, we will come back to the notion of the democratic peace with this twist: stable democracies may be less likely than other states to use force, but countries undergoing democratization are *more* likely to use force than other states.

## CHAPTER REVIEW

- Efforts to link state type with particular foreign policy behaviors go back to the founding of foreign policy analysis and the "pre-theories" work of James Rosenau.
- Except for the contested theory that democracies do not go to war with other democracies, there is little evidence that state type is linked to particular foreign policy behavior.
- National self-image helps to build a loyal population that will not evaluate leaders' decisions too critically.
- National self-image is like nationalism; both have positive and negative sides.
- The political institutions of a self-governing people should reflect the dominant political culture of that people.

*Chapter Six*

# Domestic Politics

## IN THIS CHAPTER

- Domestic Politics: The Critical Side of the Nested Game
- Accommodate, Insulate, or Mobilize
- Democratization and War
- Chapter Review

## CASES FEATURED IN THIS CHAPTER

- The decision by the United Progressive Alliance coalition of India to almost let a nuclear treaty with the United States slip away in order to keep the coalition together and in power.
- The domestic political problems confronted by Palestinian leader Yasir Arafat and Israeli leader Ehud Barak that stopped them from concluding a significant accord regarding Palestinian sovereignty.
- The domestic political dispute between the Palestinian political groups Fatah and Hamas that led to a Palestinian civil war and three Hamas-Israel wars after the first-ever Palestinian legislative elections.
- The unruly domestic political situation that encouraged Russian leaders Boris Yeltsin and Vladimir Putin to adopt neoimperial, belligerent policies, sending Russian democracy off course.

## DOMESTIC POLITICS: THE CRITICAL SIDE OF THE NESTED GAME

In 2004, the Indian National Congress Party, led by Sonia Gandhi, formed an alliance with four communist parties to govern India. The coalition was called the United Progressive Alliance (UPA). Manmohan Singh was selected by the Congress Party leadership to be the prime minister. In August 2007, the leader of the largest communist party threatened to bring down the coalition government on a critical foreign policy agreement with the United States. The main opposition party, the Bharatiya Janata Party (BJP), also opposed this agreement and might have benefited if the communists pulled their support from the UPA and caused the government to collapse. The agreement at issue did not require parliament's approval, but the Congress Party–UPA needed the communist parties to stay in the coalition in order to get any legislation passed.

The Singh government found itself in a potentially embarrassing foreign policy situation because of Indian domestic politics. Although the Indian prime minister did not offer to resign over the intracoalitional dispute, he almost let the agreement with the United States collapse in order to keep the communists in the UPA and thereby keep the UPA in power. This was no standard-issue agreement for India, yet Singh and the Congress Party apparently were willing to see it die rather than lose political power.

The agreement at issue was a nuclear treaty signed between India and the United States in 2005. India never signed the Nuclear Non-Proliferation Treaty (NPT). Indian leaders state that until the world is nuclear weapons free, India will retain its sovereign right to arm and defend itself in whatever way it can. In 1974, India successfully tested a nuclear weapon. Since then, India has been prohibited by the United States and other countries from buying civilian nuclear fuel and technology. Despite this ban, India's nuclear weapons program continued, as did Pakistan's in response. In 1998, India and enemy Pakistan engaged in tit-for-tat nuclear weapons tests. The following year, India and Pakistan fought a war in India's Kargil region.[1] Additional US sanctions were put in place against both countries in response to the nuclear weapons tests, but these sanctions were altered after the 9/11 terrorist attacks on the United States and the start of the US global war on terror.

According to the terms of the 2005 treaty, India still would not sign the NPT, but it would be given the right to buy civilian nuclear fuel and technology. In return, India would allow inspections of its designated civilian nuclear facilities by the International Atomic Energy Agency (IAEA). Its military nuclear facilities would be separated from its civilian facilities and *not* subject to IAEA (or any other) inspection. India also bargained for and won the right to reprocess nuclear fuel for energy generation—and potentially for building more nuclear weapons. For India, the treaty validated its position as a nuclear weapons power and would help its booming economy. For the United States, the treaty would open the door for US companies to build nuclear reactors in India and put US-India relations on a different footing (as discussed in chapter 9). Before the treaty would come into effect, India would ask for "India-specific" exemptions and safeguards from the IAEA and then seek the approval of the Nuclear Suppliers Group (a coalition of forty-five countries that export nuclear material but only to coalition-approved countries). On the American side, Congress needed to approve the treaty in its final form.

The Indian communist parties—coalition partners in the same government that negotiated the treaty—objected to the treaty because it might lead to a close relationship between India and the United States. In August 2007, the communist parties threatened to leave the government unless the Congress Party rewrote the treaty. If the communists withdrew from the coalition, early elections would be called with no guarantee that the Congress Party could win enough seats and coalition partners to retain control of the government. In mid-October, Prime Minister Singh said he would not risk a general election for the sake of the treaty. That is, holding on to power at home was more important than consolidating a treaty that was a win-win situation for India, diplomatically, militarily, and economically.

Political fortunes change, however, and the strength of coalition members can also change. A few weeks after the Congress Party capitulated to the communist parties, the communist parties removed their objections to the treaty process. In mid-November, the Indian government began its negotiations with the IAEA for the "India-specific" safeguards. Attempting to reassert their position, the communist parties warned that all they had agreed to were negotiations, not a final deal.

The leaders of the UPA coalition in India found themselves in a classic nested game. On the other side of the deal, the Bush administration had to move the treaty through a less-than-enthusiastic US Congress in late 2006 and early 2007 and would need to take the treaty back through Congress in 2008 right before national elections in the fall. For the Bush administration, however, the dual game was less threatening since Bush was prohibited from seeking a third term in office. Congress did approve the treaty in October 2008, despite concerns about the treaty undermining nuclear nonproliferation efforts.

The dual or nested game, as discussed in chapter 1, is one in which national leaders (however leadership may be configured) find themselves working between domestic and international politics, generally putting domestic goals ahead of international. As Peter Trumbore and Mark Boyer explain, "At the national level, domestic groups pressure the government to adopt policies they favor, while politicians seek power by building coalitions among these constituents." Meanwhile, at "the international level, governments seek to satisfy domestic pressures while limiting the harmful impact of foreign developments."[2] The critical point is that the domestic political game is primary for any government, regardless of government type. "No leader, no matter how **autocratic**, is completely immune from domestic pressure, whether that takes the form of rival political parties seeking partisan advantage, as in a democratic setting, or rival factions jockeying for influence and power in a bureaucratic-authoritarian system."[3]

## ACCOMMODATE, INSULATE, OR MOBILIZE

Government type is important in that it tells us which political actors and resources are legitimate and the processes by which policy decisions are made. But regardless of government type, what is more important is identifying the domestic political process by which winners and losers are determined on any given foreign policy issue. The process involves some interaction between members of the governing regime and other critical actors, interaction that is characterized by formal and informal rules. The motivation of the actors, in the most basic terms, is to retain or gain political power within these rules (and sometimes despite these rules when their aims are revolutionary). Political power is not necessarily the end point, as most actors also have policy agendas they want enacted. Thus, the actors are also motivated to build and maintain **policy coalitions**, as Joe Hagan explains.[4] How actors manage the domestic political game—bargaining with opponents and/or supporters or not, attempting to make decisions as if they are not bargaining when they are, pushing through a dominant solution or attempting to strike a compromise position, or taking actions that lock all the actors into a stalemate or deadlock—has consequences in both the immediate and longer term.

Building and maintaining policy coalitions and retaining political power are particularly difficult in highly politicized contexts in which a large and vocal opposition exists. When the issue at hand is a foreign policy matter and it becomes linked to questions about the **legitimacy** of the leadership, Hagan proposes that leaders might resort to three different political strategies to manage the challenge posed by the domestic opposition: (1) accommodation, (2) insulation, or (3) mobilization.[5]

The **accommodation strategy** involves bargaining with the opposition and controversy avoidance. Here "leaders seek to contain opposition, and thus retain political power, by avoiding publicly disputed policies and actions that make the country appear weak in international affairs or are closely associated with a widely acknowledged adversary."[6] Restraint in foreign policy is the expected result of an accommodation strategy, but at times efforts intended to avoid controversy can result in foreign policy deadlock. In the **insulation strategy**, the leadership attempts to deflect attention from foreign policy issues by suppressing or overriding the opposition, or, if all else fails, by neutralizing the opposition with favors and promises. The goal is to maintain a chosen foreign policy course by reducing the domestic constraints.[7] Finally, a **mobilization strategy** involves the manipulation of foreign policy to one's own political advantage, usually through greater risk taking. Leaders assert their legitimacy by confronting the opposition through appeals to nationalism or imperialism, or by **"scapegoating"** foreigners.  Leaders claim that they—and not their domestic opponents—have a "special capacity" to maintain the country's security and status abroad. When successful, this strategy works by "diverting attention from divisive domestic problems."[8]

Let's apply these strategies to a case study to see how the use of each has implications for future foreign policy choices. In 1996, Yasir Arafat was elected president of the Palestinian National Authority (shortened here to the Palestinian Authority, or PA), the governing body of the Palestinian people living in the West Bank and Gaza. Arafat was also the leader of Fatah, one of several Palestinian organizations that joined together under the umbrella framework known as the Palestine Liberation Organization (PLO). Arafat served as chairman of the PLO in its long struggle to (re)claim territory subsumed by the state of Israel in its 1948 unilateral declaration of independence and in subsequent wars with Arab states. In the 1967 war, the West Bank and Gaza were captured by Israel from Jordan and Egypt, respectively.

The government of Israel and the PLO signed a peace treaty in 1993. This treaty set in place mechanisms for future negotiations regarding the transfer of authority and land in the West Bank and Gaza to the PA. The amount of territory to be transferred to the PA, the enumeration of details regarding whether the PA was to be partially or fully independent of Israel, the rights of displaced Palestinians, and the resolution of competing claims to Jerusalem (especially the Old City) were left to subsequent negotiations.

In 1996, Benjamin Netanyahu was elected prime minister of Israel in a landslide election, defeating sitting Labor prime minister Shimon Peres. Although a hard-liner by reputation and the leader of the conservative Likud Party, Netanyahu began the transfer of some territory to the PA as part of the continuing peace process. But after a series of deadly suicide attacks against Israelis, Netanyahu stopped some troop withdrawals from and lifted a freeze on Jewish settlements in the disputed territory in contravention of the peace process. Then, in October 1998, more negotiations between the Israelis and Palestinians resulted in a three-stage agreement for the transfer of more lands. Netanyahu completed the first stage of this transfer and then was defeated in Israeli elections by Ehud Barak in 1999.

Barak led a coalition called One Israel to a landslide victory over Netanyahu and Likud. One Israel was a fragile coalition of divergent parties, including Barak's own Labor Party. In a demonstration of the fragility of Barak's coalition and hold on power, the Knesset (the Israeli parliament) elected to the powerful role of speaker a Likud party leader. Barak and Yasir Arafat signed the Wye River Agreement under the mediation of US president Bill Clinton in September 1999. Barak transferred land and released two hundred political prisoners in the second part of the three-stage peace process. In July 2000, President Clinton sponsored another series of talks at Camp David in order to initiate the third stage of the peace process. These talks failed to produce an agreement, and both Barak and Arafat indicated that the position of their respective sides had hardened. Arafat threatened that the PA would make a unilateral declaration of independence in September absent further agreement with the Israeli government.

Although Arafat postponed the unilateral declaration, events in late September 2000 brought the peace process to a deadly halt. Ariel Sharon, one of the leaders of the opposition Likud Party, and a group of followers and Israeli troops went to a disputed site in the Old City of Jerusalem, a place the Jews call the Temple Mount and the Muslims call Haram al-Sharif (Noble Sanctuary). Sharon's goal was to demonstrate Israeli commitment to maintaining full access to the Old City. His very public display on a Friday, a day of special religious observation for Muslims, prompted a Palestinian crowd to form in protest. Rocks were thrown and bullets were fired—the rocks from the Palestinian side, the bullets from the Israeli side—and months and years of active low-intensity conflict began. Over the next twelve years, the low-level conflict ignited into a Palestinian civil war and three Israeli-Palestinian wars.

The Hagan framework can be used to explore responses to this conflict on both the Palestinian and Israeli sides. On the Palestinian side, Arafat governed with the assistance of a small council of appointees from his political party Fatah. Arafat had a major domestic opponent in the person of Sheikh Ahmed Yassin, the spiritual leader of Hamas. Hamas was formed in 1987 at the start of the **intifada,** or Palestinian uprising, in Gaza and the West Bank. Hamas could be considered an indigenous organization as opposed to Fatah and the PLO, who spent decades outside of the disputed territories and thus outside of Israeli occupation. Hamas's purpose was twofold—to provide humanitarian assistance to Palestinians in Israeli-occupied territory and to coordinate military/terrorist activities aimed at the Israelis. Sheikh Ahmed Yassin spent eight years in Israeli prison until released in 1997 in a deal made between Israel and Jordan. Yassin had declared that Israel was attempting to destroy Islam, and because of this, loyal Muslims had a religious obligation to destroy Israel. Arafat and the PLO had also been committed to the violent elimination of the state of Israel, but this position was reversed in 1989 (the same year that Yassin was imprisoned by Israel). It should go without saying that Yassin and Hamas opposed the subsequent agreements made between Arafat/Fatah and the Israeli government.

In the first week of fighting after the September 2000 Sharon visit to Haram al-Sharif, seventy Palestinians were killed in the streets while confronting Israeli security forces. During that week, the Israeli government demanded that Arafat reestablish order in the West Bank. Arafat made no move to deploy an effective Palestinian police presence to quell the uprising. As Israeli leaders demanded that Arafat assert control, his leadership was called into question: either Arafat could not control the uprising, or he did not want to control it. The former suggested that the political balance had shifted in favor of a dangerous element in the Palestinian community; the latter suggested that Arafat condoned the use of violence to force Israeli concessions in negotiations. Neither explanation meant good things for the peace process.

One explanation of Arafat's lack of effective police response was that political power had shifted in the Palestinian community, putting into doubt Arafat's ability to retain political control much less to retain a strong coalition in support of further agreements with the Israelis. After the first week of conflict, Hamas declared that the following Friday would be a "day of rage" against Israeli rule—the first of many to come. The first "day of rage" call was answered by a mass outpouring in the West Bank and Gaza, with the end story being more Palestinians killed and injured. Significantly, Arafat's Fatah issued support for the "day of rage" after it was under way.

Once begun, the street uprising and violence continued. International efforts to broker a cease-fire were met at times with obstinacy from both Arafat and Barak and, at other times, with agreements that subsequently were broken. Arafat kept insisting that the Palestinian people were only defending themselves against the Israeli military and that a multinational investigation should be conducted into the causes of the violence.

Arafat's hard line toward Israel had started months before at the Camp David talks. Arafat's approach to Camp David and his later threat to unilaterally declare the independence of Palestine might have been manifestations of his decision to employ a mobilization strategy as per Hagan's model. Perhaps Arafat calculated that in the face of growing opposition by Hamas and his own worsening public opinion standing, he needed to assert a hard line toward the Israelis. This hard line would demonstrate his continued commitment to the Palestinian people and his special capacity to lead them to statehood. Taking a tough negotiating stance with the Israelis might slow down the peace process in the short term, but reinvigorating his regime against domestic opposition and retaining political power were Arafat's priorities. Arafat's initial refusal to order an effective Palestinian police presence to stem the riots might be seen as the continuation of this risky behavior. There was a symbolic Palestinian police presence in the streets, but Arafat insisted that the uprising was a spontaneous response of the people that would stop when the Israelis stopped using violence and conceded to a multinational investigation.

Arafat's mobilization strategy manifested in the failed summer negotiations worked to his great disadvantage. He had put his credibility on the line against the Israelis at Camp David to win political advantage against Hamas. But then Hamas forced Arafat's hand in calling for the days of rage. Arafat had to adopt an even more belligerent stance toward Israel or risk being seen as unsupportive of the Palestinians' right to defend themselves against Israeli aggression.

On the Israeli side of this violent event, Arafat's support for the second intifada provided evidence to Israeli hard-liners of his true intentions and untrustworthiness. Barak's One Israel coalition was fragile back in the summer at the time of the Camp David talks. By late November, after two months of violence in the West Bank and Gaza, Barak was forced to call for early elections in the face of mounting domestic political attacks on his government. Before Barak made the call for new elections, he had issued ultimatums to Arafat, approved significant escalations in the use of military force, and desperately courted Ariel Sharon to join a new emergency government. Barak's bid to woo Sharon failed, while peace with the Palestinians— still Barak's long-term foreign policy goal—seemed more unattainable with each passing day.

Applying the Hagan concepts, we can say that Barak's use of military force against the Palestinians was a manifestation of a mobilization strategy. Barak was demonstrating that he and his government were willing and able to defend the state of Israel against all threats, implying by comparison that his political opponents possessed no special capacity to do so. Barak's subsequent efforts to bring Ariel Sharon into an emergency government can be seen as an accommodating, co-opting move signaling Barak's desire to preserve some maneuvering room for his long-term foreign policy agenda. Significantly, Barak maintained throughout the crisis that the peace process was not dead and could be recommenced.

The Barak government did not survive the crisis despite efforts to co-opt or neutralize Sharon. Early elections in February 2001 brought Ariel Sharon to power. Sharon served as Israeli prime minister from this point until he was debilitated by a stroke in January 2006. His successor, Ehud Olmert, facing his own difficulties retaining political power and maintaining a policy coalition, brought Labor back into his cabinet. In mid-2007, Barak returned to the cabinet as defense minister and head of the Labor party, threatening to pull Labor out of the coalition if Olmert and Likud did not comply with Labor's demands regarding an investigation into Israel's 2006 war with Hezbollah in Lebanon.

## DEMOCRATIZATION AND WAR

Let's continue with the narrative and then add some additional conceptual material to understand the dynamics of the case. The Hamas-Fatah political struggle continued in the Palestinian territories, sometimes eclipsing the Is-raeli-Palestinian conflict. There were some indications that the Palestinian territories were moving to incorporate democratic institutions by 2005 and 2006. In January 2005, Mahmoud Abbas of Fatah was elected to the Palestin-ian presidency in an election that Hamas supporters boycotted. Then the Bush administration decided to push for broader legislative elections in order to demonstrate its commitment to democracy promotion in Arab lands—and as a counter to the democracy promotion demonstration of the Iraq war. Israeli and Fatah officials had misgivings about holding the elections because Fatah wasn't "ready."[9] Afterward, Bush administration officials came to the same conclusion.[10]

In January 2006, elections were held for a Palestinian legislature. Hamas won 76 seats in the 132-seat body; Fatah won only 43. At the start of 2006, the new government was sworn in. In April, the United States and European Union cut financial assistance to the PA, and Israel suspended payment of tax and customs receipts that it collected for the PA. In late June, Hamas gunmen from Gaza launched a raid into Israel and took hostage a young Israeli soldier. Three days after that, Israel invaded Gaza. Within a few more days, Hezbollah rocket strikes into Israel from Lebanon provoked Israel into invad-ing Lebanon. This war in Lebanon continued for another month. In Novem-ber 2006, Israel declared a cease-fire in Gaza and withdrew its troops.

In the meantime, the Bush administration was dismayed about Hamas's electoral victory and conspired with Fatah to get rid of the Hamas govern-ment. The plan involved two parts: Abbas would find a way to dismiss the Hamas government, and then when violence erupted in protest, Fatah secur-ity forces would overrun and destroy Hamas. Fatah would do this using covert military aid given to it under a special initiative run by Secretary of State Condoleezza Rice and Deputy National Security Advisor Elliott Ab-rams. The administration had told Congress that it was only supplying nonle-thal aid to Fatah, but this was a deception.[11]

The chief Middle East advisor to the US vice president later described what happened as "an attempted coup by Fatah that was pre-empted before it could happen" by Hamas.[12] In the middle of June 2007 in a series of pitched battles, Hamas took over Gaza, leaving the West Bank to be controlled by Fatah. That June marked the period now called the Palestinian civil war, but armed confrontations between Hamas and Fatah forces continued afterward albeit at a low level. Various efforts to reconcile the two were attempted and failed. Israel and Hamas continued their own hostilities, and these escalated into two more Gaza wars in December 2007–January 2008 and November

2012. At the cease-fire that ended the November 2012 Israeli-Hamas/Palestinian war, Hamas and Fatah attempted to reconcile.

Let's bring back in some conceptual material. Fatah's Abbas apparently tried to form unity governments with Hamas even as Fatah's security personnel were arming against Hamas. Had Abbas's accommodation efforts succeeded, Hamas might have been co-opted and the civil war averted. Accommodation may have limited Hamas's actions vis-à-vis the Israelis, avoiding the 2008 Gaza war, if not the 2012 war. But accommodation failed, and Hamas's own mobilization strategy—which involved provoking the Israelis into three wars—kept the issue of Fatah's legitimacy in question while asserting Hamas as the better choice for defending Palestinian interests against Israel. Meanwhile, additional Palestinian elections were suspended amid the conflict. The next general elections were to take place in October 2013.

The last chapter ended with a consideration of the "law" of international relations that democracies do not engage in war with other democracies—the democratic peace theory. This theory is based on an expectation of a strong relationship between stable democratic norms or culture and stable democratic institutions. Getting to this point, however, may involve a difficult transition period in which changing norms, expectations, and institutions combined with threatened old elites and rising new elites create dynamics that lead to war. The transition to democracy may be a period in which a state is *more* likely, not less likely, to go to war with other states, regardless of whether the targeted state is a democracy or not. This offers both a note of caution to the democratic peace idea and an elaboration on the domestic political processes being discussed in this chapter.

The definitive research on the dangers of the democratic transition comes from Edward Mansfield and Jack Snyder. Building on the work of other scholars, they conceptualize democratization as a process in which societies move toward open, competitive, and well-regulated political competition; open competition and recruitment for the position of chief executive; and constitutional constraints on the exercise of power by the chief executive. Analyzing data often used to support the democratic peace theory, they find that "an increase in the openness of the selection process for the chief executive doubled the likelihood of war"; "increasing the competitiveness of political participation" increased the chances of war by 90 percent; and "increasing the constraints on a country's chief executive" increased the chances of war by 35 percent. States moving from full autocracy to full democracy "were on average about two-thirds more likely to become involved in any type of war."[13]

Transitions involve phases, and countries may get stuck in a phase; or the process may even get reversed as the country returns to autocracy. Mansfield and Snyder conclude that states "stuck" in the first phase of democratization, "during which elites threatened by the transition are often still powerful and the institutions needed to regulate mass political participation tend to be very weak," are especially bellicose.[14] This would describe the Palestinian situation since the first legislative elections of 2006.

What accounts for these findings? Mansfield and Snyder suggest that the dynamics of democratization combine to form an unstable mix of "social change, institutional weakness, and threatened interests."[15] As citizens are freed to participate in politics through political party and interest group activities, they begin to make demands on the central government. These demands must be met or quelled, even as the central government's power is being intentionally diminished by constitutional design. The government, then, must build and maintain a policy coalition among diverse and vocal interests—some old actors in the system, some new actors in the system—while hanging on to its crumbling power and authority. Mansfield and Snyder conclude that "one of the simplest but riskiest strategies for a hard-pressed regime in a democratizing country is to shore up its prestige at home by seeking victories abroad."[16]

Let's put this into the context of culture or norms and institutions. Democratization is a period in which a society must acquire liberal norms and identity. At the same time, the society experiences institutional change including the "establishment of stable institutions guaranteeing the rule of law, civil rights, a free and effective press, and representative government."[17] The relationship between democratic culture and institutions is of course weak in this period, but each is critical to the deepening of the other. The transition can be completed—democratic norms and institutions can be consolidated—without war. But sometimes the transition period (and the still-to-come democracy) so threatens the position of elites that they attempt to retain control by substituting populist or nationalist norms for liberal democratic norms in order to win the support of mass publics and stay atop the political game. To the extent that elites can get mass publics to buy into a populist and/or nationalist ideology, they may be able to suspend the process toward fuller democratization.[18]

How does this lead to international military disputes? Mansfield and Snyder offer three "related mechanisms" that are similar in process and result to Hagan's strategies discussed above. First, Mansfield and Snyder say that elites may engage in "nationalist outbidding: both old and new elites may bid for popular favor by advancing bold proposals to deal forcefully with threats to the nation, claiming their domestic political opponents will not vigorously defend the national interests."[19] This should sound similar to Hagan's mobilization strategy in which elites attempt to stay in power by claiming a special ability to defend the national interests.

Next, Mansfield and Snyder offer a second mechanism they call "blowback from nationalist ideology: nationalists may find themselves trapped by rhetoric that emphasizes combating threats to the national interest because both the politicians and their supporters have internalized this worldview."[20] This blowback is similar to what happens in Hagan's accommodation strategy when elites attempt to accommodate the nationalist rhetoric of opponents only to become trapped into limited policy choices by their own talk.

Finally, Mansfield and Snyder say that elites may engage in "logrolling." In this, various elites form a nationalist coalition weakly held together by a protracted external problem, usually military engagement abroad. Here, we might consider Hagan's insulation strategy with a twist: a coalition of elites can agree that they wish to stay on top, but the only way they can do so is if they create an external situation that diverts attention from them, insulating them from critical domestic opponents and popular demands. Protracted military conflict becomes the method by which elites "logroll" and put off further steps toward the consolidation of true democratic change.

Mansfield and Snyder use historical as well as recent examples to illustrate their statistical findings. One example is particularly compelling—post-Soviet Russia. This example can be expanded upon to demonstrate how elites may be tempted to use force abroad and at home to deal with the threat and chaos of democratization.

Fifteen countries were formed at the collapse of the Soviet Union, but there might have been at least one more. One month before the collapse of the Soviet Union, Chechen nationalist leaders declared the independence of Chechnya. Chechnya, one of twenty-one Russian republics (administrative units), sits in southwestern Russia, along the northern border of the former Soviet Republic of Georgia (now an independent country). The Chechen people are Sunni Muslims, and their land contains considerable oil reserves.

Russia did not recognize the Chechen unilateral declaration of independence, but it also made no move to do anything about the breakaway republic until late 1994. In December 1994, the Russian government launched a massive military invasion of Chechnya. Most of the Russian firepower was concentrated on the capital city of Grozny, the home of almost half of the republic's population. Grozny was nearly flattened by the Russians, yet it did not fall to them for almost two months. Fighting in the first Chechen war raged on until 1996, despite the overwhelming force employed by the Russians against the Chechen guerrillas.

Why did Russian leaders delay responding to the Chechens in 1991? Why was there no response even when Russian troops were expelled from Chechnya a short time after the unilateral declaration of independence? It is safe to argue that the Russian leadership was too preoccupied with managing all the other changes in Russia—as well as those in some of the former Soviet republics—to give Chechnya much notice. When the Russian leaders did move to reestablish control of Chechnya, it was probably part of an effort to reestablish control in all of Russia and its "near abroad," not just in Chechnya.

What kinds of challenges were confronting the government at this time? We might call them the challenges that spring from the potentially volatile process of democratization. Fourteen months before the Russian troops launched the invasion of Chechnya, Russian troops were ordered to fire upon the Russian Duma (parliament). Russian president Boris Yeltsin had been feuding with the Duma over constitutional changes he wanted. The Duma was full of various and sundry parties and factions, many of whom were left over from the Soviet days and were opposed to Yeltsin's overall political agenda, especially his economic reforms. Fed up with the Duma, Yeltsin called in the troops and launched a two-day shelling of the White House where the Duma sits. The action killed as many as 150 people but was fairly popular among the Russian public and went without much official notice by foreign governments. Yeltsin did get the constitutional changes he wanted, but the reconstituted Duma remained fairly defiant and argumentative. Such was the difficult domestic political context facing the Yeltsin government.

Recall Mansfield and Snyder's warning: "One of the simplest but riskiest strategies for a hard-pressed regime in a democratizing country is to shore up its prestige at home by seeking victories abroad." When Yeltsin decided to send troops into Chechnya in December 1994, it was in the context of a volatile Russia and unwieldy democratization. Mansfield and Snyder write that,

> One interpretation of Yeltsin's decision to use force in Chechnya is that he felt it necessary to show that he could act decisively to prevent the unraveling of central authority, with respect not only to ethnic separatists but also to other ungovernable groups in a democratizing society. Chechnya, it was hoped, would allow Yeltsin to demonstrate his ability to coerce Russian society while at the same time exploiting a potentially popular issue.[21]

Of course, Chechnya was an internal security problem for Russia, not a foreign policy issue. But the same forces that propelled Russian leaders to use force in Chechnya were apparent in Russian relations with the other former Soviet republics in this same time period. Neil MacFarlane points out the degree to which Russia was engaging in aggressive foreign policy behavior at this time:

> Elements of the Russian military assiduously manipulated the civil conflicts in the [Transcaucasus] region (notably the Nagorno-Karabakh conflict between Azerbaijan and Armenia and the conflicts between Ossets and Abkhaz on the one hand and Georgians on the other in the Republic of Georgia) in order to return the governments of the region to a position of subservience. . . . Azerbaijan is the only country in the Transcaucasian region with no Russian forces within its border, but it has been under significant Russian pressure to allow a return of the Russian military, coordination of air defense systems, and joint

border control. Many have interpreted Russian support of the Armenian side in
the Nagorno-Karabakh dispute as a means of bringing Azerbaijan to heel. [22]

Rajan Menon, in an article that appeared in print the summer before the
Russians launched their invasion of Chechnya, gave this same basic domestic
political calculation for determining whether Russia would assert its neoimperial face in the former Soviet Central Asian republics. [23] The likelihood of
neoimperialism—a "risky" foreign policy behavior using Hagan's term—
depended upon the strength of proimperial coalitions versus the "democratic
reformers" led by Yeltsin. The proimperial coalition was composed of
groups nostalgic for the old Soviet empire. This same coalition was part of
the problematic Duma that Yeltsin had shelled in October 1993. Shelling the
Duma might be considered a type of insulation strategy as described by
Hagan (an effort to neutralize the Duma), but it might be difficult to maintain
the guise of democratic reformer if one uses military force against one's own
parliament too often!

Instead, Menon proposed that Yeltsin engaged in an accommodation
strategy to deal with the proimperial groups:

> More important than the existence of such coalitions is the extent to which
> Russia's governing democratic elites feel compelled by their weakness to en-
> gage in appeasement and accommodation toward these coalitions. They have
> done so to avoid being outflanked by ultra-nationalists, who have successfully
> manipulated the symbolic appeal of a virile defense of Russian interests and
> ethnic Russians in the former Soviet republics. [24]

Menon warned that, in adopting an accommodation strategy, "forces within
the state capable of countering neoimperial elites and offering alternative
paradigms of statecraft have been weakened." [25] The reformers became
trapped by co-opting neoimperial rhetoric, increasing the possibility of neoimperial behavior.

Unable to neutralize the opposition, Yeltsin switched strategies and co-
opted the powerful symbols of the opposition in order to assert his own
regime's special capacity to preserve the security and prestige of Russia.
Yeltsin's strategic policy spoke of the former Soviet republics as the "near
abroad" in which Russia had special rights, "obligations," and "responsibilities." And democratic reformers noted that Russia had a security interest in
their "own foreign countries" that sometimes would require the use of Russian "peacekeepers" therein. [26]

Yeltsin's military campaign in Chechnya in 1994–1996 did not play out
the way he had hoped. Domestic and international opposition to the campaign arose quickly. Indeed, Yeltsin could blame the new climate of democratization with its requisite political openness and mass participation in politics for the failure of his Chechnya policy, at least in part. Russian journalists

quickly exposed the campaign for its barbarity, stupidity, and costliness. Other actors in the newly created Russian civil society actively opposed the war. One group, the Committee of Soldiers' Mothers of Russia, was a particularly vocal opponent, organizing demonstrations and the March of Mothers' Compassion from Moscow to Grozny in spring 1996. As reported by the Inter Press Service, "Hundreds of mothers went to Chechnya to take their sons away from the battlefront. Some carried out negotiations themselves with the Chechen army to secure the release of sons held as prisoners of war."[27] Once the protests began, they did not end until a cease-fire was arranged in August 1996.

However, in 1999, Yeltsin restarted the military campaign in Chechnya after a number of unsolved "terrorist" bombings of civilian apartment buildings and public spaces in Russia. By this time, Yeltsin had instituted political change that made his office into a super-presidency rather than a restrained chief executive. Perhaps because the economic and social fabric of Russia was still so unstable and perhaps because the government successfully scapegoated the Chechen rebels for the bombings, the public rallied behind the military campaign. At the start of 2000, Yeltsin's handpicked acting president and soon-to-be-elected successor Vladimir Putin also enjoyed considerable public support for his own military campaign in Chechnya. In one campaign stunt designed to take advantage of popular support for the new nationalist war in Chechnya, Putin visited troops in Grozny aboard a two-seat Sukhoi-27 fighter bomber.[28] In time, Putin would do even more than Yeltsin to reverse course and return Russia to near autocracy.

## CHAPTER REVIEW

- National leaders play a two-level or nested game between international and domestic politics.
- National leaders in any type of political system are motivated by two similar goals: retaining political power and building and maintaining policy coalitions.
- Leaders sometimes try to accommodate and neutralize domestic political opposition in order to preserve their preferred foreign policy.
- Leaders sometimes engage in mobilization strategies that involve the use of risky foreign policy behaviors in order to undercut the nationalist rhetoric of opposition elites and prove their own government's legitimacy.
- Democratization is a transitional phase that can get stuck or reversed when threatened elites use nationalist mobilization strategies to stop the erosion of their power.

*Chapter Seven*

# Public Opinion and Media

## IN THIS CHAPTER

- Public Opinion and the Media Matter, but How?
- Different Views on the Public
- Managing Public Opinion
- Public Opinion, the "CNN Effect," and Managed News
- A Complicated Relationship: Government, Elite, Media, and the Public
- Chapter Review

## CASES FEATURED IN THIS CHAPTER

- The apparent alignment of Canadian public opinion, the "newspaper of record," and Prime Minister Stephen Harper on how Canada will defend its sovereignty in the Arctic.
- The decision in 1992 by US president George H. W. Bush to ignore calls to put troops on the ground in Somalia in order to avoid the voting public.
- The way that centralized political authority and social fragmentation in France limits the impact of public opinion on foreign policy making.
- British government efforts post–World War II to shape a single media portrayal of the Soviet Union.
- The use of "independent" Al Jazeera to promote the foreign policy goals of the emir of Qatar.
- The Reagan administration's successful framings of the shoot-downs of a Korean Air Lines flight by the Soviet Union and an Iran Air flight by the US Navy that stopped opponents and the media from producing alternative explanations for each event.

# PUBLIC OPINION AND THE MEDIA MATTER, BUT HOW?

The *Globe and Mail,* Canada's newspaper of record, ran a stunning article in January 2011. The article reported the results of a cross-national public opinion poll conducted for the Munk School of Global Affairs at the University of Toronto. The article was titled, "Canadians Rank Arctic Sovereignty as Top Foreign-Policy Priority," and the first lines reported that

> a majority of Canadians see Arctic sovereignty as the country's top foreign policy priority and believe military resources should be shifted to the North from global conflicts, according to a new opinion poll.
>
> The survey also found that Canadians are generally far less receptive to negotiation and compromises on Arctic disputes than Americans. [1]

The story went on to say that "Prime Minister Stephen Harper regularly reminds Canadians that his Conservative government is determined to defend this country's sovereignty in the Far North." "Other" findings of the poll were reported, including that "the environment ranks as the primary Arctic concern among Canadians, especially for northerners." This finding seems perplexing given the breathtaking news in the article's first lines and title.

The next day, as if to beat the drum louder, the *Globe* ran another article by the same author titled, "In the Arctic, Canada Willing to Fight to Keep the True North Free." [2] The article reported that although Harper's government had "recently embraced diplomatic solutions" and a "conciliatory approach" to Arctic disputes, "a new poll finds that Canadians are generally far less receptive to negotiation and compromises on disputes than their American neighbours." The report noted that,

> unlike his Liberal predecessors, Mr. Harper has made the Arctic a major political platform, taking every opportunity to remind Canadians that his government is determined to defend this country's sovereignty in the Far North. The poll's findings would suggest that Canadians have embraced his rhetoric.

Thus although the government was engaged in diplomacy it stood ready to defend the Canadian Arctic as the Canadian people demanded.

Stephen Harper's Canada seemed a different place than the land of peacekeepers and helpful fixers! Harper became prime minister in 2006 presiding over a minority conservative government. In 2007, he stood in front of "docked warships and was flanked by about 120 sailors in white dress uniforms" to announce that he would build eight Arctic patrol boats to "reassert the country's northern sovereignty." Harper avowed that

> Canada has a choice when it comes to defending our sovereignty in the Arctic; either we use it or we lose it. And make no mistake this government intends to

use it. Because Canada's Arctic is central to our identity as a northern nation. It is part of our history and it represents the tremendous potential of our future.[3]

The defense minister chimed in, "Today's announcement is the first step toward realizing the government's goal of a three-ocean navy." Defending Canada's sovereignty in the melting Arctic became Harper's signature policy goal. Harper's Conservative Party won more seats in the next election in 2007 and then formed the first majority party government after elections in 2011.

The reports about Canadians willing to fight over the Far North ran in the *Globe* in January in the middle of the 2011 federal elections campaign. "The campaign of 2011—so vicious and often vapid—should not be remembered fondly," noted the *Globe* editorial board in April right before the elections. The editorial continued, "If the result is a confident new Parliament, it could help propel Canada into a fresh period of innovation, government reform and global ambition. Stephen Harper and the Conservatives are best positioned to guide Canada there."[4] In response to this endorsement, the *Globe* received overwhelming public feedback—most of it negative. In response to the response, the *Globe* posted its endorsements since 1926, claiming that it had always struck a balance between liberal and conservative.[5] The balance of endorsements seemed to be about three to one in favor of conservatives, but maybe that was the balance desired.

Despite readers' dismay over the *Globe*'s endorsement of Harper, the poll results showed that Harper's "use it or lose it" policy regarding the Arctic resonated with Canadians—at least according to the *Globe* reports. The poll itself shows a somewhat different picture of Canadian opinions than those reported in the *Globe*.

The poll was conducted by a polling firm for the Canada Centre for Global Security Studies at the Munk School of Global Affairs and a Canadian foundation. There were nine thousand random interviews conducted in the eight member states of the Arctic Council and in the Arctic indigenous communities. The Arctic Council is a circumpolar forum founded in 1996 and composed of members Canada, Denmark, Finland, Iceland, Norway, Russia, Sweden, and the United States, and with representatives of the indigenous peoples of the Arctic.

The survey findings did start with the admission that "Canadians see the Arctic as our foremost foreign policy priority and one which should be resourced accordingly (most favour shifting military resources here rather than deploying them to other conflict zones)."[6] From this statement, the reported results show far less militancy than reported by the *Globe*. Here are some of the key findings presented at length in order to make a certain point:

- Canadians from all geographical regions "see the Arctic as highly important and feel that it is deserving of a dominant place in our foreign policy. Environment issues consistently rank as the primary concern."[7]
- "Unprompted, the top-of-mind conceptions of Arctic security is [*sic*] dominated by 'classical' security. . . . This sort of imagery is somewhat more common in the South than the North."[8]
- In "reflected" consideration, "sovereignty and threat are still public priorities, but it is the environment that overwhelmingly dominates. Of almost equal significance (and more so among Northerners), are concerns about human capital infrastructure. This dominance of the environment and climate change is a common feature of international outlook on the Arctic."[9]
- "When faced with limited resources, the trade-off analysis shows that when making hard choices, infrastructure and human capital investment are the clear winners. Despite agreement that military resources should be shifted to the Arctic, in the trade-off analysis, increased military presence was a very low priority for the South and the lowest priority for the North. Even though there is some support for increasing military presence, they would not choose to do so at the expense of other priorities. The preference is for resources to be invested in the non-military aspects of security. A similarly low trade-off ranking for mining and exploration suggests that current Canadian outlook is more in line with 'don't drill baby don't,' which may be a reaction to the disastrous Gulf Oil spill."[10]

Reading the poll summary directly makes one recognize those old familiar Canadians rather than the bellicose Canadians of the *Globe*'s reporting. The point of presenting so much of the poll summary here is to show how the *Globe*'s focus on the militancy of the views was not accurate. The poll summary did report that Canadians "were least open to negotiation and compromise"[11] among the peoples polled, but this could just as easily be because Canadians don't trust any others—especially Russians and Americans as the poll indicates—to put environmental concerns first, and *not* because Canadians have become more militant than Americans as was implied.

So what's going on here? What seemed to be a great alignment of views among the public, national media, and policy makers might instead be a great effort by that media to sell the story of great alignment. Whether working autonomously or with the Harper government, or just working from the same mind-set, the image of Canadians presented to Canadians supported the ruling government's story of the Arctic. Public opinion matters here, but how? The media has an autonomous voice on foreign policy issues, but how much? These are the issues to be explored in this chapter.

## DIFFERENT VIEWS ON THE PUBLIC

We will disaggregate the triangulated relationship between public opinion, media, and foreign policy makers. To begin, the relationship between public opinion and foreign policy makers and foreign policy making is complicated. Scholars and policy makers offer different views on this relationship, but not views that are always compatible. Some of the early foreign policy studies on public opinion focused on whether the public held a structured, coherent view on foreign policy matters. In a 1950 study, Gabriel Almond contended that American citizens were ignorant of foreign policy issues and that their opinions lacked structure and content. [12] Because of this the public was subject to volatile mood changes. Other scholarship in the 1970s took the position that there was structure, coherence, and stability to the public's foreign policy views. Scholars taking this position set out to identify the public's belief sets on foreign policy. [13] For our purposes, studies that analyze the structure of the public's foreign policy beliefs are less important than studies that offer insight into how public opinion either shapes foreign policy making or is shaped by policy makers. We are interested here in any purported impact rather than cognitive structures.

There are two basic views on the relationship between public opinion and policy making. The first suggests a strong impact, and the second denies any real impact. The first view derives from the pluralist model of policy making. This view is "a 'bottom-up' approach [which] assumes that the general public has a measurable and distinct impact on the foreign policy making process. In sum, leaders follow masses." [14] The second view "representing the conventional wisdom in the literature suggests a 'top-down' process, according to which popular consensus is a function of the elite consensus and elite cleavages trickle down to mass public opinion." [15] This view is consistent with realism, as it envisions a persistent national interest pursued by elites and a passive, acquiescent, or inconsequential mass public.

Foreign policy scholars of this second approach take care to distinguish between three different publics. The first is the mass public that is not interested in foreign policy matters, holds no or only poorly informed views on foreign policy, and therefore has no impact on policy making. The second is the attentive public, which, by its name, is attentive to or interested in and informed about world affairs. But this group only has an impact on foreign policy making if its views are articulated by interest groups whose power resources are greater than an amorphous public. Finally, there is the elite, that small section of the public that is interested, informed, and influential in the shaping of public opinion.

Ole Holsti's studies of the impact of public opinion on American foreign policy cautions that the relationship between policy and public opinion is more complex than that suggested by these earlier views. Using data on public opinion, Holsti dispels the notion that the American public is un-knowledgeable about or indifferent to foreign affairs; but he proposes that the public acts like a cognitive miser, making use of mental shortcuts when confronted with international issues. Recall from chapter 3 that when schol-ars conceptualize individuals as cognitive misers, they suggest that people do not exert great cognitive energy—that is, they don't think very much—when confronted with new information. Instead, the new information cues preexist-ing shortcuts so that it matches information already "stored." The new infor-mation is remembered in a way that is consistent with the individual's preex-isting belief set. Holsti concludes that the American public makes use of cognitive shortcuts that follow a pragmatic **internationalist** orientation.[16]

The linkage between public opinion and policy formation is more diffi-cult to demonstrate. Holsti says that although American policy makers tend to be more inclined to internationalism than the American public, the policy makers are restrained by their perception of what the public will tolerate. Policy makers believe the public is harder to convince about internationalist policies—especially policies that involve international cooperation and/or the possible deployment of US troops abroad—and the lack of public support could jeopardize any undertaking.[17] Holsti concludes that there is no direct linkage between public opinion and policy formation, but that policy makers' *perceptions* of public opinion—in the immediate and future sense—set the parameters for foreign policy behavior.

Surveying their own public opinion polling, Steven Kull and Clay Ram-say describe this same phenomenon (prior to the war on terror):

> In the post–Cold War period, U.S. troops have been used in a variety of operations for which the link [to national interests] is less direct or even arguably marginal. In such cases, it is widely believed among the U.S. policy elite, public support for operations is, at best, tenuous and likely to collapse in the face of U.S. troop fatalities. The public response to the deaths of eighteen U.S. Rangers in Somalia in October 1993 is viewed as a key example. Most significant, this belief about the public appears to have had a significant impact on U.S. foreign policy, leading policy-makers to hesitate from using force when they might otherwise have done so, and when using force to do so in a more cautious fashion than would be ideal from a military perspective.[18]

Kull and Ramsay call this the "myth of the reactive public." After the drawn-out wars in Iraq and Afghanistan, this worry about the reactive (and tired) American public may have contributed to Barack Obama's decision to offer only limited US air support to the NATO operation in Libya in 2011 and to the French intervention in Mali in 2013. (These cases are discussed in chap-ters 8 and 9.)

## MANAGING PUBLIC OPINION

The "myth of the reactive public" puts elites in the position of fathoming public sentiment prior to engaging in foreign policy actions. This makes sense if public policy is supposed to represent the interests of the public. However, this model suggests that there is a degree of separation between the public and public policy because elite *perception* seems to be more important than actual public views. Elite perception of public opinion may distort actual public opinion in the way that human perception always distorts an accurate reading of any phenomenon.

The reactive public idea also suggests that public opinion is an exogenous and independent variable, or one that is outside the policy-making process and one that operates autonomously. The policy maker observes the public *out there* and tries to fathom what the public likes or doesn't like (based on the policy maker's own beliefs about the public) in order to make a foreign policy decision that won't upset the public. This notion runs counter to the view of the public offered in the last chapter.

In chapter 6, we examined a model in which elites mobilize the public in favor of a foreign policy action that is designed to enhance the legitimacy of the elite vis-à-vis opponents. This model portrays the public as one of many resources that elites may manipulate for their own purposes. In this, public opinion is endogenous to or inside the process by which elites compete with one another for control. Public opinion itself is controllable. But the mobilization model discussed in the last chapter also suggests that public opinion can become like Frankenstein's monster and break out of the control of the elites who try to use it.

Matthew Baum's study of public opinion complements this last point. For Baum, public opinion or public attentiveness to a policy is both unreliably controllable and limiting. Betting on being able to control public opinion as a necessary resource in bargaining when policy makers can't even be sure they can arouse it in the first place is risky. As Baum explains in his study of American presidents, "regardless of their rhetorical strategies, presidents cannot unilaterally *command* public opinion, including the *extent* of public interest."[19] Not only can't policy makers count on the public to pay attention, but rousing the public is risky too. "All else equal, a policy fashioned under intense public scrutiny reduces the president's freedom to develop an optimal foreign policy, free from domestic pressures to compromise."[20] Leaders don't want to face the political costs of appearing to "lose" in a foreign policy interaction to which the public is paying attention. Thus, since attention can't be used reliably as a resource in bargaining and since public attention can limit the leader's flexibility and choice of actions, the best options for the policy maker are to do nothing to attract attention or to act when no one is paying attention.

Baum offers the example of George H. W. Bush (Bush 1) in the presidential election year of 1992. In January of that year, senators from both political parties sponsored resolutions demanding that the United States intervene in the humanitarian disaster unfolding in Somalia. The year before, the Somali government had collapsed and the country was plunged into a multisided civil war. At the same time, famine struck the country. Humanitarian relief organizations were having trouble getting aid into the country because the warring factions would hijack the relief supplies and threaten the workers. President Bush was being pressured by different internal and external actors and groups to intervene in Somalia throughout that election year,[21] but the pressure was not coming from the media since the media wasn't covering Somalia. Baum notes that media coverage did increase slightly in August when it was announced that the US military would provide airlift support for humanitarian operations staged from Kenya, but that increase in media coverage peaked only modestly and then dropped again.[22] More, advisors to the president thought that a boots-on-the-ground intervention could be conducted fairly easily and with a high probability of success.[23] Despite all this, the president decided that an intervention with the possibility of American casualties could alienate the public and hurt his reelection prospects. After Bush lost his reelection bid, he didn't need to worry about the public limiting his flexibility in the intervention because he could suffer no political costs; thus he ordered twenty-six thousand American military personnel into Somalia in Operation Restore Hope.

This example shows a democratically elected leader ignoring the "attentive public" concerned about Somalia until he felt safe to act. The president could ignore the attentive public in order to avoid waking the sleeping mass—or voting—public. Indeed, had he chosen to do so, Bush might have continued to ignore the attentive public as he moved out of the White House.

Bush was facing voters, so the question to be asked is whether there is any evidence that the mass public has an impact on foreign policy making outside of an electoral cycle. Thomas Risse-Kappen examines the relationship between public opinion and foreign policy making in France, the United States, and other democracies. He concludes that "mass public opinion mattered" in each case, in that it "set broad and unspecified limits to the foreign policy choices."[24] Public opinion has an important indirect effect as it appears that "the main role of the public in liberal democracies is to influence the coalition-building processes among elite groups."[25] Risse-Kappen maintains that "for both the political elites and societal actors, mass public opinion proves to be a resource for strengthening one's position in the coalition-building process."[26] This is not the mobilization method discussed earlier but a more nuanced argument that mass public opinion serves as the compass guiding elites as they form policy coalitions.

Additionally, Risse-Kappen concludes that understanding the degree of both societal fragmentation and centralization of political authority is critical to understanding the impact of public opinion on foreign policy. In countries with great societal political fragmentation, such as France, no mass public opinion exists on foreign policy issues. French social fragmentation is complemented by the highly centralized nature of political authority; both conditions combine to limit sharply the impact of public opinion on foreign policy making. For example, in a 2003 Brookings Institution report on French foreign policy, Justin Vaïsse explores the factors that influenced France's opposition to the 2003 Iraq war. Vaïsse concludes that President Jacques Chirac welcomed the support his policy received from the public but he was not motivated by what might seem to be a natural desire to unite a public experiencing major divisions between Muslims and non-Muslims. The unified public support was nice, but Chirac's decision was the result of consensus elite opinion on how the Iraq war would harm the larger war on terror.[27] The decision not to support the war in Iraq was made without regard to public opinion. A 2011 Congressional Research Service report on the shaping of French foreign policy describes divisions between the French government and public on many domestic issues, but foreign policy issues are left to the elite and the elite are united behind the idea that France is a global power that should act like a global power.[28] We might conclude that any impact on foreign policy making by the French mass or attentive public would only be apparent when the elite deviate substantially from the established great power path, which the elite are not inclined to do.

## PUBLIC OPINION, THE "CNN EFFECT," AND MANAGED NEWS

Now we should bring back in the other member of the triangle—the media. There exists in the minds of some observers and policy makers a phenomenon called the **"CNN effect."** Political scientist and former US assistant secretary of defense for international security affairs Joseph Nye explains the CNN effect in this way:

> The free flow of broadcast information in open societies has always had an impact on public opinion and the formation of foreign policy, but now the flows have increased and shortened news cycles have reduced the time for deliberation. By focusing on certain conflicts and human rights problems, broadcasts pressure politicians to respond to some foreign problems and not others. The so-called CNN effect makes it harder to keep some items off the top of the public agenda that might otherwise warrant a lower priority.[29]

Nye sees the CNN effect as real and potentially harmful to reasoned policy making. Because the news broadcasts "24/7," the media sometimes force issues onto the public policy agenda, issues that policy makers would be happier to keep off. This, in turn, lessens deliberation time and the search for the most reasonable policy response.

Those who believe that the CNN effect is real propose that it makes use of public opinion. Once the media broadcast images of mass starvation, ethnic conflict, or some other sort of mass suffering, the images arouse strong emotions in the public. The public then turn to their elected officials and demand some strong response. That is, the public, aroused by images of suffering portrayed in the media, demand that officials "do something." Elected officials, wanting to stay in the public's favor for all sorts of obvious reasons, respond with some sort of **humanitarian intervention**, military intervention, or whatever action is needed in the immediate term.

Is there a CNN effect? In his study of how George H. W. Bush avoided doing anything in Somalia in order to avoid incurring political costs, Baum reports that in interviews with administration officials some insisted that the media played an important role in administration policy on Somalia.[30] At the same time, *other* administration officials said that the media showed little interest in Somalia until after ground troops had been deployed there, and thus the media had no impact on policy making.[31] Rather than the media driving public opinion and thereby driving foreign policy, the policy brought the media and the public to the story.

If perceptions are stronger than reality and the perception is that the CNN effect is real, then the media play a powerful role in setting the public agenda. What is the nature of that role? Jonathan Mermin poses this question about the American media: "Journalists necessarily engage in agenda setting, in deciding out of the vast universe of events what to report and what to ignore. But in setting the news agenda, what rules do journalists follow?"[32] How do the media decide when to cover a story out of the many, many stories that might be covered? Mermin offers two possible answers. First, the media act independently, and "independent journalistic initiative" puts stories in the headlines.[33] Mermin cites the story of one NBC correspondent who decided on his own to publicize forgotten stories. He single-handedly put the story of the 1984 Ethiopian famine on the airwaves (a story previously covered by the BBC but not American media), prompting an outpouring of US aid to Ethiopia. But this independent journalistic initiative is the exception rather than the rule.

The second possible explanation for how the media come to cover what they cover is that "American journalists turn to politicians and government officials for guidance in deciding what constitutes news."[34] American journalists—and arguably journalists from around the world on issues of global importance—take their cues from Washington for practical reasons. First, given limited budgets and staff, reporters are assigned to newsworthy places—Washington, D.C., would rank among the top newsworthy places on almost anyone's list. Second, on foreign policy issues, Washington generates a plethora of information every day. Third, "considerations of the need to establish the legitimacy of information reported and the need for protection against the liability for inaccurate reports also encourage the use of official sources."[35]

At the same time that Washington—or any national capital—makes practical sense as a location for budget- and personnel-strapped media outlets, Washington also produces far too much news for the media to cover. As Mermin puts it, "Far more stories are pitched to reporters than end up making the news."[36] Members of the media, then, do exercise some independent judgment about which stories to cover. Mermin suggests this about what ultimately is reported: "The news agenda in this view is a joint production of sources and journalists."[37]

Mermin supports his conclusions with evidence of news coverage of the famine and conflict in Somalia in the eleven months leading up to the US humanitarian intervention already discussed above. US intervention in Somalia was not the result of the CNN effect, Mermin contends, but instead "journalists worked closely with governmental sources in deciding when to cover Somalia, and how to frame the story, and how much coverage it deserved. The lesson of Somalia is not just about the influence of television on Washington; it is equally about the influence of Washington on television."[38]

When considering the "joint" agenda setting between government officials and media, can we say the balance of influence leans more toward one side or the other? We might conclude with some degree of certainty that the "power" tilts in favor of those with information—officials—although not overwhelmingly so. We can find support for the idea that the media are driven more by policy makers than policy makers are driven by the media outside the case of the United States. Tony Shaw examines the British popular press coverage of the early Cold War period in order to learn how the press contributed to the eventual consensus that developed between policy makers and the British public. At the immediate conclusion of World War II, Shaw notes, the British press were diverse in terms of political ideologies and portrayals of the Soviet Union, the United States, and the United Nations.[39] In 1947, Shaw asserts, the British press exhibited widely different views on the Truman Doctrine, the Marshall Plan for the reconstruction of Europe, and whether Soviet troops were correct to stay throughout Eastern and Central Europe.

The British government had a different opinion regarding the Soviet Union and the United States, and it decided that the press would need to be brought around to the correct view:

> All heads of Foreign Office political departments were instructed on ways to make "subtler use of our publicity machine" to ensure the publication of anti-

Soviet material, including various ways of leaking information to friendly diplomatic correspondents and inspiring questions that the Foreign Office could pretend it did not want to answer.[40]

Similarly, the Foreign Office orchestrated a pro–United States, pro–Marshall Plan campaign aimed at changing press views. The acuity of the government's view regarding the Soviet Union was "demonstrated" by the Soviet-inspired communist takeover of Czechoslovakia in 1948. By 1949—just two years into a concerted government effort to manage the press message on the Cold War—the British press was unified in its portrayal of the emerging Cold War, and this portrayal was in line with the government's view.

Al Jazeera presents a case of direct government management of the media. Al Jazeera was begun in 1996 with the financial support of the new Qatari emir Sheikh Hamad bin Khalifa al-Thani. The satellite and cable television channel has the widest viewership in the Middle East and claims total journalistic independence. However, in 2009 US State Department cables published by WikiLeaks, the US ambassador commented that Qatar used Al Jazeera coverage as a "bargaining chip" in its foreign policy. Al Jazeera coverage was used to reward friendly countries and punish unfriendly countries, and all coverage was harnessed to the promotion of Qatar as a regional diplomatic power.[41] *Spiegel* reports that since the 2011 Arab Awakening, Al Jazeera has "fawned upon the new rulers" even as it minimized coverage of public protests in neighboring Bahrain.[42]

Policy makers can find ways to ignore events that are covered by actual independent media when those policy makers have already decided not to "do something." Encouraged by humanitarian nongovernmental organizations (NGOs) on the scene, the media *did not* ignore the unfolding genocide and refugee crisis in Rwanda in the summer of 1994. Despite media attention, with the exception of France and to a lesser extent Canada, no major powers called for any type of intervention, and in fact the major powers worked within the UN Security Council to cut the presence of UN peacekeepers within weeks of the start of the genocide. The French call for action, it should be noted, was in *opposition* to any UN operation. Media coverage of Rwanda in the horrible year 1994 made no difference because policy makers in important countries had decided that intervention did not serve their interests.

Similarly, international media coverage of Russian human rights violations in Chechnya during the first and second Chechen wars evoked little formal condemnation (and no action) by the United States. US humanitarian aid workers attempted to cajole or shame the American government into a more forceful stand on Chechnya, but US policy makers had determined already that they would not jeopardize US-Russian relations on behalf of the people of Chechnya.

The role media play in setting the public agenda is primarily determined by the conditions created by officials themselves, according to journalist Warren Strobel.[43] Strobel examines the impact of media on the United States' decision to participate in peacekeeping and **peace enforcement operations**, operations to which media have freer access and thus might be able to generate more pressure among publics for the government to act. Strobel proposes that push-and-pull factors might be at play: the media might push governments into launching peace operations, or the media might pull governments away from certain courses of action or even cause the termination of participation in peace operations. From his study, Strobel concludes,

> Images and written accounts of the horrors of the post–Cold War world that stream into the offices of government officials do not dictate policy outcomes. Sometimes they suggest policy choices, but there is ample reason to believe that officials can reject those choices if they feel it necessary. At other times, media reports become an ally for an entire administration, or individual members of it, seeking to pursue new policies.[44]

Media, like other societal actors, can take control of a government's policy only when that government loses control:

> If officials let others dominate the policy debate, if they do not closely monitor the progress and results of their own policies, if they fail to build and maintain popular and congressional support for a course of action, if they step beyond the bounds of their public mandate or fail to anticipate problems, they may suddenly seem driven by the news media and its agenda.[45]

This discussion is not meant to suggest that media have no power to mobilize opinion against a government's policy and cause some change to occur to that policy. Russian media and other interest groups were instrumental in forcing the Russian government to end the first Chechen war. Similarly, US media played a crucial role in mobilizing antiwar sentiment in the United States during the Vietnam War by offering interpretations of events that did not fit the official presentation. Strobel cautioned that we should refrain from making blanket statements about the balance of power between media and government in wartime, since the United States had not yet fought a war that involved a high number of casualties in the era of real-time television coverage.[46] Strobel issued his warning before the 2003 US-led invasion of Iraq. The second Chechen war may be instructive here since media access to Chechnya was controlled tightly by the Russian government to avoid an ending similar to that of the first Chechen war. Media and public views of the second Chechen war tended to stay in line with the official view. The lesson seems to be that policy makers—once set on or against a foreign mission— usually can control or ignore the media when they stay in full control of the policy-making process. The American air campaign against the Taliban and al Qaeda in Afghanistan in late 2001 and the subsequent military operations there as well as the US-led invasion of Iraq seemed informed by this lesson. The use of "embedded" journalists limited the media coverage to producing those images that fit the government's depiction of events.

## A COMPLICATED RELATIONSHIP: GOVERNMENT, ELITE, MEDIA, AND THE PUBLIC

This last insight—that once set on a foreign policy course, leaders can usually control or ignore media messages—can be expanded to include other actors. Robert Entman offers a model for understanding the complicated relationship between policy makers, opposition elites, the media, and the public that combines many of the elements of state-level foreign policy analysis discussed in these last three chapters. In a nutshell, his research suggests that, "in practice, the relationship between governing elites and news organizations is less distant and more cooperative than the ideal envisions, especially in foreign affairs."[47]

The basic setup is this: When a foreign policy problem arises, someone attempts to explain the problem and its solution. That someone might be the governing elite, the opposition elite, or even the media. Explaining a problem and proposing a solution to it is called **"framing."** Sometimes the governing elite get out in front of a problem and frame it in such a way as to deny others the ability to offer a competing frame. When this happens, opposition elite and media often choose to support and reinforce the frame. The single frame then "cascades" down to the public in a small and recognizable package. The public hears from multiple sources that the problem can be understood in a single way, and being cognitive misers the public is content to buy the single frame and support it.[48]

Framing is not so easy, and it is in the framing that governing elites may get behind on an issue, opening the door to competing frames from the opposition and/or the media. Framing is the act of "selecting and highlighting some facets of events and issues and making connections among them so as to promote a particular interpretation, evaluation and/or solution."[49] Frames that work best are those that have cultural resonance, that is, frames that evoke words and images that are "noticeable, understandable, memorable, and emotionally charged" in the dominant political culture.[50]

Successful frames depend upon the stimulus: when the foreign policy event is recognizable and congruent with the political culture, the national response is based on habit. If the governing elite have successfully matched the event with a habitual schema, it requires "almost no cognitive effort [by the public] to make the connections promoted by the administration's frame of the event."[51] In the aftermath of the September 11, 2001, attacks on the United States, the Bush administration framed the problem as a surprise terrorist attack on innocent US civilians. The terrorists were evil and irrational. Those who responded to the attacks were brave heroes. The images in this frame were so easily acceptable to the American public that other elites stayed silent or echoed the administration's frame, and the media also repeated the frame. Because Entman assumes that all elites and members of the media are motivated by self-interest and survival, few would dare to offer competing frames for 9/11 (for example, a frame that concedes that American foreign policy might incite individuals to take extreme actions). Commentators who sought to understand the reasons behind the attacks were marginalized and shunned as unpatriotic.

When an event is totally incongruent with national self-image and habitual response, the public's response is to block information about the event. Elites who get out in front of the framing can capture the public's support by offering an explanation that evokes images that are more reconcilable with the national self-image. Entman proposes that the governing elite's control of the frame is the highest in situations in which the event is totally congruent or totally incongruent with the political culture. He gives two compelling examples to make his case.

In the first case, a Soviet fighter jet shot down Korean Air Lines (KAL) Flight 007, killing all 269 people on board. This occurred in September 1983. In the second case, in July 1988, a US Navy ship shot down Iran Air Flight 655, killing 290 people. "In both cases, military officials misidentified a passenger plane as a hostile target; in both cases, the perpetrating nation's officials claimed that circumstances justified the attacks."[52] In the first case, Reagan administration officials got out in front of the story, depicting the events in a "murder" frame. The story of evil Soviets (from the habitual Cold War schema) murdering innocent civilians was not hard for the American public to accept. Political survival for opposition elites and sales for the media meant that the frame was never questioned, just repeated and magnified.

In the second case, the events did not fit any habitual schema and indeed were "thoroughly at odds with Americans' national self-image." This incongruent event blocked thinking about the event, allowing the Reagan administration's explanation that the shoot-down occurred due to a technical glitch to dominate the public understanding.[53] Standard expectations about opposition elite and the media hold in this case: both simply supported and maintained the administration's frame. Indeed, the media devoted more print pages and broadcast time to discussing the "murder" frame involving the shoot-down of KAL 007 than it did to the "technical glitch" frame involving Iran Air 655.[54]

Clearly Entman is proposing what some of the scholars discussed above contend: a government can control its own response to a foreign policy event when it stays on top of the event, framing and explaining the event and the appropriate response to it. When policy makers let others—domestic political opponents, media—define the event, policy makers lose control of the event. Foreign policy choices in such a case are determined by actors outside the regime if the regime cannot succeed in distracting the public in order to maintain its own foreign policy frame. Ultimately, the regime that loses control of the frame loses control of the policy.

When a foreign policy event is ambiguous and the dominant culture has no immediate, habitual response, opposition elites and the media may be able to offer alternative frames that win critical support among parts of the public. Entman warns that the governing elite tread dangerous waters here and may mismanage and lose control of the foreign policy event (that is, let others frame the situation and the solution), "especially if it cannot find compelling schemas that support its line."[55] Ultimately, this means that understanding the general orientation of public sentiment is critical to the shaping of policy that will be supported by the public. A public that is disorganized in terms of its dominant political narrative will not respond in any uniform way to a foreign policy venture. This could be costly to the regime that attempts a foreign policy action that does not resonate as true or right with the public.

## CHAPTER REVIEW

- There is little scholarly agreement on the impact of public opinion on policy making other than that the impact is probably indirect.
- The pluralist view of the impact of public opinion on foreign policy is that the public has a distinct impact on policy making. An opposing view is that elites set policy and drive public opinion.
- The public is often discussed in terms of the mass public that is uninformed about foreign policy, the attentive public whose opinion is channeled through interest groups, and the elite.
- Some scholars believe that elite perception of what the public will tolerate sets the parameters for foreign policy making.
- There is little scholarly and practitioner agreement on the "CNN effect," but policy makers seem to believe the effect is real.
- Scholarship on the "CNN effect" shows that it has no impact on policy once decision makers have already agreed on a course of action.
- The media and government officials engage in the joint production of news, with the balance of control on the side of government officials.
- When a government stays in control of the "framing" of a foreign policy event, it generally can control the views of the opposition, media, and public on that event.

- When a government lets others define and explain a foreign policy event, it stands to lose control of its own response to that event.

*Chapter Eight*

# Great Powers in General, the United States Specifically

## IN THIS CHAPTER

- The System Level of Analysis
- The Elusive Concept of Power
- Who Gets to Be a Great Power?
- The Great Powers and the International System
- The International Order That Uncle Sam Built
- American Grand Strategy
- Chapter Review

## CASES FEATURED IN THIS CHAPTER

- How the UN Security Council permanent five—the United States, Great Britain, France, Russia, and China—use their power to deny other states permanent status in the Security Council.
- How the United States, acting as hegemon, constructed a durable international order based on the rule of law and multilateralism.
- The lack of grand strategy in the George H. W. Bush presidency, the first of the unipolar era.
- The Bill Clinton soft power grand strategy designed to keep the United States at the center of the international "wheel," permanently engaged with all the other major powers.
- The George W. Bush global dominance grand strategy that blended neoconservative and realist use of power to maintain unipolarity indefinitely.

• The Barack Obama grand strategy that asserts the continued importance of the exceptional America leading a world transformed by globalization.

## THE SYSTEM LEVEL OF ANALYSIS

The National Intelligence Council (NIC) is the US intelligence community's center for medium- and long-term strategic thinking. The NIC's purpose is to produce National Intelligence Estimates and unclassified "over the horizon" reports about trends in world politics. These "over the horizon" reports make use of the collective understanding of trends in the world derived from experts from different agencies of the government and from nongovernmental experts from around the world.

*Global Trends 2030: Alternative Worlds* is the name of the NIC's "over the horizon" report published at the end of 2012 and the first Barack Obama administration. The report begins with this pronouncement:

> The world of 2030 will be radically transformed from our world today. By 2030, no country—whether the U.S., China, or any other large country—will be a hegemonic power. The empowerment of individuals and a diffusion of power among states and from states to informal networks will have a dramatic impact, largely reversing the historic rise of the West since 1750, restoring Asia's weight in the global economy, and ushering in a new era of "democratization" at the international and domestic level.[1]

As in earlier reports, one significant megatrend predicted involves a power shift from West to East and a diffusion of power among many actors. Europe and Russia will continue their decline relative to other powers, along with Japan, while countries formerly from the developing world—China, India, Brazil, Colombia, Indonesia, Nigeria, South Africa, and Turkey—will become important world powers.[2] New technologies will have a transformative impact on the global landscape, helping the United States remain "first among equals."[3] The report purports that "with the rapid rise of other countries, the 'unipolar moment' is over and Pax Americana—the era of American ascendancy in international politics that began in 1945—is fast winding down."[4] Yet "the replacement of the United States by another global power and erection of a new international order seems the least likely outcome in this time period."[5]

*Global Trends 2030* is an example of analysis at the system level. At the system level of analysis, we study interactions that occur bilaterally or multilaterally, regionally or globally. This is the level of analysis that is most commonly used in media reports of global affairs ("Europe Backs French Mali Mission with Strong Words, Modest Means"), and thus it should seem more familiar to the reader. This level of analysis might also seem familiar because the discussion is focused more on policy outcomes—specifically behaviors—than on policy process. The primary purpose of analysts using this level is to get "outside" national borders in order to discuss the interactions of states with other states, with transnational actors, and within international organizations.

There are two fundamental questions (or two sides to a single, fundamental question) underlying much of foreign policy scholarship. Do states act the way they act in the world because of who they are (as defined within the state)? Or do states act the way they do because of where they sit in the world (as defined by their relationships with other actors in the international system)? Scholars studying foreign policy at the system level stress the latter but cannot escape from the former. Foreign policy makers, too, confront this reality, as they engage in what scholars call the two-level, dual, or nested game.

System-level analysis that focuses on power and position derives primarily from the realist worldview, but Marxist-based accounts also are informative here. Later in this chapter we'll discuss US foreign policy after World War II—a discussion informed by neoliberalism. The dominant perspective used first in this chapter is realism with its focus on how a state's position in the international system is related to its foreign policy. Sometimes the suggested relationship is causal—a country's position is said to determine its foreign policy—but, most typically, the suggested relationship is a matter of explaining which options are open to states in certain positions and what those states must and/or will do to preserve or enhance their status.

To realists, the nature of the international system sets the conditions for certain kinds of foreign policy behaviors, although it does not determine specific behaviors. A classic statement on the impact of the system level on a state's foreign policy comes from neorealist Kenneth Waltz:

> With many sovereign states, with no system of law enforceable among them, with each state judging its grievances and ambitions according to the dictates of its own reason or desire—conflict, sometimes leading to war, is bound to occur. To achieve a favorable outcome from such conflict a state has to rely on its own devices, the relative efficiency of which must be its constant concern. [6]

And,

> In anarchy, there is no automatic harmony. . . . Because each state is the final judge of its own cause, any state may at any time use force to implement its policies. Because any state may at any time use force, all states must constantly be ready either to counter force with force or to pay the cost of weakness. The requirements of state action are, in this view, imposed by the circumstances in which all states exist. [7]

In a realist world, anarchy requires a foreign policy stance that is always watchful for encroachments on one's security and power, and for opportunities to advance one's security and power.

Realists place their primary, if not exclusive, emphasis on the study of powerful states. The system level of analysis is the level of choice for realism, and the subject of choice is that group of states that have some shaping impact on the system. This is true for classical realists as well as for those neorealists who study international relations through the lens of international political economy. These scholars focus on the states at and near the top of the power hierarchy. For instance, Charles Kindleberger contends that a state's size determines its ability to stabilize or disrupt the international economic system. "Large" countries have the capability to stabilize the system, "middle" countries can damage or disrupt the system, and "small" countries have no impact at all on the system.[8] Because the focus is on expected systemic impact, the study of small countries yields no interesting lessons and so lacks analytical value to realist scholars. Not all foreign policy scholars take this position, but those who study foreign policy at this level admit that position in the system opens opportunities for some states—the more powerful—and closes opportunities for others.

The terms used here—large, middle, and small countries, or great, middle, and small powers—can be misleading. For example, when foreign policy scholars speak of "small states," they are not necessarily suggesting anything about the geographical size of the state, its population, or the level of the institutional development of its governance structures. Instead, something is implied about how the country's attributes—size, population, economy, and so forth—position the state in respect to other states. Similarly, foreign policy discussions of "weak states" may not necessarily suggest anything about the internal features of countries and the effectiveness of their governments (as is suggested by the terms "failed state" and "failing state," for example). Instead, the state is weak in relation to other state actors. System-level analysis focuses on the power-based relationships between international actors.

Another knotty aspect of the use of categories such as great, middle, and small is that there is rarely agreement among scholars or policy makers about which states fit which categories because the categories themselves are often a little "fuzzy." For instance, recall the "pre-theory" of foreign policy proposed by James Rosenau and discussed in earlier chapters. In Rosenau's pre-theory, he offered eight ideal nation-types that he developed from a simple "large country" versus "small country" starting point. Rosenau's purpose, remember, was to get the ball rolling on systematic, comparative foreign policy research, and so he did not offer any definition of large and small. He had in mind that the United States, Soviet Union, India, and China were large countries, while Holland (the Netherlands), Czechoslovakia (long before the country split into two), Kenya, and Ghana were small countries. Unfortunately, other analysts have been content to offer similarly impressionistic designations of state type without any greater definitional precision.

## THE ELUSIVE CONCEPT OF POWER

Much of the imprecision in the definition of great, middle, or small powers comes from a fundamental problem that resists resolution: there is no agreement among analysts about the definition of the elemental, fundamental concept of "power." Power is one of the defining features of international politics, according to realists, liberals, and Marxists. But none of these perspectives has ever reached consensus about what this critical concept means. This failure is not limited to international politics; one of the more prominent international relations scholars, Robert Gilpin, noted that this is endemic to the broader study of politics. Gilpin declared that the "number and variety of definitions (of power) should be an embarrassment to political scientists."[9]

When Rosenau divided states into large and small, developed and underdeveloped, and open and closed, he had in mind the idea that we can categorize states based on measurements of certain attributes or resources. More powerful states, for instance, are those with larger, more industrialized national economies and larger, better-equipped, better-trained national militaries. We might also add that more powerful states have healthier, better-fed, better-educated citizens. Indeed, we could keep adding different measurable attributes to this list, depending on what we as analysts believe to be important. From this, we can say that power derives from or is the summation of these tangible resources of the state. Tangible aspects of power create a certain level of state capability.

But capability does not translate directly into influence. A powerful state measured in tangible capabilities may not be able to influence the foreign or domestic policies or behaviors of other states. *How* states translate material capability into the ability to make other states modify their behaviors is a long-standing puzzle.[10] Indeed, history provides many examples of very powerful states—again, as measured in military and economic attributes—that lost wars to far less powerful actors. The US failure to defeat the opponent in Vietnam during the 1960s and early 1970s and the Soviet failure to defeat the opponent in Afghanistan in the 1980s are two prominent examples. To be sure, powerful states sometimes can have *their* behavior changed by actors whose power capabilities seem minuscule in comparison. Despite this cautionary note about the nature of power, it is the fact that some countries are considered to be and are more powerful than others, and being more powerful permits a country a much wider range of policy options than is permitted to the less powerful.

# WHO GETS TO BE A GREAT POWER?

Despite the elusive nature of power, we continue to define great, middle, and small powers in terms of measurable power capabilities. So, which countries get to be great powers? We might be inclined to use membership in certain "elite" international organizations as proof of a country's ranking and position. For example, we might decide that the permanent members of the UN Security Council—the United States, Russia, Great Britain, France, and China—are the states that properly should be designated "great powers." These states were the victors of World War II (with the French resistance earning France its title as victor) and created for themselves a privileged position in the new United Nations with the special power of the veto. Some modifications within this group have been allowed by the group. The China seat was held by the Republic of China or Taiwan until 1971 when the People's Republic of China took over that seat. Similarly, the Soviet Union was an original member of the "Big Five," but upon its dissolution its seat went to Russia and not to any of the other independent countries created out of the former Soviet Union.

These self-made modifications notwithstanding, the possibility of adding permanent members to the Security Council has been and remains a controversial topic. Other countries have become powerful actors on the world stage—and certainly are great powers by some definitions—yet they remain outside permanent membership. Japan has been the second-largest financial contributor to the United Nations, yet it is only periodically a member of the Security Council, sometimes occupying one of the ten two-year, rotating, nonpermanent seats. India is the world's largest democracy by population, it is a major participant in UN peacekeeping activities, and it possesses nuclear weapons, yet it holds no permanent Security Council seat. Indonesia is the world's fourth-largest country by population, the largest Muslim country, and a country that seems to have weathered the world financial crisis that started in 2008 much better than most. Nigeria is a powerhouse in West Africa and a leader of the Economic Community of West African States (ECOWAS). Neither Indonesia nor Nigeria should have much hope of acquiring a permanent seat in the Security Council.

We could continue to name strong candidates for permanent membership to the Security Council and great power designation—none of which are ever likely to achieve the same status as the permanent five. Why? Because adding permanent members to the Security Council requires a change to the UN Charter, and all changes to the UN Charter require the approval of three-quarters of the General Assembly membership and the agreement of all of the permanent five. Each of the permanent five maintains opposition to the possibility of admitting certain other states to the permanent membership, and all maintain opposition to sharing the veto with any other state. This is what great powers do—they block rising great powers using whatever means available.

What if we decided to use other criteria besides Security Council permanent membership for great power designation? For example, what if possession of nuclear weapons earned a state great power status? Then the great powers would include the Security Council permanent five—the United States, Russia, Great Britain, France, and China—as well as Israel, India, Pakistan, and North Korea. There would be very little beyond the possession of nuclear weapons to characterize the membership of this group. Few analysts would be comfortable speaking about the nuclear weapons club as the club of great powers. Indeed, the problem discussed earlier about translating capability into influence is particularly acute when thinking about nuclear weapons. North Korea routinely claims great power status and threatens other countries—especially the United States, its "archenemy"—with attack, but North Korea's nuclear weapons do not constitute "real" power enough to cause much if any change in other countries' foreign policy behaviors. The "power" that comes with possessing nuclear weapons doesn't seem to have made North Korea very powerful at all. For that matter, the possession of a massive nuclear weapons arsenal did not protect the territorial United States from terrorist attacks in 2001.

The report discussed at the start of this chapter, *Global Trends 2030*, attempts to designate some countries as great powers largely based on the size of national economies and share of world wealth. After consulting experts in and out of government from around the world, the list that the NIC develops is still more impressionistic than definite: the United States is still a great power, but Europe, Russia, and Japan will be diminished powers (but how diminished and will they still be considered powerful states?), and others—China, India, Brazil, Colombia, Indonesia, Nigeria, South Africa, and Turkey—will have ascended in the ranks. Will this change the international architecture? The discussion above about the UN Security Council permanent membership suggests the contrary, and this may be more fundamental to understanding the term "great power" than material capabilities.

## THE GREAT POWERS AND THE INTERNATIONAL SYSTEM

The *Penguin Dictionary of International Relations* explains this about great powers:

> In addition to military and economic strength, great powers normally have global if not universal interests and are usually characterized as possessing the political will to pursue them. The United States, for example, although long regarded by others as a great power, has not always displayed the political will to behave like one, especially during the period until 1917 and between 1921

and 1941. It was only after the Second World War that the United States consistently and self-consciously adopted this posture.[11]

And,

> The term [great power] itself can be traced back to fifteenth-century Italian politics but the first time it was adopted as an orthodox diplomatic concept was with the signing of the Treaty of Chaumont in 1817. As a result of the Congress of Vienna (1815) five states, Austria, Britain, France, Prussia and Russia, had informally conferred on themselves great power status. The intention was that these states acting in concert would adopt a managerial role in relation to the maintenance of order in the European state system.[12]

Great powers by this accounting are states with significant military and economic capabilities (that slippery thing called power), global political interests, *and* the will to protect and maintain those interests. The Congress of Vienna great powers designated themselves as great powers and linked this designation to the job description of maintaining the European state system. These great powers did not act out of altruism but out of their own broadly defined self-interests.

That great powers have interests beyond their own immediate interests and are willing to use their power—especially military force—to promote those broadly defined interests is what sets great powers apart from others. Consider Edward Luttwak's distinction between small and great powers:

> To struggle for mere survival was the unhappy predicament of threatened small powers, which had to fight purely to defend themselves and could not hope to achieve anything more with their modest strength. Great powers were different; they could only remain great if they were seen as willing and able to use force to acquire and protect even non-vital interests, including distant possessions or minor additions to their spheres of influence. To lose a few hundred soldiers in some minor probing operation or a few thousand in a small war or expeditionary venture were routine events for the great powers of history.[13]

Moreover, Luttwak adds, "great powers are in the business of threatening, rather than being threatened. A great power cannot be that unless it asserts all sorts of claims that far exceed the needs of its own immediate security, including the protection of allies and clients as well as other less-than-vital interests."[14]

Luttwak defines great powers as those states with overwhelming power resources who display "a readiness to use force whenever it [is] advantageous to do so and an acceptance of the resulting combat casualties with equanimity, as long as the number [is] not disproportionate."[15] And, Luttwak explains, "great powers [are] strong enough to successfully wage war without calling on allies."[16] With this, Luttwak cuts the potential membership of this group down to very few states.

Not only are great powers defined by their willingness to use force, but great powers *arise* through the use of force. The great powers of the twentieth century, explains Ian Lustick, engaged in large-scale **state-building** wars in their formative years. Lustick expands on Charles Tilly's description of state building in the West, a description summarized in the idea that "war made the state, and the state made war."[17] In the European state-building experience, political units were engaged in an ongoing fight to survive. The need to raise money to field armies necessary for basic protection and the defeat of opponents, and ultimately for the acquisition of increasing amounts of territory, led the early European states to institutionalize. Taxation and conscription could only be successfully accomplished through the consolidation of internal control, and both were necessary for the consolidation of external power.

Lustick asserts that European and North American states were free of international constraints such as UN Charter prohibitions against the use of force, and thus they were able to amass the necessary power capabilities to be strong internally and externally. The unrestricted use of force was necessary for building great power capabilities and achieving great power status. By the twentieth century, international prohibitions against such use of unrestricted force—prohibitions designed by the existing great powers and embodied by international institutions—kept other great powers from rising in other places.[18]

Indeed, twentieth-century institutions and norms, particularly those embodied in the mid-century creation, the United Nations, have been used to *justify* the use of force by great powers against potential rising challengers. For example, Iraq's invasion of Kuwait in 1990 resulted from the inability of the two countries to reach agreement on key points of contention regarding Kuwaiti loans to Iraq. When the Iraqi leader Saddam Hussein could not persuade Kuwait to accept more agreeable repayment terms, he decided to settle differences with Kuwait through invasion and occupation. Perhaps the Iraqi leader had in mind how the US invaded Panama in December 1989 after the US government could not get the Panamanian leader Manuel Noriega to comply with American wishes. But Iraq is not the United States. The Iraqi invasion of Kuwait was condemned by the members of the United Nations as a violation of key principles of the UN system. When Iraq refused to comply with UN demands to vacate Kuwait, the UN Security Council gave its blessing to the United States and a multinational coalition to use force against Iraq to compel it to act by the established rules.

This description of great powers thus far is essentially derived from realist accounts, but we need only modify it slightly to make it read as a Marxist account or an account positing that economic interests are primary to understanding foreign policy choices. Marxists would argue that states described as great powers are the product of global elite economic interests. Global economic elites—acting through their agents the states—form a global core that protects established wealth and assists in the acquisition of even greater wealth. International institutions are built by this rich club to impose restrictions on others to keep them out, down, and dependent. States on the periphery that attempt to challenge this system—or gain entrance into the rich club—are punished by international organizations. The use of UN principles to justify the war against Iraq is an example of this. Had Iraq managed to maintain control of Kuwait, Iraq would have controlled too much of the world's oil reserves to be kept out of the club of the elite. The old great powers did not want to open the doors of the club, and so they used their power in the United Nations to justify war against Iraq.

Thus, great powers are states with enormous power capabilities and the demonstrated willingness to use those capabilities whenever necessary. Great powers are attuned to potential threats to their status and must constantly guard against rising powers and potential competitors. And because these are realist ideas, great powers are not fully committed to their own friends or allies because allies might restrain the great powers from doing what they want to do or trap them into doing what they don't want to do.

One other realist idea needs to be introduced here before we turn to our next topic. Much of what we've discussed so far can be discussed in terms of strategy. Because great powers are global actors with global interests, realists explain that they develop and employ grand strategies (and of course only great powers have grand strategies). And because realists are realists, most of them insist that grand strategies are about the use of military power to achieve broad national (and global) political goals. For example, Robert Art explains that "a grand strategy tells a nation's leaders what goals they should aim for and how best they can use their country's military power to attain these goals."[19] Christopher Layne states that "grand strategies must be judged by the amount of security they provide; whether, given international systemic constraints, they are sustainable; their cost; the degree of risk they entail; and their tangible and intangible domestic effects."[20] Although both Art and Layne are realists, each advocates a different grand strategy for the United States in the new millennium, a subject to which we will return at the end of the next section.

## THE INTERNATIONAL ORDER THAT UNCLE SAM BUILT

The account of great powers given so far has been derived primarily from realism, with a little Marxist interpretation here and there. However, to understand the current international order, the power that built it, and the grand strategy involved in protecting that order from threats, we need to make use of liberalism, or neoliberalism to be precise.

The current international order—the rules, organizations, and expected behaviors—is the same **hegemonic order** constructed after World War II despite changes in relative capabilities among countries at and near the top of that order. A hegemon is a *preponderant* power defined in terms of military and economic power. After World War II, the United States was the world's preponderant power, and acting in hegemonic form, it constructed an international order that suited its interests. John G. Ruggie explains that a hegemonic power "will seek to construct an international order in *some* form, presumably along lines that are compatible with its own international objectives and domestic structures."[21] As it turned out, that international order also suited a wide-range of interests, as it still does today.

Soon after World War II, the international distribution of military power in the world sorted into the two camps associated with the Cold War, the US-led Western bloc and the Soviet-led Eastern bloc. This was the bipolar era named for the two-pole distribution of military power. American grand strategy during the Cold War was directed at containing the Soviet threat through the construction of peacetime military alliances, the fighting of numerous proxy wars, and the building of a massive nuclear arsenal, among other things. After the end of the Cold War, the international distribution of military power was concentrated primarily in one superpower; thus we say the system entered a unipolar phase. *Global Trends 2030* envisions the world as a modified **multipolar** world with the same preponderant (but diminished) power, the United States, leading the same post–World War II international order.

It is useful to think about the Cold War as a story within a story. The overarching story of the international system after World War II consists of how the United States built a **liberal international order** that continues today, while the story within a story is about the United States protecting that liberal international order from its most significant threat in the form of the Soviet Union and its allies. Thus, it is correct to characterize the world from 1947 or so until 1989 or so as a **bipolar international system** (defined by military power), and it is also correct to characterize the world since 1945 as a continuous single hegemonic order. American policy toward the Soviet threat—or any threat to the order—was a manifestation of the American grand strategy. It is useful to think about any great power system (multipolar, bipolar, or unipolar) as existing within a context that we can call the hegemonic or international order. The order is the overarching context for great power relations, and only one hegemonic order exists at a time.

Before the United States entered World War II (thus before it emerged as the world's hegemon), American planners were already thinking about restructuring the world order. Anne-Marie Burley tells us that the formal process for this began just two weeks after the United States was attacked at Pearl Harbor. President Franklin Delano Roosevelt tasked a planning committee with the job of constructing a blueprint for "every aspect of international relations, in all areas of the world."[22] Walter McDougall proposes that the American political elite of this era possessed a sense of "global meliorism" that aimed "to make the world a better and safer place through the promotion of economic growth, human rights and democracy." Global meliorism was informed by the lessons learned by the Great Depression's "relief agencies, the New Deal, and Keynesian economics."[23] Making the world a better place was the best way to preserve and protect the "exceptional country" that was—and remains today—America.

Earlier, Ruggie was quoted about a hegemonic power seeking "to construct an international order in *some* form, presumably along lines that are compatible with its own international objectives *and domestic structures*."[24] When American planners began to think about fixing the world, they decided to project outward the liberal polity that was the US domestic order. Burley explains,

> Just as the New Deal government increasingly took active responsibility for the welfare of the nation, U.S. foreign policy planners took increased responsibility for the welfare of the world. It was widely believed that they had little choice. The United States was going to be a world power by default. It could not insulate itself from the world's problems. As at home, moreover, it could not neatly pick and choose among those problems, distinguishing politics from economic, security from prosperity, defense from welfare. In the lexicon of the New Deal, taking responsibility meant government intervention on a grand scale.[25]

The United States would construct an international order modeled on its domestic order, and this would require US intervention "on a grand scale," building, funding, and protecting that order. Protecting that order would sometimes require the use of military force against enemies of the order. The expectation was that over time the order would be sustained by the development of good and proper democratic politics within other states that would honor and sustain cooperation between states. Steve Weber explains that President Roosevelt "believed that the process of politics—the coordinating and the compromising of interests among the great powers—would do good things over time to the *internal* characteristics of these states and that this, in turn, would make them act in more peaceable and cooperative ways."[26]

The desire to project the value of democratic processes onto international politics and into other states derived from the lessons learned by necessity in American domestic politics. Within the United States, the rule of law helped to "push downward" ethnic and religious identities while creating a civic national identity within the political arena.[27] Within domestic politics, institutionalized multilayered checks and balances put limits on the exercise of power by the majority and guaranteed the rights of minorities, reinforcing the shared civic identity and keeping all the stakeholders more or less happy and more or less inside the rules of the domestic order. [28] The international order should also be rule based and process oriented in order to keep all the stakeholders more or less happy. Further, the international order should contain checks and balances to reassure others, especially the significant powers, that the preponderant power would observe rules that might sometimes limit its unilateral exercise of power.

Scholars of different sorts seem to agree that the American hegemon's decision to use multilateralism as the overarching framework for the postwar world was a distinctly American decision. Ruggie proposes that "to the extent it is possible to know such things, other leading powers would have pursued very different world order designs." [29] Had Germany come out of World War II as the new hegemon, it would have constructed a world order of "imperial design." The Soviet Union as hegemon would have extended its political control through a Comintern, using "administered economic relations among its subject economies." And a British hegemon would have continued its established practice of colonialism and discriminatory trade practices. [30]

Weber agrees that as a policy choice for balancing power toward the goal of securing interests, multilateralism is one of many available to the hegemonic power and is not by itself the most "obvious institutional form for these purposes." [31] As Weber points out, "a priori, there is at least one alternative [to multilateralism] for an alliance system made up of one extremely powerful state and several smaller states. The alternative is for the large state to cut a series of bilateral deals with each of the subordinates." [32] Yet the United States chose multilateralism, creating a much different kind of world. In support of his position, Weber asks us to compare the choices made by the United States to those made by the Soviet Union in relation to the European allies of each:

> The structural position of the United States vis-à-vis Western Europe was different certainly from that of the Soviet Union vis-à-vis Eastern Europe [because the Soviet Union was so much more powerful than the countries of Eastern Europe], which means that an American version of bilateralism would have looked necessarily more balanced than Stalin's version. But that structural position did not produce NATO. The United States could have interpreted bipolarity and the Soviet threat as a license to develop a more coercive and extractive subsystem for security that the West European states would have been nearly obliged to accept. [33]

Even in the alliance that was designed to counter the Soviet threat to the international order, the United States chose multilateralism over bilateral exploitation.

For Ruggie and others, in the postwar era "it was less the fact of American *hegemony* that accounts for the explosion of multilateral arrangements than of *American* hegemony."[34] Ruggie asserts that the breadth and diversity of multinational arrangements after 1945 was because of American hegemony, and the only logical explanation for this choice of world order must be derived from an understanding of American domestic politics and political identity. Burley agrees and proposes that the relative inexperience of American planners in foreign policy led them to construct a world order from a domestic analogy. The Europeans, conversely, had "centuries of diplomatic interaction [that] impelled leaders to view the international world as distinct and separate from the domestic one."[35] The Europeans were skeptical of applying liberal ideas beyond their national borders, while American planners were convinced that because the liberal model worked at home, it would work for the American-built international order.

The liberal international order built by the American hegemon was designed to bring all the other major powers into a common system that would end restrictive trading practices that US planners saw as a key factor causing both world wars. That is, a fundamental value that would be promoted and protected in the international order would be the "free" market of capitalism. That system would also have to recognize the aspirations of nations to be self-governing and be respectful of the sovereign rights of other countries/people so that they could freely participate in and benefit from the capitalist system. More, the system would have to provide basic safety for and channels by which other *major* powers could prosper so that they would have no realist-based objections to participating in a US-led order. That is, the other major powers would see that they could benefit from the order, and so they wouldn't seek to build their military power as a counter or balance to the power of the United States. The operating principle of the order was multilateralism.

Multilateralism is a notion that is fundamental to the neoliberal institutionalist worldview. Neoliberal institutionalism is a variant on liberalism that sees international cooperation as a "natural" result of world politics. Unlike liberals, however, neoliberal institutionalists see this cooperation coming out of the pursuit of self-interests; thus neoliberals make peace with realists on this issue. Self-interested actors acknowledge that through cooperation with other actors they can achieve more security, wealth, and well-being than through unilateral action. That cooperation is assisted and sustained by multilateralism.

Neoliberal institutionalists define multilateralism as the "international governance of the 'many.'"[36] Multilateralism helps many self-interested actors achieve the benefits of cooperation by institutionalizing diffuse reciprocity for good behavior and punishments for bad behavior into international affairs. If rewards and punishments are built into the institutional arrangement of an international organization, states no longer need to worry about whether other states are trustworthy. Trust in the benefits of the system (not necessarily trust in other states) is achieved over time on a variety of issues as events demonstrate that the institutional arrangement benefits all good actors without discrimination and compels all actors to be good partners most of the time. Moreover, over time actors expect that all kinds of international problems are best solved through multilateralism, and thus multilateralism becomes the "deep organizing principle of international life."[37]

The United Nations, the International Monetary Fund, the World Bank, the General Agreement on Tariffs and Trade (GATT) and the World Trade Organization, and NATO are chief components of the American hegemonic order, and this is not an exhaustive list. All of these institutions work on the notion of multilateralism. Countries are bound by rules but also can expect to benefit from the rule-based system, and this applies to small powers as much as major powers and even to the hegemonic power, the United States. People can argue and have argued about whether these institutions have benefitted some states more than others, and they can and do argue about how much the United States is actually bound by the rules; but most states derive some benefit from these institutions, and *most of the time* even the United States plays within the rules or at least uses the rules to justify its own foreign policy behaviors. Moreover, although many of the contemporary rising powers did not have a voice in the construction of the international order (think the People's Republic of China, India, Indonesia, or democratic South Africa), and although they may demand that the institutions of that order be made more representative of the entire world (think democratizing the Security Council by increasing the number of permanent members), these rising powers do not seem interested in creating an alternative order. The order is enduring because it serves more than the interests of the hegemon that established it.

For a time, some observers worried about the durability of this American-built international order. In the 1980s particularly, some analysts were concerned about the potential impact of the relative decline in US power on the continuation of the international order. The theory was that international order needed to be maintained actively by the hegemon, and a hegemon with waning power would be less able to maintain the order against alternative visions and rising powers. The collapse of the Soviet Union and its empire at the end of that decade ended these discussions. Other discussions started over whether the United States should use its singular power ("restored" to new apparent heights) to sustain its international **primacy** or whether the United States should use its power to manage the rise of a new multipolar international system. These discussions were *not* about altering the international order but were instead about how to adjust US grand strategy within that international order to manage the effects of falling and rising great powers. This will be the final subject of the present chapter.

## AMERICAN GRAND STRATEGY

The international order built for the postwar world still exists today. However, since the end of the Cold War and the dawn of the new millennium, the order has been the scene of some significant changes: the rise of new great and emerging powers, global networked terrorism, and the world financial crisis that hit in 2008, to name the most significant. There have been more than enough shocks to the components of the international order to cause the best-laid grand strategies to require adjustment.

In this section, we will discuss the grand strategies of the four US administrations since the era of unipolarity began. Recall that a grand strategy is an articulation of a great power's broad goals and the operational plans that harness the country's military power to the pursuit of those goals. The subtext of American grand strategy since the end of the bipolar era is whether the United States should attempt to maintain its predominant power and stay atop a **unipolar system,** or whether it makes more sense to reserve US power and manage the rise of other great powers in anticipation of a multipolar system. In this last scenario, the goal would be to keep the United States slightly more powerful than the other great powers, similar to Britain's position relative to the European great powers of the late nineteenth and early twentieth centuries.

*George H. W. Bush.* The presidency of George H. W. Bush was marked by four major world events, three of which had nothing to do with administration policy: the 1989 Chinese crackdown of the prodemocracy demonstrators in Tiananmen Square, the end of the Soviet bloc starting in 1989, the December 1991 dissolution of the Soviet Union, and the January 1991 Gulf War. The list is presented slightly out of chronological order because only the last event on the list—the Gulf War and the start of what Bush proposed to be a UN-based "new world order"—was the result of intentional policy decisions by the president. With the important exception of the Gulf War, the first Bush administration's grand strategy seemed to be about watching world events rather than shaping them. Bush did seem to embrace a sense that world politics should be multipolar in some way and that the United Nations would be the appropriate vehicle for great power management of world events. After his failed reelection bid, Bush committed the US military to lead a UN-approved multinational enforcement operation in Somalia.

Because this Bush administration only lasted one four-year term and despite the fact that Bush seemed more tuned to world events than domestic problems, characterizing the nature of the grand strategy involved is difficult. Anne-Marie Slaughter writes that "first [presidential] terms are about justifying your place in office. Second terms are about justifying your place in history."[38] Maybe this can help us understand the absence of grand strategy since Bush was a one-term president. Clearly the administration saw the United States as a world leader, but not the only significant world power, and so Bush reserved criticism of the Soviet Union/Russia and China regarding their domestic affairs and sought their approval and a Security Council go-ahead for military action against Iraq. In the end, we might safely conclude that Bush was inclined to see the world as it had been, and his grand strategy wasn't much inclined to be different than his predecessors. Bush's experience as the US ambassador to the United Nations from 1971 to 1973 no doubt shaped his preferences about using the United Nations for great power global management as well as for humanitarian interventions such as the one he started but did not stay to see the end of in Somalia.

*Bill Clinton.* Some of the Clinton administration foreign policy toward China was discussed in chapter 1. Clinton's economic goals made his administration more interested in engaging with existing and rising great powers, and the administration seemed inclined to embrace a multipolar world (while ignoring conservative critics who had started dreaming of preserving unipolarity at the end of the Bush 1 administration). Early bad experience with peacekeeping in Somalia made Clinton issue Presidential Directive (PD) 25 on May 3, 1994, in which he announced that "peace operations are not and cannot be the centerpiece of U.S. foreign policy. However . . . properly conceived and well-executed peace operations can be a useful element in serving America's interests." PD 25 effectively put the world on notice that the Clinton administration would not continue his predecessor's use of UN-authorized peace operations or humanitarian interventions. The timing of PD 25 put an exclamation point on this, being released in the midst of the Rwandan genocide, which the administration continued to deny until it was over.

The Clinton grand strategy was more about enlarging the circle of market democracies, a policy that continued old American themes while emphasizing economic priorities. Rather than harnessing military power to this, Clinton made use of "soft power" as explained by Undersecretary of State Joseph S. Nye Jr.[39] To some admirers like Josef Joffe, the use of soft power made the United States an attractive rather than a repellent great power to all the major actors in the world. "America is different," he wrote during the Clinton administration,

It irks and domineers, but it does not conquer. It tries to call the shots and bend the rules, but it does not go to war for land and glory. . . . Those who coerce or subjugate others are far more likely to inspire hostile alliances than nations that contain themselves, as it were. [40]

Joffe contended that the United States had a monopoly on soft power. "This type of power—a culture that radiates outward and a market that draws inward—rests on pull, not on push; on acceptance, not on conquest. Worse, this kind of power cannot be aggregated, nor can it be balanced." [41]

The Clinton grand strategy was to be the center of the wheel, the hub among the spokes, as Joffe put it, making the United States the good friend and partner of many countries. The military brass sent its tentacles out along the spokes, establishing a vast US military presence throughout the world, disproportionate to the civilian presence of the State Department. [42] This military presence was about securing world energy sources, making the US military indispensable to the world economy. Clinton policy also oversaw the enlargement of NATO, and Clinton made active use of NATO, such as in the bombing of Serbian positions to end the Bosnian war and the air campaign against Yugoslavia over the Kosovo crisis in 1998. Clinton military actions also included continuous joint US-British air strikes against Iraqi air defenses throughout the decade, US intervention in Haiti in 1994–1995, and the 1998 airstrikes against Sudan and Afghanistan in retaliation for al Qaeda's attacks on the US embassies in Kenya and Tanzania.

Despite the popular myth that the United States was at peace during the Clinton administration, it was a time of vast military expansion and frequent use of US military force. It was a time similar to what Joffe says when comparing Clinton's grand strategy to Bismarck's hub-and-spokes strategy: Bismarck, like Clinton, chose "not intermittent intervention, but permanent entanglement." [43]

*George W. Bush.* When George W. Bush ran for office, he expressed the view that the United States should be a humbler country and less involved in world affairs. The Bush (2) administration, by its own admission, experienced a sea change on some aspects of its grand strategy from pre– to post–September 11. The pre–September 11 Bush 2 administration appeared to be following a stay-at-home and go-it-alone strategy. After 9/11, Bush adopted a "you're with us or you're with the terrorists" or a "my way or the highway" primacy or global dominance grand strategy that contained elements of neoconservatism and realism. Both periods, however, were marked by the Bush administration's preference for unilateralism.

We should pause at this moment and think about whether the preference for unilateralism meant that the Bush 2 administration was undoing the US-built multilateral international order. That the United States built an international order on the principle of multilateralism did not ever mean that

American policy makers abandoned unilateralism. Margaret Karns and Karen Mingst offer evidence that the United States always mixed multilateralism and unilateralism from 1945 until 1990, using different methods in different issue areas and regions.[44] Neoliberals agree that the United States was willing to restrain itself and act multilaterally with some key others—particularly when dealing with Europeans in Europe—while always maintaining the right to pursue unrestrained unilateral pursuits outside of Europe.[45] In specific response to the unilateral preference of George W. Bush, John Ikenberry suggests that the administration's "opposition to multilateralism represents in practical terms an attack on specific types of multilateral agreements more than it does a fundamental assault on the 'foundational' multilateralism of the postwar system."[46] Thus, despite the strong unilateralism, the Bush 2 administration did not intend to revise the entire international order built on multilateralism.

After the 9/11 terrorist attacks, the administration favored the view that unipolarity could be maintained indefinitely and that the military was the proper means by which to ensure this. The administration used what some called a primacy or global dominance strategy. Stephen Walt explains:

> In this strategy, the United States sets the agenda for world politics and uses its power to make sure its preferences are followed. Specifically, the United States decides what military forces and weapons other states are allowed to possess and makes it clear that liberal democracy is the only form of government that the United States deems acceptable and is prepared to support.[47]

The Bush strategy was influenced by two camps within the administration. The first was the neoconservative camp, which thought 9/11 was an opening for the United States to use might to create right in the world. They believed that democracy and human rights could be coercively imposed and saw the post-9/11 world as a blank canvas for the United States to paint upon (if painting can be done with cruise missiles). The second camp was the realist camp led by Vice President Dick Cheney. These realists co-opted the neoconservative democracy-promotion goals in order to pursue raw power aimed at enhancing US primacy and the unipolar era far into the twenty-first century.

The merger of these two views created the Bush Doctrine announced in the September 2002 National Security Strategy (NSS) of the United States of America and elaborated in Bush's second inaugural address. The doctrine, in brief, was that the United States had the unilateral right to engage in preventive war to eliminate *potential future* threats. The real-world results of this grand strategy involved protracted wars in Afghanistan and Iraq, and constant threats of a "World War III" with Iran over its nuclear weapons program. In time Bush's neoconservative supporters started to abandon him for misunderstanding and poorly executing their ideas, especially in the botched occupation of Iraq. They were also disappointed by the lack of carry-through on the democracy-promotion mission in places like Saudi Arabia. Meanwhile, the realist preoccupation with Middle Eastern oil resulted in the accommodation of North Korea as it developed operational nuclear warheads. The other real-world result of fighting two wars was the critical undermining of the US economy. In August 2008, the world financial crisis hit, putting the United States on course for the Great Recession.

*Barack Obama.* When Barack Obama was first elected president in 2008, he took office under monumentally bad circumstances: the world financial crisis, the national economic recession in which seven hundred thousand jobs were being lost each month, and two draining wars under way with the end games not yet in sight, to name some of the problems. We'll leave out any discussion of the extraordinary refusal of much of the opposition party to work with the new president on almost all issues of governance. Added to these problems were monumental expectations placed on Obama from people at home and abroad. As David Sanger explains,

> Not quite nine months into his presidency, Barack Obama woke to the news that he had won the Nobel Peace Prize—not for anything yet accomplished, but for the promise that he would end the war in Iraq, win the "war of necessity" in Afghanistan, move toward the elimination of nuclear weapons, tackle climate change and engage America's adversaries.[48]

Monumental problems and monumental expectations create so much more of each!

At the start of the second Obama administration, analysts asked the question, does Obama have a grand strategy? Sanger proposes that the "bitter experience" of Obama's first administration drove him to "a strategy in which Mr. Obama [would] try to redirect world events subtly, rather than turning to big treaties, big military interventions and big aid packages."[49] Slaughter, who worked in the top ranks of the State Department in the first years of the first Obama administration, intones that "Obama's choice of a grand strategy for his second term could help drive a more proactive foreign policy, defining a legacy that is more than the sum of responses to crises."[50] Slaughter thinks Obama needed to find a different grand strategy for his second term, rejecting his first strategy's theme of "domestic renewal and global leadership" as proposed in the National Security Strategy of 2010 and illustrated in the American contribution to the intervention in Libya. Other observers were less kind and suggested that Obama lacked a grand strategy and that this was paramount to "strategic incompetence," which would put the United States and the world on course for disaster.[51] The analysts—pro and con—seemed almost universally unable to accept Obama's explanation of his grand strategy as a real grand strategy, perhaps because of their own expectations (good or bad) for his presidency.

The Obama vision of the United States in the world is not different from the first two post–Cold War American presidents, nor is it different from the presidents of the Cold War era. I suspect that some of the grand expectations put on Obama are there because of his historical position as the first African American president and because of the general repulsion that occurred to the Bush presidency.

What was the Obama grand strategy articulated in his first administration? What kind of world—unipolar or multipolar—does he envision, and how will he harness American power—military, but other power as well—to the pursuit of his goals? The administration answers these questions in the National Security Strategy of 2010 and in the address given by Obama on the issue of Libya on March 28, 2011. In brief, the world is in transition, but clearly global power is being redistributed and a kind of multipolar world is taking shape. The power players in this world will include the traditional European and Asian ones (presumably Britain, France, Germany, Japan, and South Korea) as well as "other key centers of influence," which include China, India, Russia, Brazil, South Africa, and Indonesia.[52]

Multipolarity is forming in part because of globalization, which provides yet another unique opportunity for the United States:

> No nation should be better positioned to lead in an era of globalization than America—the Nation that helped bring globalization about, whose institutions are designed to prepare individuals to succeed in a competitive world, and whose people trace their roots to every country on the face of the Earth.[53]

America the exceptional nation stands alone as the country most suited to lead the world, and leading the world is the best way to ensure the security and well-being of the exceptional nation.

The Obama grand strategy is in its briefest formulation "a strategy of national renewal and global leadership." This requires first taking a variety of steps to put the national economy, infrastructure, educational system, and society on a stronger course toward the goal of returning to the place where "American innovation" is the "foundation of American power."[54] This is not a call to turn inward at the cost of vacating global leadership as some commentators have suggested and does not signal a withdrawal of America from the world.[55] American power and security requires restoring the bases of both at home, as America's "adversaries would like to see America sap our strength by overextending our power."[56]

As to global leadership and the use of US military power in the world, Obama says what we'd expect any American president to say in the first sentence below, and then in the second sentence he makes a shift in worldview from the Bush administration, using language from a United Nations report on common security:

> Going forward, there should be no doubt: the United States of America will continue to underwrite global security—through our commitments to allies, partners, and institutions; our focus on defeating [al Qaeda] and its affiliates in Afghanistan, Pakistan, and around the globe; and our determination to deter aggression and prevent the proliferation of the world's most dangerous weapons. As we do, we must recognize that no one nation—no matter how powerful—can meet global challenges alone. As we did after World War II, America must prepare for the future, while forging cooperative approaches among nations that can yield results.[57]

This last line is critical to understanding the form of American global leadership. Where some commentators have disparaged Obama's "leading from behind" strategy, they fundamentally miss the point. Under the Obama grand strategy, America isn't leading from behind as much as it is finding ways to help others step up to the obligations that they incurred some time ago when the post–World War II international architecture was created.

It is remarkable the degree to which the Obama strategy makes use of the lessons of the postwar era for the world today:

> In the aftermath of World War II, it was the United States that helped take the lead in constructing a new international architecture to keep the peace and advance prosperity—from NATO and the United Nations, to treaties that govern the laws and weapons of war; from the World Bank and International Monetary Fund, to an expanding web of trade agreements. This architecture, despite its flaws, averted world war, enabled economic growth, and advanced human rights, while facilitating effective burden sharing among the United States, our allies, and partners.[58]

Rather than walk away from those multilateral institutions and commitments, the goal should be to strengthen those institutions. The American role, then, will be assisting others to see how they can step up to help maintain those institutions and protect the values that are commonly shared.

> Constructive national steps on issues ranging from nuclear security to climate change must be incentivized, so nations that choose to do their part see the benefits of responsible action. Rules of the road must be followed, and there must be consequences for those nations that break the rules—whether they are nonproliferation obligations, trade agreements, or human rights commitments.[59]

The intervention in Libya that started in March 2011 is the event that best exemplifies the Obama grand strategy in action. (It is, of course, also the event that fed critics and frustrated supporters.) When the Arab Awakening that swept North Africa and the Middle East came to Libya, Muammar Qaddafi responded in typical ruthless fashion with military repression. Protests turned into armed rebellion, to which Qaddafi responded with threats to make the streets run with the blood of anyone standing against his regime. Knowing his history and seeing his military force already in action, on March 17, 2011, the UN Security Council authorized states to take all necessary measures to protect civilians, establish a no-fly zone, and intensify an arms embargo against the government (S/RES/1973). This was the first overt civilian protection mandate issued by the Security Council.

Two days later, on March 19, the US Marines, Air Force, and Navy began an air campaign against the Libyan government to degrade its military capacity to hurt civilians. The campaign was commanded by the US Africa Command and joined by the forces of Britain, France, Canada, Norway, and Denmark. On March 31, mission command was handed over to NATO. The armed rebels and some British special operations forces on the ground took the fight to the capital with significant NATO air support. At the end of October, NATO forces hit a ground convoy carrying Qaddafi, ending his forty-two-year control of Libya.

When the United Nations was started in 1945, some of the working details were left to be decided later. One important detail was what kind of military force would be assembled to enforce a UN Security Council resolution on collective security. The US view was that an international force should be devised that would make use of the relative strengths of each of the permanent members. Specifically, in the immediate postwar era, the United States was the world's air power, Britain was an important naval power, and the Soviet Union possessed a huge land army. When necessary, in the American view, this division of military labor should be employed to enforce United Nations mandates. This notion was quickly rejected by the Soviet Union, but the idea of making use of different countries' military specialties became incorporated to some degree in NATO. This notion, like other American notions from the postwar era, are revived in the Obama grand strategy, as Obama explained in his remarks on Libya: "I said that America's role would be limited; that we would not put ground troops into Libya; that we would focus our unique capabilities on the front end of the operation and that we would transfer responsibility to our allies and partners."[60]

The international response to Libya worked within the "rules of the road" and involved others stepping up. In Obama's words,

> In just one month, the United States . . . worked with our international partners
> to mobilize a broad coalition, secure an international mandate to protect civil-
> ians, stop an advancing army, prevent a massacre, and establish a no-fly zone
> with our allies and partners. To lend some perspective on how rapidly this
> military and diplomatic response came together, when people were being bru-

talized in Bosnia in the 1990s, it took the international community more than a
year to intervene with air power to protect civilians. It took us 31 days.[61]

President Obama never claimed that Libya was in the strategic interests of
the United States, but that it was the kind of challenge that threatened "our
common humanity and our common security."

> In such cases, we should not be afraid to act—but the burden of action should
> not be America's alone. As we have in Libya, our task is instead to mobilize
> the international community for collective action. Because contrary to the
> claims of some, American leadership is not simply a matter of going it alone
> and bearing all of the burden ourselves. *Real leadership creates the conditions
> and coalitions for others to step up as well; to work with allies and partners so
> that they bear their share of the burden and pay their share of the costs; and to
> see that the principles of justice and human dignity are upheld by all.*[62]

This is a clear statement of the Obama grand strategy.

In late December 2012, the UN Security Council, alarmed by a humanitarian crisis and widespread human rights abuses in northern Mali, authorized an African-led military mission in support of the transitional authorities
in Mali (S/RES/2085, December 20, 2012). The African-led mission was
authorized to use all necessary measures to help Malian authorities recover
the north from criminal networks, terrorist groups (including elements of al
Qaeda in the Maghreb, or AQIM), and armed separatist groups, and assist the
authorities, among other tasks. The mission was not expected to deploy until
later in 2013. However, when the armed groups escalated their actions, the
French intervened on behalf of the Malian transitional government on January 11, 2013.

The United States Air Force assisted by airlifting French troops, equipment, and vehicles into Mali as the French deployed the first of what were
slated to be up to twenty-five hundred ground troops. While other European
states "appeared reluctant" to help, the US secretary of defense explained
that America had a "responsibility" to assist France and that the partnership
would be a "model" for meeting future challenges.[63] As the French and
Malian troops quickly recovered some of the northern cities, the UN secretary general declared the French military intervention to be courageous, and
the British government announced it would send special forces and reconnaissance aircraft. The leadership model and grand strategy employed by the
Obama administration seemed to be in evidence again, with the French quick
to step up and the British following behind. The readers of this book will be
able to supply the ending for this foreign policy event.

In summation, the Obama grand strategy appears to be a reassertion of the
themes of the post–World War II era but this time with a practical focus on
burden sharing and encouraging other states to step up to international obli-

gations. The Obama strategy seems to be content with the rise of other powers and the eventual formation of a multipolar world.

Or perhaps we might bring the political realists back into this discussion. "American primacy in the global distribution of capabilities is one of the most salient features of the contemporary international system," write G. John Ikenberry, Michael Mastanduno, and William C. Wohlforth. "The end of the cold war did not return the world to multipolarity. Instead the United States—already materially preeminent—became more so."[64] Perhaps Obama's grand strategy is better understood as evidence in support of one of two possible hypotheses regarding "the inclination of the now singularly dominant state to provide international public goods."[65] First, the United States might "take on an even greater responsibility for the provision of international public goods" because it has relatively more power and because it has the opportunity to "lock in" others into "a durable international order that reflects its interests and values."[66] This "locking in" looks more like a George W. Bush goal than a Barack Obama goal, however.

So, this leads Ikenberry, Mastanduno, and Wohlforth to propose a contradictory hypothesis:

> We should expect a unipolar power to underproduce public goods despite its preponderant capabilities. The fact that it is unthreatened by peer competitors and relatively unconstrained by other states creates incentives for the unipole to pursue more parochial interests even at the expense of a stable international order. The fact that it is extraordinarily powerful means that the unipole will be more inclined to force adjustment costs on others, rather than bear disproportionate burdens itself.[67]

This hypothesized behavior by the **unipole**—the United States—seems to describe the Obama strategy as well as the earlier, neoliberal institutionalist description does. And this realist interpretation sets the stage for the following chapter on the behavior of other states in the unipolar system.

## CHAPTER REVIEW

- Realists focus on the great powers in the international system because these states have the ability to shape the system and write the rules for all other states.
- Great powers are states that use force to promote interests beyond their own vital national interests.
- Great powers arise through the use of force, and since the start of the twentieth century the existing great powers have used international institutions to try to block the rise of other great powers.

- A grand strategy is a policy employed by a great power in which military power is used to promote national interests and global goals.
- A hegemon is a preponderant power defined in terms of military and economic power.
- Since the end of World War II, the United States has been the world's hegemon. As hegemon, the United States built an international order based on the rule of law and multilateralism.
- International distributions of power can be described in terms of the number of power centers in a system: multipolar, bipolar, or unipolar. Since the collapse of the Soviet Union, the international distribution of power is unipolar, and the United States is the unipole.

## Chapter Nine

# Competitors, Rising Powers, and Allies

IN THIS CHAPTER

- Gauging the Options in Unipolarity
- Potential Balancers and Competitors
- Major Allies
- Rising Powers
- Middle Powers
- Weak Powers and Client States
- Chapter Review

CASES FEATURED IN THIS CHAPTER

- The 2010 British-French defense treaty as a way to remain important to the United States in a time of unipolarity.
- The Shanghai Cooperation Organization seen as either a potential Russian-Chinese counterbalance to the United States or a nonthreatening regional forum.
- The division over military intervention among the major European allies.
- Brazil's global ambitions and ambivalent relations with the United States.
- India's ambivalence about global ambitions.
- Australia's efforts to rethink its middle power role to be a deputy to the United States.
- Canada's efforts to rethink its middle power role as a reaction to the United States.
- The patron-client relationship of the United States and Saudi Arabia and why the Obama administration fired Hosni Mubarak of Egypt as a client.

## GAUGING THE OPTIONS IN UNIPOLARITY

In November 2010, the United Kingdom and France signed a defense treaty. The declaration on the new relationship included the bold statement that the two countries did "not see situations arising in which the vital interests of either nation could be threatened without the vital interests of the other also being threatened."[1] In order to meet the common threats, and for the more practical purpose of sharing costs and "eliminating unnecessary duplication," the treaty called for a joint expeditionary task force, cooperation on the deployment of aircraft carriers, the integration of air and logistical support, and a jointly owned and maintained nuclear weapons facility to be located in France.[2]

In the press conference announcing the treaty, British prime minister David Cameron was asked how the treaty would affect the British relationship with the United States. Cameron responded,

> I think in terms of the relationship we have with Washington, which is obviously a very strong relationship—it is the special relationship—they want European countries like France and Britain to come together and share defense resources so we actually have greater capabilities. Often it is the case that the Americans and other NATO partners will be acting together and they would like us obviously to have the biggest bang for our buck that we possibly can. . . . I think this will get a very warm welcome in Washington.[3]

Cameron declared that the treaty was about helping the two countries meet their global responsibilities as well.

How should we understand this military treaty between countries that already were military allies in the North Atlantic Treaty Organization (NATO) and were bound together in the European Union (EU)? Maybe this treaty—which seemed redundant in many ways—was designed to make Britain and France better partners to the United States, as Cameron suggested.

But there might be other ways to understand this treaty. Perhaps Cameron and French president Nicolas Sarkozy were "pooling their own capabilities" in order to "reduce their dependence on the unipole."[4] This might be an act of "leash-slipping" in the view of realists Christopher Layne and Stephen Walt—that is, an act designed "to gain a measure of autonomy and hedge against future uncertainties" in their relationship with the United States.[5]

We might also understand this treaty in terms of British and French geopolitical concerns in the face of the possibility of declining American commitment to them. Britain and France are part of the Eurasian landmass (albeit on the edge) where the other major powers of the world are located (with the exception of the United States). That is, Britain and France sit on the edge of a landmass brimming with powerful potential competitors. They might need to find a way to keep the United States invested in their security and position.

In a unipolar world, "other states cannot be as certain that the United States would back them out of its own self-interest and must therefore work harder to keep U.S. commitments intact."[6] By this view, Britain and France needed to pool their resources to maintain their military capabilities in order to prove their importance to their indispensable ally.

Or recall the end of the last chapter when Ikenberry, Mastanduno, and Wohlforth predicted that one expected behavior of the extraordinarily powerful United States would be "to force adjustment costs on others, rather than bear disproportionate burdens itself."[7] Perhaps Britain and France were preparing for the United States to make a more starkly self-interested move. As Walt describes it, "one can imagine a unipole choosing to pass the buck (or free ride) on various regional powers, instead of letting them pass the buck to it."[8] Protecting the vital interests of Britain and France may fall more squarely on their shoulders in the future without the assistance of the United States.

The British-French security treaty of 2010 is the first of many major power policies and actions to be discussed in this chapter—policies and actions designed to help the major powers navigate in uncertain times. There are some certainties in this second decade of the new millennium: Asia's middle class is growing exponentially, putting pressure on limited and dwindling natural resources and hastening global warming and climate change. Additionally, states everywhere are faced with a plethora of nonstate actors, some of which are good partners and collaborators while others seek to inflict harm and instability. And the international system is unipolar:

> America's daunting capabilities are a defining feature of the contemporary international landscape, the debacle in Iraq and its various fiscal deficits notwithstanding. U.S. primacy shapes the perceptions, calculations, and possibilities available to all other states, as well as to other consequential international actors. Although other states also worry about local conditions and concerns, none can ignore the vast concentration of power in U.S. hands.[9]

As in the previous chapter, this chapter focuses on how a state's position in the international system is related to its foreign policy. The primary lens used here will be realism, and the dominant context is American unipolarity in an era of globalization. Given this context, what options and potential behaviors might we expect to see from the major powers and others?

Realists suggest that we should expect two basic behaviors: **balancing** or **bandwagoning**. Balancing involves creating a countercoalition designed to contain the power of the United States. Bandwagoning involves taking sides with the United States in order to appease it, neutralize the threat it poses, or gain something desired in the future from a closer association with it.[10] Countries might also try to hedge between balancing and bandwagoning.

As discussed in the last chapter, it sometimes is difficult to come up with a list of great powers (or middle or small powers) that satisfies everyone for every purpose. For our purposes here, we can use military spending and size of economy to sort out powerful states and then apply other factors to categorize these states in the international system. As will be shown, being a top military spender or having a large economy does not necessarily mean that a state is considered a great power.

In 2011, the United States accounted for 42 percent of the world's military spending (and 22 percent of the world's gross domestic product, but only 4 percent of the world's population).[11] The Stockholm International Peace Research Institute (SIPRI) is arguably the best source for military spending data. In 2011, SIPRI ranks these states as the top ten military spenders measured in billions of dollars:

1. United States $711 billion
2. China $143 billion
3. Russia $71.9 billion
4. United Kingdom $62.7 billion
5. France $62.5 billion
6. Japan $59.3 billion
7. India $48.9 billion
8. Saudi Arabia $48.5 billion
9. Germany $46.7 billion
10. Brazil $35.4 billion [12]

The United States outspends all of the other states on this list combined by $132.1 billion. Even if US military spending should decrease significantly with the removal of combat troops from Afghanistan in 2014, the United States would maintain its outsized military spending compared to the other top-spender states on this list.

The top-ten list shifts slightly when we consider size of economy as measured in trillions of US dollars for 2011 (to use comparable years). The source for these data is CNNMoney using figures from the International Monetary Fund.

1. United States $15.1 trillion
2. China $7.3 trillion
3. Japan $5.9 trillion
4. Germany $3.6 trillion
5. France $2.8 trillion
6. Brazil $2.5 trillion
7. United Kingdom $2.4 trillion
8. Italy $2.4 trillion
9. Russia $1.9 trillion
10. India $1.8 trillion [13]

The most obvious differences between the lists are Saudi Arabia's absence from the list of largest economies and Italy's appearance on that list. The United States and China stay first and second on both lists. Indeed, the forward projections to 2015 show this same ranking, with not much change in the relative size of each economy compared to the other. In 2011, the US economy was 2.1 times larger than the Chinese economy, and in 2015, the US economy will be 1.6 times larger than the Chinese economy. From 2011 to 2015, the ranking of the top four economies stays the same as above. France is displaced from fifth on the list in 2014 by Brazil. Russia maintains the ninth spot from 2011 through 2015.

Viewing these lists through the prism of foreign policies and ambitions, and through relations with the United States, five categories can be discerned: potential balancers and competitors (China and Russia); major allies (Great Britain, France, Japan, and Germany); rising powers (India and Brazil); and clients (Saudi Arabia). We'll use these categories—and add middle powers to the list—to discuss the expected behaviors of states in the unipolar system.

## POTENTIAL BALANCERS AND COMPETITORS

Great powers are divided here into two groups: those who aren't allies of the United States and those who are. Potential balancers and competitors China and Russia are not allies of the United States, although Russia is a NATO Partnership for Peace affiliate. China is commonly named as the primary future competitor of the United States while Russia is a competitor of diminishing importance.[14]

Since 2001, China and Russia have been members of the Shanghai Cooperation Organization (SCO). As of the start of 2013, the other full members of the SCO are Kazakhstan, Kyrgyzstan, Tajikistan, and Uzbekistan. Official observer states to the SCO are Afghanistan, India, Iran, Mongolia, and Pakistan. Dialogue partners include Belarus, Sri Lanka, and Turkey.

In 2005, the United States asked for observer status and was turned down. Also in 2005, the SCO was blamed for the closing of an American air base in Uzbekistan involved in supporting American military operations in Afghanistan.[15] These actions and joint military exercises run by China and Russia led to some speculation that the SCO was designed as a counterbalance to the United States.

In 2008, the National Intelligence Council's *Global Trends 2025* looked at joint SCO military exercises led by China and Russia, burden fatigue in the United States and some NATO countries over Iraq and Afghanistan, and growing antipathy and economic nationalism shown by America toward China and proposed a possible future called "A World without the West."[16] In this scenario, the United States and its European allies pull out of Afghanistan leaving a power vacuum that is filled by the SCO. Once the SCO moves into the role of stabilizing Afghanistan, its members—not natural allies by most accounts—get pulled together into a power bloc. An important question for the National Intelligence Council was whether the SCO would persist as a bloc and clear counterweight to a diminishing NATO.

But is the SCO really a counterbalancing alliance of China and Russia against the United States? One answer might come again from the National Intelligence Council. In the NIC's *Global Trends 2030* released late in 2012, the SCO doesn't even get mentioned. Indeed, in that report, Russia is largely dismissed (along with Europe and Japan) as a greatly diminished power. [17]

Not only is the SCO dismissed by the NIC as a potential competitor worth mentioning, but most of the members of the SCO are NATO affiliates. "All of the SCO countries, except China, have signed Partnership for Peace (PfP) framework documents with NATO and the Central Asian SCO members are past participants in PfP defense training and exercises." [18] This suggests that the SCO members aren't balancing against the United States and NATO as much as they are bandwagoning.

Walt suggests that if the SCO is an attempt at hard balancing—that is, forming a military counterweight—against the United States, it is a "tentative and half-hearted" effort at most. [19] For Walt, hard balancing against the United States in this international system is a formidable task because "when one state is far stronger than the others, it takes a larger coalition to balance it, and assembling such a coalition entails larger transaction costs and more daunting dilemmas of collective action." [20] Further, China and Russia face each other and other great power competitors on the same landmass with more immediate potential security concerns. Fundamentally for Walt, the United States doesn't pose a significant enough threat to potential balancers to make the effort worthwhile:

> The relative dearth of hard balancing is consistent with the view that alliances form not in response to power alone but in response to the level of threat. States will not want to incur the various costs of balancing (increased military spending, loss of autonomy, punishment by the unipole, and so on) unless they believe doing so is truly necessary. In particular, states will not engage in hard balancing against the unipole if its power is not perceived as posing an imminent threat to their security. [21]

Walt concludes that even the George W. Bush administration was not perceived as aggressive enough to cause hard balancing.

To judge whether a group like the SCO constitutes a balance of any sort, we should ask "what security problem the alliance was intended to address and why particular leaders opted for a specific policy choice." [22] The SCO is designed to address three security problems: terrorism, extremism, and separatism. Each of the SCO countries has internal terrorist, extremist, and/or separatist threats, and these are linked to similar threats in the broader region. None of this is linked to the United States or its predominant power. India, no fan of large military alliances, wants to join the SCO because of its focus on common regional security issues generally and worries about Afghanistan specifically. If the SCO were a counterbalance to the United States, we wouldn't expect to see India joining it. [23]

## MAJOR ALLIES

In the list above of the top ten military spenders, the United Kingdom is fourth, France fifth, Japan sixth, and Germany ninth. All of these are major allies of the United States. We would not expect to see hard balancing at all by these countries, but we might see efforts to demonstrate the continued importance of these countries to the United States. Japan's foreign policy orientation was discussed in chapter 5, so here we'll focus on the three EU countries.

During the George W. Bush administration, the secretary of defense was notorious for making a distinction between the old Europe and new Europe. A split among the European allies was apparent at that time—if not exactly as the observer suggested—in the British full-on support for the Iraq war, while the French and Germans (and Russians) attempted **soft balancing**. Walt explains that "soft balancing accepts the current balance of power but seeks to obtain better outcomes within it, by assembling countervailing coalitions designed to thwart or impede specific policies." [24] The soft balancing of the French, Germans, and Russians in the Security Council stopped the Bush administration from getting approval for the Iraq war, but the Americans and British and their new Eastern European allies went to war anyway. [25]

The Obama administration has not attempted to split the Europeans, which is just as well since by the start of 2013 they were busy splitting themselves into camps (but different camps than during the Bush years). The Eurozone crisis was one reason for this split. While Sarkozy was still the president of France, the French and Germans enjoyed unusually warm relations based on shared leadership views on fiscal policy and the need for greater austerity among the countries facing debt crises. In 2011, Sarkozy and German chancellor Angela Merkel proposed that greater political integration of the Eurozone would provide stronger tools for imposing fiscal discipline among member states in order to avoid the many crises that had developed since 2009. Before this could occur, the French people rejected austerity and voted in pro-growth socialist François Hollande. With this major change in the French perspective, the Eurozone countries agreed to a banking union in December 2012 and a common insurance fund for investors. This, in turn, caused British PM Cameron to declare that he would seek a British referendum on whether to continue in the European Union—even though Britain was not a member of the Eurozone (the Conservative Party has always been the party of Euroskeptics). Anger toward the Germans, and resentment over German control of the debt crisis debate within many Eurozone countries, and French and German disagreement over the proper role of government in the economy had put continued European integration into question by the start of 2013.

Another factor driving a split among the European allies was a difference of opinion regarding the use of military intervention. This dispute put the French and British on one side and the Germans on the other. Recall that the French and Germans had opposed the war in Iraq. As discussed in chapter 5, German opposition to the war in Iraq marked an evolution in Germany's post–World War II self-image, an evolution that involved the Germans standing with NATO to stop genocide in Kosovo and then sending military personnel to Afghanistan to stand with America in collective defense and unity after the 9/11 terrorist attacks. But German opposition to the Iraq war signaled a maturing of German foreign policy such that it could say no to its ally America when America engaged in wars of choice. Toumas Forsberg explains Germany's policy on Iraq as one grounded in "emancipation." Germany demonstrated "a new sense of self-esteem and independence" in its Iraq stance. This independence was still within the Western alliance framework, Forsberg contends, as "German assertiveness is better understood as a desire to not only be part of the West but also to define what 'the West' is."[26] For France, the Iraq war demonstrated how the uncontrolled "hyperpower" of the United States needed to be countered in some way.

In early 2011, a strong fissure appeared between Germany on one side and France and Britain on the other regarding the use of military intervention to stop imminent mass killings in Libya. France and Britain were important early supporters of military action to protect the people of Libya from Qaddafi. When the Security Council voted to approve military intervention for the purposes of civilian protection (discussed in chapter 8), Germany (as a nonpermanent member) abstained from voting, along with Russia, China, Brazil, and India. Germany wasn't the only NATO country that refused to participate in the intervention, but its opposition to the action was public and brought it significant criticism.[27] France, conversely, launched a second intervention in support of a civilian protection mandate in Côte d'Ivoire within a month of starting the Libyan intervention.

When the French decided to intervene to compel various armed groups to leave northern cities in Mali in January 2013, Germany expressed strong public disapproval again. This put Germany in opposition—again—to the United States. The Americans offered air and logistical support to the French in Mali, calling it their responsibility to assist France and indicating that this could be a model for the future. The British followed the Americans and assisted the French.

After the divisions of the Bush era, France and the United States seemed to be enjoying a renaissance in their relations. The readers of this book will be able to judge whether the ideological affinities between French president Hollande and US president Obama draw the two countries even closer, and whether the division between the major European allies gets greater. The French seem to have embraced the idea of demonstrating France's importance as a willing, able, and useful partner to the American unipole. This seems to fit well with the French national self-image as described by one French official in January 2013: "We still have a foreign policy, a capacity to act beyond our borders, a capacity to make a difference." After all, the official said, "if you don't have the military means to act, you don't have a foreign policy."[28]

## RISING POWERS

An analyst at Goldman Sachs is credited with coining the term "BRIC" when looking at the fastest-emerging economies at the start of the millennium. The countries included in the term are Brazil, Russia, India, and China. Later, an "S" was added to include South Africa. Other groupings and acronyms have also been developed, but none have stuck quite like BRICS. Leaving the major powers China and Russia out, India, Brazil, and South Africa established the IBSA Dialogue Forum in 2003. The dialogue was based on these three countries' positions as democratic countries from the developing world that were capable of global action. And, before we leave acronyms behind, in 2009 before the Copenhagen climate talks, China organized a draft proposal on behalf of the BASIC group—Brazil, South Africa, India, and China. The BASIC group agreed to stage a walkout at Copenhagen if there was any discussion of their nonnegotiables.[29]

The framework being used in this chapter is that unipolarity sets the conditions in which other actors operate, and relations with the United States are the baseline for foreign policy choices among the more powerful states. As if to make this point, the BASIC group had its private meeting at Copenhagen crashed by an unhappy President Obama and Secretary of State Hillary Clinton who then co-opted BASIC's efforts in a quick news conference just before the Americans headed for the airport.[30] Let's consider the foreign policies of rising powers Brazil and India, particularly vis-à-vis the United States.

Brazil is a country that does not have a strong or even a good relationship with the United States, and it is a country with global aspirations. According to Peter Hakim, these two things work together. On the first issue, Hakim says, "it would certainly be hard to say the U.S. and Brazil are adversaries or in conflict, but the fact is, they disagree more than they agree." And on the second point,

> Brazil is in many respects still learning what it means to be a global power. And the way it's been successful, ironically, is not by joining with the United States, which would have been one route, but rather in opposition to the United States, that it sort of has gained its international prestige precisely by showing its independence of the United States. [31]

Hakim also believes that a major problem is that the "U.S. rarely consults with Brazil on the important global issues." Which leads to the obvious question: would Brazil try to partner more with the United States if the United States gave Brazil more respect? But, sticking with our unipole framework, what incentive does the United States have to partner with Brazil?

Brazilian president Luiz Inácio Lula da Silva and his successor President Dilma Rousseff both engaged in high-profile foreign policy bids demonstrating Brazil's global ambitions and difficult relations with the United States. The first at Copenhagen in 2009 has been mentioned. The second came just months after Copenhagen. In May 2010, da Silva and Turkish prime minister Recep Tayyip Erdogan engaged in dramatic negotiations with Iranian authorities over a nuclear fuel swap. They tried to revive a deal that had been proposed the year before and supported by the United States and the major powers in the UN Security Council. The Iranians had changed their position on the deal several times even as they continued to enrich uranium. [32] Because of this, the United States was collecting votes in the Security Council in favor of more stringent sanctions. US secretary of state Hillary Clinton announced the agreement on the sanctions even as the Brazilian-Turkish deal was being announced. Clinton criticized the Brazil-Turkey plan as one that would make the world "more dangerous," singling out Brazil for special criticism. [33] In response, Brazilian authorities released a letter reported to be from US president Obama laying out the very plan that Brazil had brokered; Turkey refused to release a similar letter. [34]

The January 2011 election of Brazil's first female president, Dilma Rousseff, did not change Brazil's global ambitions and antipathy toward the United States. For Rousseff, a defining moment was when the UN Security Council approved the civilian protection mandate for Libya in March 2011. Brazil joined Russia, China, India, and Germany in abstaining from the vote, and Rousseff and the other leaders expressed alarm over what they considered a distortion of the mandate to justify regime change.

Rousseff used her address to the UN General Assembly that September to claim that the Libyan intervention allowed terrorism to flourish "where it previously did not exist, gave rise to new cycles of violence and multiplied the number of civilian victims." Then she indicated the direction Brazil was about to take in international discussions: "Much is said about the responsibility *to* protect; yet we hear little about responsibility *in* protecting."[35] In November, the Brazilian permanent representative to the United Nations presented a letter/concept paper to the secretary general on "Responsibility While Protecting." In it, Brazil stated its position that the responsibility-to-protect (RTP) idea (the idea behind civilian protection) was being used for political purposes to enact regime change.[36] The concept paper then set out a series of problems Brazil saw in the responsibility-to-protect idea, a list that suggested an incomplete appreciation of the RTP.

Brazil went on to host international discussions of the "responsibility while protecting" (RWP) at the United Nations and in Rio de Janeiro. At the Rio discussions, Brazilian authorities threatened soft balancing when they said they would work with India and South Africa through the IBSA framework to oppose any future UN civilian protection actions. One participant at the discussions noted that the IBSA countries complained repeatedly that "their diplomats were treated dismissively throughout the [Libyan] operation and were left uninformed. This sense of personal humiliation at the hands of the P3 (the U.S., France, and the U.K.) appears to be the most significant proximate cause of RWP."[37] The RTP was the outgrowth of significant middle power diplomacy; thus, by attacking the RTP, Brazil seemed to be positioning itself against the middle powers as much as against the United States and major allies France and Great Britain.

At the same time that Rousseff was striking a blow against civilian protection, she was riding to the rescue of the Eurozone. After consulting with Russia, China, and India, Brazil backed away from a plan to buy European debt directly. Instead, the Brazilian president donated $10 million to the International Monetary Fund to assist Eurozone countries.[38] Brazil threatened to withhold future funds from the IMF if the IMF imposed austerity measures on Greece in exchange for assistance. The IMF and the European Union ignored Brazil's threats and imposed strict austerity conditions anyway. Every time Brazil tried to assert itself in global affairs, it never seemed to receive the respect it wanted.

Brazil's partner in the BRICS, BASIC, and IBSA, India, has not appeared as bold or as decisive in establishing its own credentials as a rising power. A 2011 Congressional Research Service report on India explains in a nutshell, "Some observers argue that the New Delhi Government acts too timidly on the global stage, and that the country's regional and domestic difficulties continue to hinder its ability to exert influence in geopolitics."[39] India's political and economic systems have long been seen as the potential bases for great power status as well as debilitating obstacles to a great power claim.

Additionally, continued border disagreements with China keep India distracted from a global power status enhancement project.

The United States has urged India to take a more prominent role in the world, especially as an "indispensable partner" of the United States and a "potential counterweight to China's growing clout."[40] (The other "indispensable partner" of the United States is Great Britain.) Both George W. Bush and Barack Obama exhorted India to act like a great power. In 2005, the Bush administration initiated and signed the US-India nuclear deal as discussed in chapter 6. The treaty, which came into force in 2008, essentially acknowledged that India was a nuclear weapons power and allowed India in effect to build more nuclear weapons if it so chooses, despite the fact that its whole nuclear weapons development program has been outside international agreements and norms. One benefit that was to accrue to the United States from the treaty was the opening of the Indian civilian nuclear energy market to American manufacturers of nuclear equipment. However, India's parliament passed a law that imposed liability on nuclear equipment manufacturers in the event of an operating accident. Because of this obstacle, American private-sector manufacturers remained outside the Indian market while Russian and French state-owned companies were happy to comply with the Indian requirements.[41] American efforts to exhort India to bring its liability laws into accord with international standards had no effect.

Complying with international norms on nuclear issues has never been India's strong suit, yet the United States continued to insist that such compliance would facilitate greater cooperation between the two countries toward the goal of transforming their relationship. The United States wanted India to act as an "anchor of regional stability" and a partner in the US strategic pivot to Asia.[42] Toward that end, American and Indian military forces have conducted more than fifty military exercises since the nuclear treaty was signed in 2005.[43] On the other hand, in 2011, India announced it would choose between two European vendors to supply combat aircraft, a decision that came against US hopes and expectations.[44] India did not appear to be acting like an indispensable partner to the United States and was not likely to become a counterweight to China in the near future.

India's relationship with China, like its relationship with the United States, defies easy description. India manifests both cooperative and adversarial attitudes toward China. India's largest trading partner by 2011 was China. India joined with China on the BASIC plan for Copenhagen, yet the Indian government was reported to be unhappy that the Chinese were credited with putting together the BASIC plan.[45] Additionally, at the end of 2012 India indicated that it wanted to become a full member of the Shanghai Cooperation Organization—which the Chinese cofounded—while at the same time India and China remained in a significant arms race around an unresolved border dispute.

The border dispute between India and China can be traced back to 1904 and is ensnarled in the Tangled Tale of Tibet discussed in chapter 1. In 1904, Britain was unable to convince Tibetan authorities to sign a border agreement between British colonial India and Tibet. In the next ten years, Britain marched its troops into what is today called Arunachal Pradesh and established the Northeast Frontier Agency, and Chinese forces took control of Tibet. But then the Qing dynasty fell in China, and the Tibetans expelled the Chinese and declared Tibet's independence.

In 1914, at the Simla Conference attended by British, Chinese, and Tibetan authorities, a British administrator drew and lent his name to the McMahon Line delineating the boundary between British India (including Arunachal Pradesh) and Tibet. Arunachal Pradesh contained within it the city and monastery of Tawang, honored as the birthplace of the sixth Dalai Lama. The agreement said that China had "suzerainty" over Tibet, but that China would refrain from interference in the administration of Tibet, including the selection of the Dalai Lama. Further, China would agree not to make Tibet a province, and the British promised not to annex Tibet. The British would retain control of Arunachal Pradesh. The Chinese did not like the agreement and so quit the conference. Nevertheless, Great Britain and Tibet signed the Simla Accord agreeing to borders between a country that had left the conference (China) and another one that was not yet independent (India).

Upon its independence, India accepted the McMahon Line; China never accepted it. Over the years there were times when the disputed territory was ignored in relations between China and India. However, in 1962 Chinese troops marched into Arunachal Pradesh starting a war that resolved nothing but which is still remembered with bitterness in India today. Various bilateral commissions on the border were formed, but none resolved the dispute. India's basic position is that China should accept the fait accompli that Arunachal Pradesh is part of India (much like Tibet is part of China).

Complicating the border dispute is the position of the fourteenth Dalai Lama regarding the ownership of Arunachal Pradesh. The Dalai Lama's old position was that Arunachal Pradesh was part of Tibet. But in 2008 the Dalai Lama changed his position and declared Tawang and Arunachal Pradesh to be Indian according to the Simla Accord of 1914.[46] Before 2008, the Dalai Lama had the same kind of territorial claim on Arunachal Pradesh (on behalf of an autonomous Tibet) that the Chinese had. After 2008, the Dalai Lama had a greater political interest in India maintaining control of Tawang—the monastery to which the Dalai Lama had fled in 1959 and one possible spot where the Dalai Lama might be born should he choose to reincarnate.

In chapter 1, we discussed the competition between India and China over the claim of being the seat of world Buddhism. Tawang is the largest Buddhist monastery in India, and thus control of Tawang is critical to India's claim. This area is also the site of massive militarization. Because of an

Indian ten-year plan for Arunachal Pradesh, India soon will be able to match China's troop deployment on the contested border so that "half a million men are eyeball to eyeball."[47] India had two fighter squadrons in the area to counter China's fighters based in a string of modern air bases in Tibet.[48]

And this is a juncture at which we can see the enormous differences between the two countries most frequently mentioned as the rising powers of the twenty-first century. Reuters describes the scene and the problem for India:

> The road to Tawang, a center of Tibetan Buddhism by the border, is one of India's most strategic military supply routes. Growling convoys of army trucks bring troops, food and fuel through three Himalayan passes on the 320-kilometer (199 mile) muddy coil to camps dotted along the disputed border.
>
> On a road trip in late May and early June [2012], Reuters found much of the 14,000-foot-high road to be a treacherous rutted trail, often blocked by landslides or snow, despite years of promises to widen and resurface it.[49]

On the other side, China had built a series of airstrips and wide, paved roads. The Chinese military practiced military attacks using laser-guided bombs. On the Indian side, "work gangs of local women chip boulders into gravel with hammers to repair the road, many with babies strapped to their backs."[50]

In this disparity between India and China in the area of India's humiliating military defeat of 1962 and where India's largest Buddhist monastery sits, we see the sharp differences between these two rising powers. Steven Rattner concludes that "China has lunged into the twenty-first century, while India is still lurching toward it."[51] Corruption, government red-tape and famous inefficiency, a mind-set that is ambivalent about whether India should play a bigger global role, and a reckless military buildup against China in an area that lacks paved roads all make America's decision to prop India up as its indispensable partner in Asia look like an exercise in fantasy. The United States sees potential where many have long seen potential, but India is not poised—and possibly not inclined—to be a great power or any kind of counterweight to China.

How might we characterize India if not as a rising power? Charalampos Efstathopoulos suggests that India's foreign policy should not be seen through a great power prism, but through a middle power prism focusing on ideational and behavioral characteristics. India is either unable or unwilling to "match the transformative agency of major powers" despite its potential. Instead, India's global orientation and multilateral preferences make it a better candidate for middle power.[52] This takes us to the next topic.

## MIDDLE POWERS

Of all the categories we discuss in this chapter, "middle power" is the best defined. Middle power diplomacy involves international mediation, peace-keeping, consensus building within international organizations, and other similarly cooperative, multilateralist, and go-between behaviors. According to some analysts, middle power diplomacy (i.e., the foreign policy behaviors of the middle powers) derives from a moral imperative found in the political cultures of the middle powers (Canada, Australia, Sweden, Norway, Denmark, and so forth). This moral imperative is to serve as international "helpful fixers," extending their own social policies on the redistribution of wealth, peaceful conflict resolution, and so on outward. To other observers, middle powers play their roles because of their position in the international distribution of power, especially vis-à-vis the great powers. Middle powers are not capable of directing the system—as are the great powers—but neither are they the weakest members of the international system. Thus their foreign policy derives from their in-between status.

"Middle power" is a self-identification taken up sometimes by Canadians, Australians, Swedes, Norwegians, Dutch, and Danes—and as of the 1990s, (South) Koreans—to explain their own countries' roles and positions in the world. The self-identification goes back to the interwar period; "middle power" was a designated category within the League of Nations system (1920–1946), but not a particularly popular one. Brazilian delegates threatened to end their participation in league activities if Brazil were designated as being in the middle of anything. Indeed, Brazil quit the league in 1926, only a few years into its existence.

At the half-century mark, Canadian diplomats set their sights on carving out a role for Canada in the architecture of the post–World War II era. "Middle power" would designate both what certain states had contributed to the Allied war effort—important, albeit secondary, resources and energies—and what these states would contribute to maintaining the postwar international system. As the United Nations took shape, Canadians and Australians began promoting the codification of middle power status into the UN Charter based on functional criteria. The great powers, the permanent five, had no particular interest in delineating categories for non–great powers. And countries relegated by the self-described middle powers to small power status had no interest in seeing another layer constructed atop them. This functionally based, status-seeking claim by the Canadians, Australians, and others was rejected, but the notion of the middle power held fast for them.

The self-identified middle powers did not go back to stand among the ranks of the non–great powers. Instead, they internalized the idea of the middle power and began conforming their external behaviors to role expectations. In time, middle power diplomacy became defined as the "tendency to pursue multilateral solutions to international problems, tendency to embrace compromise positions in international disputes, and tendency to embrace notions of 'good international citizenship.'"[53] In line with this, middle powers were self-defined as states that committed their relative affluence, managerial skills, and international prestige to the preservation of international peace and order. Middle powers were the coalition builders, the mediators and go-betweens, and the peacekeepers of the world. Middle powers, according to the diplomats and scholars of these states, performed internationalist activities because of a moral imperative associated with being a middle power—middle powers were the only states that were able and willing to be collectively responsible for protecting the international order, especially when smaller states could not and greater powers would not.[54]

How did this moral imperative get imported into what, in the first instance, was a status-seeking project? One quick answer is that the imperative was already present. The self-declared middle powers already possessed a sense of moral superiority and certitude that required a unique foreign policy stance. Going hand in hand with this do-gooder impulse was the equally strong impulse to demonstrate to the world that middle powers were *like* great powers, but were *not* great powers. As J. L. Granatstein explains, in regard to Canada,

> Canadian policy in the postwar world would try to maintain a careful balance between cooperation with the United States and independent action. This was especially true at the United Nations. And peacekeeping, while it often served U.S. interests, to be sure, nonetheless had about it a powerful aura of independence and the implicit sense that it served higher interests than simply those of the United States, or even the West.[55]

The packaging of middle power diplomacy in a moral wrapping was not intended to obfuscate the essentially interest-based, status-seeking nature of the middle power project. Middle power scholars, particularly, never shied from this element of middle power diplomacy. Middle powers were devoted to the preservation of international norms and principles because they clearly benefited from a routinized international system. Further, middle power internationalism earned these states much deserved prestige. Even as middle powers proclaimed that their internationalism made them different from the great powers, middle powers also acknowledged that they generally were *active followers* of the great powers. Middle power scholars Andrew Cooper, Richard Higgott, and Kim Richard Nossal have coined a term to describe this behavior: "followership." This phrase is chosen to be both similar and dissimilar to the term "leadership."[56]

Middle power, then, is a self-declared role that contains both status-seeking, self-interested behavior (securing a coveted international position) and moralistic/idealistic elements (being a good international citizen). Thus middle power contains realist and liberal characteristics. Post–World War II efforts to attain international recognition for the "middle power" label failed, yet the middle powers maintained the identity and elaborated on the role expectations attendant to it. It is not difficult to find statements from the prime ministers or foreign ministries of middle powers saying, "Middle powers act in certain ways, and therefore we must act in certain ways." Yet the middle power imperative did not blind these states to real-world constraints and dangers, and so it also is not difficult to find statements that take the following form: "Middle powers act like this; we are a middle power so we naturally want to act like this, but unfortunately this is not a prudent time for such actions." Imperative—a sense of duty coming from within the country's national culture to do some good in the world—and position—where one is positioned or where one desires to be positioned in the international hierarchy of states—have long been two sides of the middle power coin, equally at play in explaining middle power diplomacy.

Middle power studies all have emphasized middle power vulnerability to changes in the central great power relationship.[57] Such changes produce uncertainty about the role middle powers should play in the world since "middle power" is a role that is both reactive against the whims of the great powers *and* dependent on partnership with a relevant great power. For example, at the conclusion of the Cold War, Australian officials began to refocus Australia's middle power orientation toward the rising Asian powers of Indonesia and China. This Asian focus was in response to the consensus that American power had waned considerably in the 1980s and Asian powers were on the rise. But American power (particularly the American economy) was resurgent in the 1990s—unparalleled in fact—so Australia began to cast itself as a deputy to the United States for managing Asian affairs. Rather than hitch itself to Indonesia's rising star, Australia led a multinational enforcement operation into the soon-to-be-former Indonesian territory of East Timor in 1999. This enforcement operation was in response to an American call for someone to do something to stop ethnic cleansing in Timor, although later Bill Clinton said he had in mind that Indonesia had a special responsibility to stop the violence there.

Australian prime minister John Howard enthusiastically announced that with the "Howard Doctrine" Australia would fulfill its special responsibility for maintaining order in Asia. The Clinton administration showed little interest in having an Australian deputy since the Clinton strategy was to be best friends with all major actors in the world including those in Asia (as discussed in chapter 8). Clinton had no desire to put Australia in between America and key Asian countries. But within another two years, another US president, George W. Bush, was happy to deputize Australia in the global war on terror. This critical role continues in a slightly different cast for the

Obama administration: Australia plays a central role in the American pivot to Asia.

The most senior of the middle powers is Canada. It holds this seniority precisely because the middle power role is one defined in terms of a special relationship with and service to the relevant great power. Canada's critical secondary role to Great Britain and America in the world wars and its critical participation in the 1991 Gulf War as a chief follower to the United States mark its place in the world.

Further, Canada's place as the premier peacekeeping country during the Cold War demonstrated its commitment to the US-led rule-based international order. When the Clinton administration announced in 1994 that America would start saying no to United Nations peace operations, Canada's own retrenchment from UN peacekeeping followed soon after.

After the Bush administration started the global war on terror, Canada played the expected role of middle power follower and NATO ally in Afghanistan. Like most coalition partners there, the Canadian presence and role was not especially large. Canada did not follow the United States into Iraq in 2003, a move that made sense given the nearly global consensus that the Bush administration was contravening international law and order.

Like its middle power counterpart Australia, Canada had been thinking about its role in the world. In 2005 in a foreign policy white paper, the liberal government of Paul Martin said this: "Our old middle identity imposes an unnecessary ceiling on what we can do and be in the world. Canada *can* make a difference, if it continues to invest in its international role and pulls its weight."[58] The new role that Canada might play was not so clear. It still had a special relationship with the United States, but Bush administration policies made it difficult to follow America. Canada's economy was fairly robust, but in 2005 it was still smaller than that of Brazil, Korea, India, and Italy; its defense spending had dropped below that of fellow middle powers Norway, Sweden, the Netherlands, and Australia; and its development assistance was at an all-time low. "In this context, the traditional notion of Canada as a middle power is outdated and no longer captures the reality of how power is distributed in the 21st century."[59]

Canada's role in the world might not be characterized as a middle power, but Martin proposed that Canada would continue to fulfill its "responsibilities as a global citizen." Toward this,

[Canada's] current economic and political standing provides the freedom to make choices about how we will contribute. By investing strategically today, we will maintain our capacity to act in the future. Our unique relationship with the United States does not alone assure Canada's influence in the world. We will set our own course, and pull our own weight.[60]

The word used most frequently in the 2005 white paper to describe Canada's foreign policy was "responsibility." And the "responsibility to protect" was noted to be Canada's primary global initiative.[61] Middle power Australia sought to hitch itself in good follower form to the United States. Middle power Canada was thinking about its responsibility for protecting the international order when the great power was predisposed not to do so. Both reactions fit the idea of the middle power.

More recently, both Canada and the United States experienced significant leadership changes. As discussed in chapter 7, conservative Canadian prime minister Stephen Harper took a belligerent tone regarding Canadian sovereignty in the Arctic. In 2007, Harper said, "Canada has a choice when it comes to our sovereignty over the Arctic. We either use it or lose it and make no mistake this government intends to use it because Canada's Arctic is central to our national identity and our future."[62] The defense minister bragged that Canada would develop a three-ocean navy to defend its claims—particularly against the Russians.

The United States, under the leadership of Barack Obama, did not seem to take Canadian Arctic bellicosity and military competition with Russia seriously. In 2011, a US diplomatic cable published by WikiLeaks commented that Canadian Arctic sovereignty claims were little more than campaign rhetoric.[63] Indeed, in an internal government memo acquired by the Canadian media, Harper worried that Canadian participation in *NATO-sponsored* Arctic military exercises would offend Russia![64] While Harper was talking tough, the Canadian government sought the help of the United States to map the continental shelf in order to make a sovereignty claim before the UN Commission on the Limits of the Continental Shelf in the true form of a good international citizen and friend of America.

There are some countries from the **global south** that have adopted the title of middle power. Efstathopoulos distinguishes between traditional Western middle powers like Canada and Australia and southern middle powers like India, South Africa, and Indonesia. Southern middle powers are similar to traditional middle powers in their use of multilateralism and their commitment to post–World War II global institutions. But where traditional middle powers tend to be more status-quo oriented, southern middle powers seek fundamental revisions of these institutions in order to address the problems of the majority of the world's states.[65]

For instance, South Africa's 2011 foreign policy white paper notes South Africa's commitment to multilateralism, especially through the United Nations, which "occupies the central and indispensable role within the global system of governance." Yet South Africa sees the United Nations as deeply flawed by "a continued over-emphasis by the developed world on issues of peace and security [which] undermine efforts to deal with the root causes of poverty and underdevelopment."[66] One way to transform the United Nations would be to democratize the Security Council by making South Africa a permanent member.

Similarly, Efstathopoulos notes that "India's world-view perceives the institutions of the current world order as representative of an outdated configuration of power constructed in the post-war period that does not reflect the new dynamics of global governance and the heightening impact of leading developing countries."[67] India, too, proposes that the United Nations be transformed by giving it a permanent Security Council seat—an idea supported by the Obama administration. Since the start of the new millennium, India has become the world's premier peacekeeper.

Beyond the desire to transform global institutions, southern middle powers play important regional roles, which serve as power multipliers to move these countries onto the global stage. Regionalism is a requirement for managing immediate foreign policy and security issues that the Western middle powers never confronted:

> Whereas traditional middle powers like Australia and Canada have been relatively more detached from their regional environment, Southern middle powers are more entangled in dynamics of regional hegemony and antagonism, and are inclined to provide leadership in projects of regional integration to manage these tensions.[68]

Southern middle power Indonesia promotes itself—and is promoted by the United States—as a country well suited to taking on a global middle power role because of its long commitment to regional multilateralism in the Association of Southeast Asian Nations (ASEAN). The United States has been assisting Indonesia as it develops its military capacity to become one of the top ten contributors to UN peacekeeping. Additionally, Indonesia seeks to make itself the "hub" of a network of peacekeeping training centers in Southeast Asia.[69]

The middle power role, whether for Western middle powers or those from the global south, is embedded with moral imperative. Western middle powers are called to be good international citizens, while southern middle powers seek to do the same while promoting the interests of countries often left behind by globalization and international politics.

## WEAK POWERS AND CLIENT STATES

The final country to be discussed from the list of biggest military spenders is Saudi Arabia. In earlier versions of *The New Foreign Policy*, Saudi Arabia was characterized as a **client state** under the heading "small powers." The starting point for any observer of small power foreign policy is the acknowledgment that the range of opportunities for independent, self-interested behavior is more limited than that for more powerful states. Small powers are boxed in by virtue of their relative weakness, but they are not powerless. Maria Papadakis and Harvey Starr contend that small states have some power over their foreign policy choices and ultimate fates, but this power is contingent on the opportunities present in the international system and the willingness of the leaders of small states to take advantage of those opportunities.[70] In this way, small states are like most states; international conditions must be ripe for action, and leaders must be inclined to act.

Davis Bobrow and Steve Chan contend that some small states are more powerful than others because they "have been able to carve out for themselves a special niche in the strategic conceptions, political doctrines, and domestic opinions of their chief ally."[71] These states derive power from manipulating the very relationship in which they are the dependent partner. Israel and South Korea are former small powers that were successful in defining their importance to the United States and taking great advantage from this.

Some small powers or weak states (weak relative to other state actors) are able to establish special relationships with larger powers called cliency. Mary Ann Tétreault defines cliency as a "strategic relationship between a strong state and a weak one."[72] The use of the word "strategic" is important here as it indicates agency on the part of both actors; although the power relationship is asymmetrical, cliency is reciprocal. The patron gains access to something valued such as a strategic route or critical resource while the client gains protection. Often the protection is for the purpose of facing an internal threat. The client plays on the fear of the patron that the client regime may be overthrown if not given sufficient resources and backing. **Patron-client relationships** seem to experience serious diminishing gains over time. And in a system characterized by unipolarity, the client may have difficulty convincing the patron to stay involved.

The patron-client relationship between the United States and Saudi Arabia serves as an example of the diminishing returns that seem to characterize this kind of relationship. The cliency relationship between these two states goes back to World War II when the Franklin Delano Roosevelt administration sought to secure access to Saudi oil reserves. In return for access to Saudi oil, the United States extended a security guarantee to the House of Saud, promising protection from external and internal challengers. The 1990 Iraqi invasion of neighboring Kuwait posed a serious external military threat, which the United States answered with a massive military response known as the Gulf War of 1991. This special relationship was cited by many different observers as a key reason for the September 11, 2001, terrorist attacks on the United States: unable to dislodge the illegitimate House of Saud, Osama bin Laden determined to poison and kill the relations between patron and client by attacking the patron.

In the unipolar international system, the possibility of the United States disengaging from many parts of the world—because it can—has implications for small or weak powers who previously were able to exploit US fears. Under unipolarity, Walt explains,

> weaker states are less able to influence the dominant power's conduct by threatening to realign or by warning that they may be defeated or overthrown if not given sufficient support by their patron. Not only do weaker states lack an attractive alternative partner, but the unipole needs them less and thus will worry less about possible defection or defeat.[73]

The American relationship with the Hosni Mubarak regime of Egypt is an interesting case in point. When Egypt signed a peace treaty with Israel in 1979, the United States rewarded Egypt with substantial foreign assistance (mostly military) and the implicit promise of support against enemies external and internal. Egypt was an important client to win in the Cold War. After the Cold War, the Mubarak regime's importance to the United States was measured in its ability to suppress Islamic fundamentalism, which was seen as a threat to Israel. After the 9/11 terrorist attacks and despite neoconservative desires to force democracy on the broader Middle East, Mubarak's value as a counterweight to militant Islam remained high. This was especially true for the Bush administration with its intense concerns about maintaining unipolarity against a variety of threats.

As discussed in the last chapter and the start of the present one, unipolarity as an enduring characteristic of the international system is more or less established, and the Obama administration is more comfortable with the idea of other powers rising. Had the Bush administration been in charge when the Arab Awakening hit Tahrir Square on January 25, 2011, Mubarak would have been guaranteed American support as a counterweight to militant Islam in the global war on terror. But for the Barack Obama administration, the threat that Mubarak might be overthrown by persons aligned with a counterweight to the United States was insufficiently balanced against other concerns. The possible threat of a Muslim Brotherhood–controlled Egyptian government could not overcome the intriguing value of nudging Mubarak out of power in order to come out on the right side of history by supporting the people of Egypt. This, of course, takes us out of a realist interpretive mode in preparation for the next and last chapter.

## CHAPTER REVIEW

- The condition of unipolarity has an effect on the foreign policy choices of many different kinds of states from potential competitors to major allies, rising powers, middle powers, and client states.

- Major allies to the United States may be enhancing their military capabilities and demonstrating their willingness to lead military interventions in order to remind the United States of their importance. This can be called bandwagoning behavior.
- Balancing behavior—the effort to create a counterbalance to the predominant power—does not appear to be happening in the present unipolar system.
- Soft balancing is the attempt to create a countervailing coalition to thwart a policy choice of the dominant power without challenging the international position of that dominant power.
- Although analysts think they know "rising powers" when they see them, some so-called rising powers have mixed global ambitions and do not always live up to international expectations.
- Middle power diplomacy involves international mediation, peacekeeping, and consensus building within multilateral organizations.
- Patron-client relations involve a reciprocal albeit asymmetrical exchange that may not be durable or maintain value over time.

*Chapter Ten*

# Conclusion: A Nested Game with Many Players

## IN THIS CHAPTER

- The Tangled Tale of Pinochet
- Linkage Actors on the Rise
- The Facebook Revolution
- A Nested Game with Many Players

## CASES FEATURED IN THIS CHAPTER

- A tangled tale in which a Spanish judge, the London Metropolitan Police, human rights groups, victims of torture, and a host of others bring Augusto Pinochet to answer for his regime's human rights abuses.
- Al Qaeda's use of linkage-actor strategies in its September 11, 2001, attacks on the United States.
- A demonstration of the power of linkage actors—of young people armed with Facebook accounts and global identities who managed to topple a dictator in Egypt.

## THE TANGLED TALE OF PINOCHET

In the summer of 1996, a Spanish group called the Association of Progressive Prosecutors filed a criminal complaint in a Spanish court against Chilean citizen Augusto Pinochet. The complaint alleged that Pinochet was responsible for the murder or disappearance of seven Spanish citizens while he was the military dictator of Chile from 1973 to 1990. The prosecutor of the case expanded the indictment to include charges of genocide, murder, and torture of Chileans and non-Chileans. Spanish judge Baltazar Garzón issued an arrest warrant for Pinochet.[1]

Twenty-five years earlier, Socialist Party leader Salvador Allende was elected president of Chile. He took power in a country suffering from economic depression; it was also deeply divided politically. Allende's economic agenda was welcomed by many and opposed by many. Some non-Chileans were especially unhappy with the election. US multinational corporations (MNCs) doing business in Chile worried about the nationalization of certain industries. US national security advisor Henry Kissinger had this to say about Allende's election: "I don't see why we need to stand by and watch a country go Communist due to the irresponsibility of its own people."

By 1972, Chile was in an economic crisis, and the streets were beset with protests and strikes. Meanwhile, the Nixon administration undertook a destabilization plan that involved, among other things, CIA support for the Chilean military's orchestration of unrest and lawlessness. A generalized strike was followed by a state of emergency declaration in the summer of 1973. Allende turned to General Augusto Pinochet to restore order to the capital, but within a month Pinochet led a military coup against the government. Chile was plunged into seventeen years of military dictatorship. More than three thousand people were tortured and murdered or "disappeared" during the dictatorship.

The Tangled Tale of Pinochet will help us return to the primary themes of *The New Foreign Policy*, reinforcing the importance of multilevel foreign policy analysis while bringing into focus the many linkage actors who play an increasingly critical role in shaping states' foreign policies.

When he overthrew the elected government of Chile in 1973, Pinochet vowed that it would be a generation before Chile returned to democracy. In 1989 Pinochet finally allowed national elections. Throughout Latin America there had been a "return to the barracks" as military juntas relinquished political control and democracy swept over the region. The Chilean military leaders, like military leaders elsewhere, negotiated "golden parachutes" to ease their way out of politics. Pinochet's golden parachute came in the form of "senator for life" status, with limited immunity from prosecution and a permanent presence in Chilean politics (albeit a decidedly low-key one). Although many Chileans and non-Chileans believed that Pinochet's deal meant that justice would be forever denied, Chilean political leaders believed the deal was the best way to move Chile into a democratic future.

In the fall of 1998, Augusto Pinochet had back surgery in London. While he was recuperating, the London Metropolitan Police arrested him on the warrant issued by Spanish judge Garzón. The British police, a domestic institution whose purpose is to uphold British law inside Britain, arrested a former Chilean head of state for crimes allegedly committed in Chile on a warrant issued by a Spanish judge in Spain. Why would the British police carry out an arrest warrant issued by a Spanish judge for crimes allegedly committed in Chile? Great Britain, Spain, and Chile were all signatories to the UN Convention against Torture and Other Cruel, Inhuman, and Degrading Treatment or Punishment. The convention became binding on all three countries in 1988. Once ratified at home, international treaties take on the force of domestic law and are upheld within national territory by the same state agents—the police and the courts—that uphold domestic law. Legal proceedings commenced in Britain to extradite Pinochet to Spain.

Spain's extradition request to the British government was joined by Switzerland, Belgium, and France, while Germany and Sweden opened their own investigations into allegations against Pinochet. Chile, on the other hand, protested Pinochet's arrest and requested that he be allowed to return to Chile. Chile's protest was based on the principle that heads of state and former heads of state enjoy immunity from prosecution. This was the same claim made by Pinochet's lawyers as they attempted to stop his extradition to Spain and win his release from British custody.

The issue of immunity for heads of state and former heads of state (or their representatives) is an extremely contentious one. New millennium efforts to establish the International Criminal Court (ICC) for prosecuting crimes against humanity, war crimes, and genocide were met with strong opposition by some states, who feared that the ICC could be turned against them as a political tool. The United States, in particular, opposed the ICC for this reason. Bill Clinton signed the ICC treaty expecting that it would never be ratified; George W. Bush "unsigned" it in 2002. Countries opposed to the ICC argue that their own domestic legal systems are adequate for ensuring justice and that an international legal authority is unnecessary. These states are reluctant to cede traditional state authority to a supranational or international organization.

Six of the European states involved in this tangled tale—Great Britain, Spain, Belgium, France, Germany, and Sweden—are members of the European Union. As EU members, these states already consented to supranational authority on particular issues. For instance, individual rights are privileged in the EU system to the extent that community citizens have legal recourse to challenge *domestic* laws that are claimed to be in conflict with EU legislation. Community citizens may bring their challenges in domestic courts or within the European Court of Justice (ECJ) framework. Great Britain, Spain, Belgium, France, Germany, and Sweden had erased an important line dividing domestic from international. Their membership in the EU and ECJ *and* their obligations under the UN Convention against Torture *required* them to investigate allegations against Pinochet.

By international accord, including the Rome Statute that gave life to the ICC, **diplomatic immunity** cannot be claimed in cases of heinous human

rights violations because even heads of state—*particularly* heads of state—
must recognize and protect human rights. In the words of one of the British
law lords who ruled on the Pinochet case,

> International law recognizes, of course, that the functions of a head of state
> may include activities which are wrongful, even illegal, by the law of his own
> state or by the laws of other states. But international law has made plain that
> certain types of conduct, including torture and hostage-taking, are not accept-
> able conduct on the part of anyone. This applies as much to heads of state, or
> even more so, as it does to everyone else; the contrary conclusion would make
> a mockery of international law. [2]

Chile's argument against Pinochet's extradition to Spain was based on the
idea of state immunity, although the government's real goal was to maintain
democracy in Chile against some strong domestic political forces. Chilean
leaders were in an uncomfortable dual or nested game. On one side were the
European states with which Chile wanted favorable economic and political
relations. Also, Chilean leaders sought to maintain a good international reputation, especially in regard to Chile's international commitments; the Chilean
government was a signatory of the 1998 Rome Statute, and under the Pinochet regime, Chile had signed the UN Convention against Torture. On the
other side of this nested game was a divided domestic political arena: many
Chilean citizens and citizens' groups demanded that justice be done in the
Pinochet case while the military and its supporters wanted the past to remain
in the past.

Chile's leaders appealed to the Spanish government to intercede and save
Chile from this difficult situation. Since the early 1980s, Spain had cultivated
a special relationship with its former colonies in Latin America, and it was on
the basis of this special relationship that the Chilean leaders made their
appeal. But the Spanish government did not intercede on Chile's behalf, out
of respect for both its own relatively young democratic system and its commitments to the European Union and the UN Convention against Torture.

Chilean leaders also appealed to another international actor with whom it
had a special relationship: the Roman Catholic Church. Since Pinochet's
arrest in October 1998, Chilean leaders had appealed to the Vatican—even
directly to the pope—to ask the British authorities to allow Pinochet to return
to Chile. In Latin American international relations, there is a long history of
mediation and arbitration by the Vatican. The Vatican holds religious and
historical importance in Latin America, giving it considerable diplomatic
power and influence. In February 1999, it was revealed that the pope and his
representatives had appealed to the British government for "leniency for
humanitarian reasons and in the interests of national reconciliation in
Chile."[3] The Vatican also endorsed Chile's claim that diplomatic immunity
barred the prosecution of Pinochet on any charges stemming from his rule.

This tale became more tangled as the case moved to British court in October 1998. What is important to note in this discussion is the variety of actors involved—state, nonstate, and individuals. Pinochet's lawyers brought an action of habeas corpus before the London High Court to win Pinochet's release. The London High Court agreed that Pinochet had diplomatic immunity from the charges, but it ruled that he would remain under arrest while an appeal was heard. The Crown Prosecution Service (an agent of the British government) brought an appeal on behalf of the Spanish government. The appeal was heard by a five-member panel convened by the House of Lords. In this hearing, several human rights organizations—Amnesty International, Redress Trust, and the Medical Foundation for the Care of Victims of Torture—were permitted to intervene in the case, as was a British doctor who had been tortured in Chile and the family of a British citizen who disappeared in Chile during the Pinochet era. Meanwhile, the Spanish government filed a formal extradition request with British home secretary Jack Straw.

The House of Lords rejected the previous court's ruling and declared that Pinochet was not protected by diplomatic immunity. The law lords, however, restricted the charges to those that occurred after 1988—the year that the Convention against Torture was incorporated into British law. The home secretary, in response, announced that the extradition would go forward. In December 1998, Pinochet appealed the law lords' ruling after it was revealed that one of the ruling judges had a formal affiliation with Amnesty International, one of the interveners. The first ruling was set aside, and the implicated judge was disqualified from the case. But, in an unprecedented move, Amnesty International was allowed to participate in the oral arguments in a second hearing. The government of Chile was also allowed to make arguments before the court. In March 1999, a seven-judge panel of law lords ruled again that Pinochet was not entitled to diplomatic immunity.

Over the course of the next year, the extradition process played out, with Pinochet's lawyers and the Chilean government making repeated requests for Pinochet's release, citing his medical condition as the reason. In early January 2000, the home secretary declared that a medical review panel had found Pinochet mentally unfit to stand trial, and so he would be released to return to Chile. Belgium and a group of human rights organizations filed an appeal against the ruling, but this only extended Pinochet's stay in London by another month or so. In March 2000, Pinochet was released from detention and returned home aboard a Chilean air force plane. Within a week of Pinochet's return to Chile, in an odd twist of fate, Ricardo Lagos was elected Chile's second socialist president, the first having been Salvador Allende.

Eventually Augusto Pinochet was stripped of his immunity from prosecution and was made to stand trial in Chile for crimes committed while in office. A 2002 Chilean Supreme Court ruling found that Pinochet was too ill to be prosecuted, but in 2006 the court reversed this ruling. Pinochet died in

December 2006 still facing pending human rights and financial corruption prosecutions. He had lived out his life in freedom once released from British arrest. A former political prisoner under Pinochet was elected to the presidency that same year—that former political prisoner was also the third socialist and first woman president of Chile, Michelle Bachelet.

Despite the fact that Pinochet was never found guilty by a legal authority for his regime's human rights abuses, international human rights groups hailed the Pinochet case as an important step forward for the protection of human rights everywhere. The case became the model for similar nongovernmental organization (NGO) efforts to bring dictators to justice, as in the case made by Human Rights Watch against Hissene Habre, the former ruler of Chad known as the "African Pinochet."[4]

## LINKAGE ACTORS ON THE RISE

Let's consider the many different actors present in the Tangled Tale of Pinochet. Like the earlier Tangled Tale of Tibet, the Pinochet case involves more actors than just states. The international actors involved in the tale of Pinochet include the following:

- Chile, Great Britain, Spain, France, Belgium, Switzerland, and Sweden
- United Nations, European Union, and European Court of Justice (all by implication)
- Roman Catholic Church/Vatican
- International human rights groups: Amnesty International, Human Rights Watch, Redress Trust, Medical Foundation for the Care of Victims of Torture
- Chile-based human rights groups
- Spain-based human rights groups
- UK-based human rights groups
- Spanish Association of Progressive Prosecutors
- Spanish legal system
- British legal system/House of Lords
- General Augusto Pinochet
- Spanish Judge Baltazar Garzón
- British home secretary Jack Straw
- British doctor tortured in Pinochet's Chile
- Family of a British citizen "disappeared" in Pinochet's Chile
- Other victims of torture and murder in Pinochet's Chile

This list is far from complete, but it demonstrates a key point: the "stuff" of foreign policy involves many different actors. It would be impossible to try to understand the issues involved in the Pinochet case just from the perspective of the involved states. The issues go beyond state interests and state actors.

NGOs played critical roles in the arrest of and the case made against Pinochet. The important roles played by NGOs increased the net power of citizen groups and forwarded the notion of a global citizenry, while diminishing the strong grip of states on their own domestic and foreign affairs. Globalization facilitates the rise of nonstate actors. Beyond the empowerment of NGOs and international organizations, globalization can be used for citizen empowerment through the efforts of "transnational advocacy networks" such as that illustrated in the Pinochet case. "Transnational advocacy networks" is the term coined by Margaret Keck and Kathryn Sikkink to refer to groups "working internationally on an issue who are bound together by shared values, a common discourse, and dense exchanges of information and services."[5] The tangled tale of Pinochet prompts us to think about the impact of these rising networks of linkage actors on states' foreign and domestic policy making and the strategies these groups employ.

Karen Mingst provides such a framework in her work on **linkage actors**. Mingst uses Rosenau's definition of "linkage" to indicate "any recurrent sequence of behavior that originates in one system and is reacted to in another."[6] She offers seven categories of linkage actors:

1. Government negotiators engaged in the nested game between domestic and international politics.
2. International organizations, whether acting as agents in their own right or as agents of states.
3. International courts, especially the European Court of Justice, which enjoys supranational jurisdiction.
4. Transgovernmental coalitions between agencies of different states acting cooperatively toward a common goal.
5. Individuals involved in "track two" or informal diplomacy, such as the representative of the Vatican or a former head of state.
6. Nongovernmental organizations.
7. Epistemic communities, which are, as Mingst quotes Peter Haas, "network[s] of professionals with recognized expertise and competence in a particular domain and an authoritative claim to policy-relevant knowledge within that domain or issue area."[7]

Linkage actors utilize four strategies to influence state policy. The first strategy is the **power approach**. This entails making diplomatic contacts at the highest decision-making levels in a high-stakes game of influence. Mingst warns that this strategy is risky because failed efforts can come at a great loss of the linkage actor's credibility. In the Pinochet case, the power approach is illustrated in Vatican efforts to convince the British government to release Pinochet on humanitarian grounds.

The second strategy employed by linkage actors is the **technocratic approach**. This entails, among other things, the use of the linkage actor's knowledge and expertise in the procedural mechanisms of domestic and international courts to force state compliance with international agreements. In the Pinochet case, a coalition of human rights groups in Chile and Spain led by a group of Spanish prosecutors used those prosecutors' expert knowledge of Spanish law to establish the grounds for the original arrest warrant. Similarly, the human rights NGOs that intervened in the hearings in the British House of Lords used expert knowledge of British and international law to argue against Pinochet's claim of diplomatic immunity.

The third linkage-actor strategy is **coalition building**. Building a coalition that contains many different linkage actors and their resources ensures a stronger, more effective tool to change state policies. The coalitions of European governments and human rights organizations and of British human rights organizations and private British citizens who had suffered under the Pinochet regime are illustrations of effective coalition building.

Finally, the fourth strategy is **grassroots mobilization**. This entails building widespread public involvement in the cause, especially when the "public" spans multiple national borders. Generally such a strategy involves the use of large-scale public education efforts designed to mobilize the public to demand a response from officeholders. Although Pinochet was not made to stand trial in Spain, the case was seen as a victory for the larger cause: publicity generated by the case educated people worldwide on their rights and on the costs of violating those rights. Moreover, the case served to educate global citizens on the notion that heads of state and former heads of state did not enjoy unlimited diplomatic immunity on human rights issues, thereby standing this old notion on its head.

As nonstate actors rise in importance and power, foreign policy analysts will need to incorporate them into foreign policy studies. The realist notion that nonstate actors are simply instruments of state interests and the Marxist notion that nonstate actors are simply instruments of economic elite interests do not cover the range of nonstate motivations, behaviors, and power we see displayed in the Tangled Tale of Pinochet. Nonstate actors use features of globalization—such as global communications—to protect individuals against states even while recognizing that globalization itself poses dangers to individuals. Globalization offers such paradoxes—it offers avenues for strengthening the hands of citizens and NGOs against the traditional state structure and against states while also offering more reasons for citizens and NGOs to be alarmed. States, too, may reap the benefits of globalization; state leaders may claim that they cannot act to protect their poor or their workers or their environment because the globalization tide is inevitable and overwhelming.

September 11, 2001, presented another paradox of globalization that cannot be ignored. For some people in the world, globalization seals the indictment against the United States and the West while it also presents one means by which the Western world system might be undermined. Osama bin Laden and his terrorist network, al Qaeda, stood in opposition to the US-dominated global economic and political systems and to the Americanization of global culture. At the same time, al Qaeda made full use of globalization to link associated groups, cells, operatives, and finances in dozens of countries.

The al Qaeda network operated in much the same way as any linkage actor. The 1993 bombing of the World Trade Center, the attacks on the US Marines barracks in Saudi Arabia in 1996, the 1998 bombings of the US embassies in Kenya and Tanzania, and the attack on the USS *Cole* in 2000 can all be characterized as demonstrations of the power approach described above. September 11 demonstrated that this particular linkage actor would do what state opponents of the United States would not. Further, the terrorist attacks of September 11 took considerable technocratic expertise—the second linkage-actor approach discussed above. How else could the hijackers fly jumbo commercial aircraft into the World Trade Center and Pentagon? Everything about the September 11 attacks required precise, long-term planning, execution, and considerable knowledge of building structures. Coalition building, the third linkage-actor approach, is the way in which al Qaeda attracted adherents and spin-off organizations. As governments attempted to undermine this terrorist network, they found it to be a diverse and tangled web of humanitarian assistance groups, governments, terrorist training bases, and various legitimate and illegitimate financial concerns. Finally, the network that took on the United States found its next round of frontline troops in grassroots mobilization, or in the "rage, poverty, and hopelessness in neighborhoods throughout the Middle East and sub-Saharan Africa."[8]

Like all other linkage actors, global terrorists work within the confines of the international state system. This is yet another paradox of globalization: it erodes the importance of states while it accentuates their power. In 1991, Saudi Arabia expelled Osama bin Laden because he had issued a fatwa against the government, denouncing the regime as illegitimate. From then until 1996, Osama bin Laden and his entourage of mujahedeen (holy warriors left over from the successful 1980s Afghan war against the Soviets) resided in Sudan. Around 1996 bin Laden chartered a jet and took his entourage and financial assets to Afghanistan.

Osama bin Laden was forced or encouraged by states to relocate several times. States—fully functional states—retain control over who resides within their borders. Afghanistan was, perhaps, a much better refuge for bin Laden, since the ruling Taliban regime was extraordinarily sympathetic to him, his cause, and his money. Plus, the Taliban did not have full control over the country, so its own position was precarious, giving it less relative power over bin Laden than the Saudi or Sudanese governments had and making it far more dependent on bin Laden's fighters and assets.

Bin Laden and al Qaeda were not the only actors in this "war" bound by the state system. The American war against international terrorism was constrained by the power retained by other states. For example, the first arrests in the September 11 attacks came in Spain. In mid-November 2001, eight men were arrested and charged with complicity in the attacks in an indictment released by Spanish investigative judge Baltazar Garzón—the same judge who issued the indictment that led to Augusto Pinochet's arrest in London. Spanish authorities had been investigating an al Qaeda cell that had formed in 1994 in Madrid. Phone intercepts indicated that the individuals in the cell had helped plan the September 11 attacks with some of the hijackers.

Although the arrest of the al Qaeda cell for complicity in the attacks should have been very good news, it actually posed some diplomatic difficulties for the Bush administration. As part of the administration's evolving plans for the war on international terrorism, Bush announced that he would use military tribunals to try any foreign nationals on charges stemming from September 11. This announcement was met with criticism from all sides of the political spectrum within the United States as well as from America's closest allies. Within days of the announcement of the arrests of the cell, the Spanish Foreign Ministry announced that "Spain could extradite detainees only to countries that offer defendants the legal guarantees provided by Spanish courts."[9] Military tribunals would not offer the same legal guarantees, making extradition to the United States highly unlikely. Moreover, none of the other EU countries could be expected to extradite suspects to the United States for the same reason. Because the death penalty would be an option in these US tribunals, extradition of suspects from Europe would violate EU policy against the death penalty. Although Spain and the broader European Union were supportive of US efforts in the war against international terrorism, they were not prepared to sacrifice their own national and EU laws and principles in the process. The war on terror, a primary American foreign policy initiative, was entangled in a complicated nested game with many actors.

The United States had not limited its war on terrorism to the literal battlefield. One official in the US Department of State, James Glassman, had been thinking about al Qaeda's use of the Internet. In his words from late 2008,

When I was speaking at my confirmation hearings back in January, I made the comment that al Qaeda has been eating our lunch—my inelegant phrase—on the internet. And I think it's true that al Qaeda has used the internet to expand its organization. But al Qaeda has historically been using the internet as [an] exhortative kind of tool, an instructional tool. This is the old way to use the internet. . . .

The internet is a place where people can practice democracy and freedom and where, in fact, organizations like al Qaeda are going to have to struggle because they can't stand the kind of criticism and discussion that takes place in a social networking environment. And what we know about young people around the world is they love this environment. They love expressing their views and talking to people around the world. This is the antithesis of what al Qaeda is all about. [10]

Glassman was speaking on the occasion of the first annual Alliance of Youth Movements Summit. The summit was inspired by a protest of some five million Colombians who took to the streets across their country and the world against the Revolutionary Armed Forces of Colombia (FARC). The protest had been organized in one month by thirty-three-year-old Oscar Morales who had simply started a Facebook page. A young dissident from Egypt attended that Alliance of Youth Movements Summit in December 2008, and although his notes from the summit were confiscated by the Egyptian security policy when he returned home, the strength and conviction of a worldwide social movement helped to empower him and his compatriots to topple a dictator.

## THE FACEBOOK REVOLUTION

In the name of God the merciful, the compassionate, citizens, during these very difficult circumstances Egypt is going through, President Hosni Mubarak has decided to step down from the office of president of the republic and has charged the high council of the armed forces to administer the affairs of the country. May God help everybody.
—Omar Suleiman, vice president of Egypt, February 11, 2011

The story of the Egyptian Revolution that started on January 25, 2011, and caused the toppling of Hosni Mubarak seventeen days later has been widely told. As mentioned in the first chapter of this book, all stories have many entrance points. We can briefly enter the story of the Egyptian Revolution six years earlier in 2005 when the Mubarak regime held meaningless multiparty elections to satisfy the US Bush administration. That same year, "a government initiative to encourage technological innovation in Egypt" resulted in a great expansion of computer and Internet use. "The new technologies and political movements grew symbiotically." [11] Bloggers who opposed the regime became popular and even had their posts printed in opposition newspapers. Meanwhile, state authorities largely ignored what was being said on the Internet—or assumed it could be controlled like everything else in Egyptian society.

In March 2008, some young Egyptian political activists decided to call themselves the April 6 Strike movement and launched a Facebook page in support of a planned textile workers strike.[12] The Facebook page drew enormous interest, gathering more than seventy thousand supporters in a month. The Egyptian police were aware of the site and had joined it. When the strike occurred, rioting and mass arrests also occurred. Some of the April 6 organizers were politically astute; some were not. One of the organizers posted her plans for the day of the strike on Facebook and told people what she would be wearing in case they wanted to find her.[13] She was quickly arrested by the police.

Later that year, in December 2008, the first summit of the Alliance of Youth Movements (AYM) met at Columbia Law School in New York City. As noted above, the summit was inspired by the Facebook organizing of the Million Voices against FARC campaign. The AYM summit was organized by the US State Department and cosponsored by Google, Facebook, Howcast, MTV, Gen-Next, AT&T, and Access 360 Media. State Department officials, members of the media, and academics moderated discussions, and the newly victorious Obama campaign's New Media Team participated too. But the guests of honor were members of Internet activist groups and "observer" groups including: Million Voices against FARC, Save Darfur Coalition, Genç Siviller (Young Civilians), Invisible Children, Illuminemos Mexico, Youth for Tolerance, One Million Voices against Crime in South Africa, Burma Global Action Network, and the People's March against Knife Crime.

Most of the invited groups were already active online; that is, the US government did not create these groups as part of a public diplomacy initiative. Glassman explained that to find invitees for the first summit, "We looked online—you know, what are the organizations that really have shown that they have been able to organize people online. So we invited those."[14] And, Glassman added, the groups that were invited were only the tip of the iceberg. The groups represented "civil society organizations popping up in places where people wouldn't otherwise be able to afford the startup costs for a civil society organization," which was made possible by social media and media-savvy young people. The purpose of the summit was to discuss the "best ways to use digital media to promote freedom and justice, counter violence, extremism and oppression."

The groups that were invited—the people that were invited—didn't wait to arrive at the summit to start their work together. One State official explained,

There's a youth organization coming from Afghanistan that had never heard of Facebook before, and didn't have Facebook accounts. . . . Already the Million Voices Against FARC movement all the way in Colombia, without ever having to go to get a visa to go to Afghanistan or vice versa, is working together to get the members of that organization in Afghanistan . . . Facebook profiles. . . . You couldn't do this five years ago.[15]

The State Department provided the logistical and financial support, and Columbia provided the facilities and "good offices" (in diplomatic speak). That is, State and Columbia—acting as linkage actors—helped facilitate coalition building among the groups. The groups themselves brought their grassroots mobilization skills and joined their technocratic know-how with that of representatives of Google, Facebook, and other social media groups. The linkage-actor power approach used by the members of this coalition had already been demonstrated and would continue to be demonstrated in the rallying of millions of people to protest against violence, oppression, and other indignities and insecurities.

AYM held two more summits of Internet activists and maintains a constant Internet presence through http://www.movements.org. Groups from around the world can link to this site and learn how to use the Internet to build awareness for their causes, plan and strategize campaigns and movements, mobilize supporters, and fund-raise.

One of the members of Egypt's April 6 movement attended the first AYM summit in December 2008. After returning to Cairo, he discussed his experience at the summit with US embassy officials. In a 2008 cable published by WikiLeaks, a State official in Cairo wrote,

> On December 23, April 6 activist Ahmed Saleh expressed satisfaction with his participation in the December 3–5 "Alliance of Youth Movements Summit," and with his subsequent meetings with USG [US government] officials, on Capitol Hill, and with think tanks. He described how State Security (SSIS) detained him at the Cairo airport upon his return and confiscated his notes for his summit presentation calling for democratic change in Egypt, and his schedule for his Congressional meetings. Saleh contended that the GOE [government of Egypt] will never undertake significant reform, and therefore, Egyptians need to replace the current regime with a parliamentary democracy. . . .
> [Saleh said that at the summit] he was able to meet activists from other countries and outline his movement's goals for democratic change in Egypt. He told us that the other activists at the summit were very supportive, and that some even offered to hold public demonstrations in support of Egyptian democracy in their countries. . . . Saleh said he discussed with the other activists how April 6 members could more effectively evade harassment and surveillance from SSIS with technical upgrades, such as consistently alternating computer "simcards." . . .
> Comment: Saleh offered no roadmap of concrete steps toward April 6's highly unrealistic goal of replacing the current regime with a parliamentary democracy prior to the 2011 presidential elections. Most opposition parties and independent NGOs work toward achieving tangible, incremental reform within the current political context, even if they may be pessimistic about their

chances of success. Saleh's wholesale rejection of such an approach places him outside this mainstream of opposition politicians and activists.[16]

Saleh was in a much wider "mainstream" than this particular official appreciated. This "mainstream" was growing quickly in the activist community in support of the peaceful end of the Mubarak regime. In 2010, another hugely popular Facebook group appeared in Egypt called "We Are All Khaled Said." This group was started by a Google executive in honor of a blogger killed by the police for exposing police abuse. When the government of Tunisia fell to protests in mid-January 2011, the Internet activists in Egypt quickly organized street protests for January 25 using their Facebook pages once again. Once the protests began, many other groups joined in, resulting in a popular revolution. Hosni Mubarak resigned seventeen days later.

We might say there were two "mainstreams" that came out into the open with dramatic urgency in the Arab world in early 2011. The young activists of Saleh's "mainstream" understood and took advantage of the power inherent in their technological sophistication and their globally shared belief in a better world. The Mubarak regime never seemed to understand what kind of power the activists wielded. The regime was part of the other "mainstream," one that had been playing an old power game with real weapons and political repression for generations. That old-school "mainstream" consisted of Hosni Mubarak and others just like him, as well as the leaders of Israel and Saudi Arabia and other countries in the region, and US foreign policy advisors who all wanted to stand by a staunchly pro-American "moderate" and "mainstream" friend.

As it turned out, Barack Obama was a member of Saleh's "mainstream." On February 1, Obama called Mubarak and told him that he must step down. Mubarak replied, "You don't understand this part of the world. You're young."[17]

## A NESTED GAME WITH MANY PLAYERS

We started this discussion of foreign policy with the Tangled Tale of Tibet and ended it with the Tangled Tale of Pinochet and the Facebook youth revolution in Egypt. In between we've examined many different ways to understand foreign policy. The study of foreign policy is a study of complex interactions and competing interests, which is easier to get our minds around when we disaggregate it into smaller parts. The study of foreign policy is still about the study of states and their foreign policies, but the "stuff" of the policies has always involved and has always had an impact on the lives of regular people. How people organize and think about themselves in this world has been changing, and policy makers can't afford to remain in the old mainstream.

And so we'll stop where we started with some simple statements about foreign policy:

- Foreign policy is made and conducted in complex domestic and international environments.
- Foreign policy results from the work of coalitions of interested domestic and international actors and groups.
- Foreign policy issues are often linked and delinked, reflecting the strength of various parties and their particular concerns.
- The "stuff" of foreign policy derives from issues of domestic politics as well as foreign relations.
- Foreign policy analysis needs to be multilevel and multifaceted in order to confront the complicated sources and nature of foreign policy.

# Notes

## 1. INTRODUCTION: THE NEW FOREIGN POLICY

1. Jonathan Mirsky, "The Dalai Lama on Succession and on the CIA," *New York Review of Books*, June 10, 1999, 48.

2. Jim Mann, "China Issue: Early Test for Clinton," *Los Angeles Times*, January 25, 1993, D1.

3. John W. Dietrich, "Interest Groups and Foreign Policy: Clinton and the China MFN Debates," *Presidential Studies Quarterly* 29, no. 2 (1999): 285.

4. Dietrich, "Interest Groups," 286.

5. Nicholas D. Kristof, "Chinese Apparently Halt Rights Talks with U.S.," *New York Times*, November 25, 1992, A12.

6. Dietrich, "Interest Groups," 288.

7. Dietrich, "Interest Groups," 289.

8. Dietrich, "Interest Groups," 292.

9. Robert D. Putnam, "Diplomacy and Domestic Politics: The Logic of Two-Level Games," *International Organization* 42, no. 3 (1988): 427–69.

10. Charles F. Hermann, "Foreign Policy Behavior: That Which Is to Be Explained," in *Why Nations Act*, ed. Maurice A. East, Stephen A. Salmore, and Charles F. Hermann (Beverly Hills: Sage, 1978), 25.

11. Hermann, "Foreign Policy Behavior," 26.

12. Hermann, "Foreign Policy Behavior," 34.

13. Bruce Russett, Harvey Starr, and David Kinsella, *World Politics: The Menu for Choice*, 6th ed. (New York: St. Martin's, 2000), 117.

14. Russett, Starr, and Kinsella, *World Politics*, 117.

15. Deborah J. Gerner, "The Evolution of the Study of Foreign Policy," in *Foreign Policy Analysis: Continuity and Change in Its Second Generation*, ed. Laura Neack, Jeanne A. K. Hey, and Patrick J. Haney (Englewood Cliffs, N.J.: Prentice Hall, 1995), 18.

16. The realist worldview has many variants, including neorealism or structural realism, as well as balance-of-power versus balance-of-threat arguments. For an interesting presentation of the variations in realism, see Ethan B. Kapstein and Michael Mastanduno, eds., *Unipolar Politics: Realism and State Strategies after the Cold War* (New York: Columbia University Press, 1999).

17. "Liberalism" is one of the many labels applied to this worldview. Its variations include idealism, pluralism, and neoliberal institutionalism. For an example of this worldview com-

pared with realism, see Daniel Deudney and G. John Ikenberry, "Realism, Structural Liberalism, and the Western Order," in Kapstein and Mastanduno, eds., *Unipolar Politics*.

18. Marxism has variants of its own: neo-Marxism, structuralism, dependency theory, and world-systems theory. For a comprehensive overview of Marxism as compared with realism and liberalism, see Paul R. Viotti and Mark V. Kauppi, *International Relations Theory: Realism, Pluralism, Globalism, and Beyond* (Boston: Allyn & Bacon, 1999).

19. Deborah J. Gerner, "Foreign Policy Analysis: Renaissance, Routine, or Rubbish?" in *Political Science: Looking to the Future*, vol. 2, *Comparative Politics, Policy, and International Relations*, ed. William Croty (Evanston, Ill.: Northwestern University Press, 1992), 126.

20. Gerner, "Foreign Policy Analysis," 126.

21. Gerner, "Foreign Policy Analysis," 128.

22. Howard Wiarda, "Comparative Politics Past and Present," in *New Directions in Comparative Politics*, ed. Howard J. Wiarda (Boulder, Colo.: Westview, 1984).

23. Laura Neack, Jeanne A. K. Hey, and Patrick Haney, "Generational Change in Foreign Policy Analysis," in Neack, Hey, and Haney, ed., *Foreign Policy Analysis*, 5.

24. Wiarda, "Comparative Politics," 12.

25. Neack, Hey, and Haney, "Generational Change," 5.

26. Neack, Hey, and Haney, "Generational Change," 6.

27. Gerner, "Foreign Policy Analysis," 130.

28. Richard Snyder, H. W. Bruck, and Burton Sapin, *Decision-Making as an Approach to the Study of International Politics*, Foreign Policy Analysis Series, no. 3 (Princeton, N.J.: Princeton University Press, 1954); Richard Snyder, H. W. Bruck, and Burton Sapin, eds., *Foreign Policy Decision Making* (New York: Free Press, 1963).

29. Charles F. Hermann and Gregory Peacock, "The Evolution and Future of Theoretical Research in the Comparative Study of Foreign Policy," in *New Directions in the Study of Foreign Policy*, ed. Charles F. Hermann, Charles W. Kegley, and James N. Rosenau (Winchester, Mass.: Unwin Hyman, 1987), 22–23.

30. Snyder, Bruck, and Sapin, *Foreign Policy Decision Making*, 65, as quoted in James E. Dougherty and Robert L. Pfaltzgraff Jr., *Contending Theories of International Relations: A Comprehensive Survey*, 5th ed. (New York: Longman, 2001), 554.

31. Hermann and Peacock, "Evolution and Future of Theoretical Research," 23.

32. James N. Rosenau, "Pre-theories and Theories of Foreign Policy," in *Approaches to Comparative and International Politics*, ed. R. Barry Farrell (Evanston, Ill.: Northwestern University Press, 1966).

33. Rosenau, "Pre-theories," 115–16.

34. Rosenau, "Pre-theories," 124.

35. Hermann and Peacock, "Evolution and Future of Theoretical Research," 23.

36. Neack, Hey, and Haney, "Generational Change."

37. Robert O. Keohane and Joseph S. Nye, *Power and Interdependence: World Politics in Transition* (Boston: Little, Brown, 1977).

38. Neack, Hey, and Haney, "Generational Change," 7.

39. Jon Western and Joshua T. Goldstein, "Humanitarian Intervention Comes of Age," *Foreign Affairs*, November/December 2011, 48–59.

40. Didi Kirsten Tatlow, "Dalai Lama Keeps Firm Grip on Reins of Succession," *International Herald Tribune*, October 6, 2011, 2.

## 2. RATIONAL ACTORS AND NATIONAL INTERESTS

1. "Japan PM Dismisses Beijing's Claim to Islands in South China Sea—Thai Daily," BBC Worldwide Monitoring, January 17, 2013.

2. "Japan PM Dismisses Beijing's Claim to Islands in South China Sea."

3. Hans J. Morgenthau, *Politics among Nations*, brief ed., rev. Kenneth W. Thompson (New York: McGraw-Hill, 1993), 5.

4. Michael D. McGinnis, "Rational Choice and Foreign Policy Change: The Arms and Alignments of Regional Powers," in *Foreign Policy Restructuring: How Governments Respond to Global Change*, ed. Jerel A. Rosati, Joe D. Hagan, and Martin W. Sampson III (Columbia: University of South Carolina Press, 1994), 69.

5. McGinnis, "Rational Choice and Foreign Policy Change," 70.

6. George Kennan, quoted in Graham Allison and Philip Zelikow, *Essence of Decision: Explaining the Cuban Missile Crisis*, 2nd ed. (New York: Longman, 1999), 28.

7. James E. Dougherty and Robert L. Pfaltzgraff Jr., *Contending Theories of International Relations: A Comprehensive Survey*, 5th ed. (New York: Longman, 2001), 553.

8. Richard Snyder, H. W. Bruck, and Burton Sapin, "Decision-Making as an Approach to the Study of International Politics," in *Foreign Policy Decision Making: An Approach to the Study of International Politics* (New York: Macmillan, 1962).

9. Allison and Zelikow, *Essence of Decision*, 17.

10. Allison and Zelikow, *Essence of Decision*, 18.

11. Allison and Zelikow, *Essence of Decision*, 19.

12. Allison and Zelikow, *Essence of Decision*, 30.

13. Glenn H. Snyder, "The Security Dilemma in Alliance Politics," *World Politics* 36, no. 4 (July 1984): 461.

14. Ben D. Mor, "Nasser's Decision-Making in the 1967 Middle East Crisis: A Rational-Choice Explanation," *Journal of Peace Research* 28, no. 4 (1991): 359–75.

15. United Nations peacekeeping troops can only be placed within a country with the permission of that country's government. This consent requirement is necessary because the United Nations recognizes the key principle that all states are sovereign. Sovereignty means that there is no higher authority than a state in its territory. Placing foreign troops in a country without the consent of the government would constitute an invasion and would only be permissible under certain narrow provisions of the UN Charter.

16. Mor, "Nasser's Decision-Making," 371–72.

17. Deborah Sontag, "No Optimism about Mideast Talks," *New York Times*, September 6, 2000, A13.

18. Robin Wright, "Attack on Iraq May Be Outcome Hussein Wants," *Los Angeles Times*, January 31, 1998, A1.

19. Uzi Mahnaimi, "Israel's Iron Shield Flashes Warning to Iran," *Sunday Times* (London), December 2, 2012, 29.

20. Christopher Layne, "Security Studies and the Use of History: Neville Chamberlain's Grand Strategy Revisited," *Security Studies* 17 (2008), 401.

21. Morgenthau, *Politics among Nations*, 5.

22. Layne, "Security Studies," 401.

23. Layne, "Security Studies," 399.

24. Layne, "Security Studies," 405.

25. Layne, "Security Studies," 427.

26. See Kenneth Waltz's side of the debate presented in Scott D. Sagan and Kenneth N. Waltz, *The Spread of Nuclear Weapons: A Debate Renewed*, 2nd ed. (New York: Norton, 2002).

27. Dougherty and Pfaltzgraff, *Contending Theories*, 562.

28. Karen Mingst, *Essentials of International Relations* (New York: Norton, 1999), 68.

29. Robert L. Jervis, "Hypotheses on Misperception," *World Politics* 20, no. 3 (April 1968): 477.

30. Jervis, "Hypotheses on Misperception," 477.

31. Jerel Rosati, "The Power of Human Cognition in the Study of World Politics," *International Studies Review* 2, no. 3 (Autumn 2001): 49.

32. Alex Mintz, "Applied Decision Making: Utilizing Poliheuristic Theory to Explain and Predict Foreign Policy and National Security Decisions," *International Studies Perspectives* 6, no. 1 (February 2005): 94–95.

33. David Brulé, "Explaining and Forecasting Leaders' Decisions: A Poliheuristic Analysis of the Iran Hostage Rescue Decision," *International Studies Perspectives* 6, no. 1 (February 2005): 99–113.

34. Mintz, "Applied Decision Making," 94.

35. Brulé, "Explaining and Forecasting Leaders' Decisions," 100.


# 3. COGNITION AND PERSONALITY


1. Stephen Benedict Dyson, "Personality and Foreign Policy: Tony Blair's Iraq Decisions," *Foreign Policy Analysis* 2, no. 3 (July 2006): 289.

2. Dyson, "Personality and Foreign Policy."

3. Louise Grace Shaw, "Attitudes of the British Political Elite towards the Soviet Union," *Diplomacy & Statecraft* 13, no. 1 (March 2002): 63–64.

4. Shaw, "Attitudes of the British Political Elite," 70.

5. Michiko Kakutani, "All the President's Books," *New York Times*, May 11, 2006, E1.

6. Margaret G. Hermann and Joe D. Hagan, "International Decision Making: Leadership Matters," *Foreign Policy,* Spring 1988, 126.

7. Hermann and Hagan, "International Decision Making," 126.

8. Hermann and Hagan, "International Decision Making," 135.

9. Patrick J. Haney, "The Submarines of September: The Nixon Administration and a Soviet Submarine Base in Cuba," Pew Case Studies in International Affairs, no. 372 (Washington, D.C.: Georgetown University School of Public Service, 1996).

10. Haney, "Submarines of September," 3.

11. Kenneth Waltz, *Man, the State, and War* (New York: Columbia University Press, 1959), chaps. 2 and 3; Jerel Rosati, "A Cognitive Approach to the Study of Foreign Policy," in *Foreign Policy Analysis: Continuity and Change in Its Second Generation*, ed. Laura Neack, Jeanne A. K. Hey, and Patrick J. Haney (Englewood Cliffs, N.J.: Prentice Hall, 1995), 51.

12. Robert L. Jervis, "Hypotheses on Misperception," *World Politics* 20, no. 3 (April 1968): 454.

13. Jervis, "Hypotheses on Misperception," 455.

14. Irving L. Janis, *Crucial Decisions* (New York: Free Press, 1989); *Groupthink: Psychological Studies of Policy Decisions and Fiascoes*, rev. ed. (Boston: Houghton Mifflin, 1982).

15. Kakutani, "All the President's Books."

16. Rosati, "A Cognitive Approach," 50.

17. Jerel Rosati, "The Power of Human Cognition in the Study of World Politics," *International Studies Review* 2, no. 3 (Autumn 2001): 50.

18. For an elaboration on five stereotypical images of outside actors, see Richard K. Herrmann and Michael P. Fischerkeller, "Beyond the Enemy Image and Spiral Model: Cognitive-Strategic Research after the Cold War," *International Organization* 49, no. 2 (1995): 415–50.

19. Ole R. Holsti, "Cognitive Dynamics and Images of the Enemy: Dulles and Russia," in *Image and Reality in World Politics*, ed. John C. Farrell and Asa P. Smith (New York: Columbia University Press, 1967), 17, as discussed in Rosati, "A Cognitive Approach," 55.

20. Kurt Eichenwald, "The Deafness before the Storm," *New York Times*, September 10, 2012, 23; see also Kurt Eichenwald, *500 Days: Secrets and Lies in the Terror Wars* (New York: Touchstone, 2012).

21. Jack S. Levy, "Learning and Foreign Policy: Sweeping a Conceptual Minefield," *International Organization* 48, no. 2 (1994): 283.

22. Janice Gross Stein, "Political Learning by Doing: Gorbachev as Uncommitted Thinker and Motivated Learner," *International Organization* 48, no. 2 (1994): 172.

23. Stein, "Political Learning," 172.

24. Matthew S. Hirshberg, "The Self-Perpetuating National Self-Image: Cognitive Biases in Perceptions of International Interventions," *Political Psychology* 14, no. 1 (1993): 80.

25. Hirshberg, "Self-Perpetuating National Self-Image," 85.

26. Hirshberg, "Self-Perpetuating National Self-Image," 91.

27. Office of the Press Secretary, "President Outlines Steps to Help Iraq Achieve Democracy and Freedom," remarks by the president on Iraq and the war on terror, United States Army War College, Carlisle, Pennsylvania, May 24, 2004.

28. Office of the Press Secretary, "President Commemorates Veterans Day, Discusses War on Terror," Tobyhanna Army Depot, Tobyhanna, Pennsylvania, November 11, 2005.

29. Office of the Press Secretary, "President Participates in Discussion on War on Terror," Kentucky International Convention Center, Louisville, Kentucky, January 11, 2006.

30. "Croatian Jets Strafe UN Observer Posts," *Reuters World Service*, August 4, 1995.

31. Keith Shimko, "Foreign Policy Metaphors: Falling 'Dominoes' and 'Drug Wars,'" in Neack, Hey, and Haney, ed., *Foreign Policy Analysis*, 73.

32. Phil Reeves, "Sharon Appeals to America Not to 'Appease' Arabs," *Independent* (London), October 5, 2001, 15; Alan Sipress and Lee Hockstader, "Sharon Speech Riles US," *Washington Post*, October 6, 2001, A1.

33. Reeves, "Sharon Appeals to America."

34. Allison Astorino-Courtois, "The Cognitive Structure of Decision-Making and the Course of Arab-Israeli Relations, 1970–1978," *Journal of Conflict Resolution* 39, no. 3 (1995): 420.

35. Peter Suedfeld, Michael D. Wallace, and Kimberly L. Thachuk, "Changes in Integrative Complexity among Middle East Leaders during the Persian Gulf Crisis," *Journal of Social Issues* 49, no. 4 (1993): 183–84. See also Philip E. Tetlock, "Integrative Complexity of American and Soviet Foreign Policy Rhetoric: A Time-Series Analysis," *Journal of Personality and Social Psychology* 49 (1985): 165–85.

36. Astorino-Courtois, "Cognitive Structure of Decision-Making," 420; Stephen G. Walker and George L. Watson, "Integrative Complexity and British Decisions during the Munich and Polish Crises," *Journal of Conflict Resolution* 38, no. 1 (1994): 3–23.

37. Astorino-Courtois, "Cognitive Structure of Decision-Making," 421.

38. Scott Crichlow, "Idealism or Pragmatism? An Operational Code Analysis of Yitzak Rabin and Shimon Peres," *Political Psychology* 19, no. 4 (1998): 684.

39. Alexander George, "The 'Operational Code': A Neglected Approach to the Study of Political Leaders and Decision-Making," *International Studies Quarterly* 13, no. 2 (June 1969): 197.

40. Stephen G. Walker, Mark Schafer, and Michael D. Young, "Presidential Operational Codes and Foreign Policy Conflicts in the Post-Cold War World," *Journal of Conflict Resolution* 43, no. 5 (1999): 613.

41. Crichlow, "Idealism or Pragmatism?" 689.

42. Ibrahim A. Karawan, "Sadat and the Egyptian-Israeli Peace Revisited," *International Journal of Middle East Studies* 26, no. 2 (1994): 249–66.

43. Karawan, "Sadat and the Egyptian-Israeli Peace," 252.

44. Margaret G. Hermann, "Explaining Foreign Policy Behavior Using the Personal Characteristics of Political Leaders," *International Studies Quarterly* 43, no. 1 (March 1980): 8.

45. Dyson, "Personality and Foreign Policy"; Vaughn P. Shannon and Jonathan W. Keller, "Leadership Style and International Norm Violation: The Case of the Iraq War," *Foreign Policy Analysis* 3, no. 1 (2007): 79–104.

46. Hermann, "Explaining Foreign Policy Behavior," 11–12.

47. Hermann, "Explaining Foreign Policy Behavior," 12.

48. Shannon and Keller, "Leadership Style and International Norm Violation," 80.

49. Shannon and Keller, "Leadership Style and International Norm Violation," 97–98.

50. Dyson, "Personality and Foreign Policy," 294.

51. Dyson, "Personality and Foreign Policy," 294–96.

52. Werner Reutter, "Who's Afraid of Angela Merkel? The Life, Political Career, and Future of the New German Chancellor," *International Journal* 61, no. 1 (Winter 2005/2006): 215.

53. Sarah Elise Wiliarty, "Angela Merkel's Path to Power: The Role of Internal Party Dynamics and Leadership," *German Politics* 17, no. 1 (March 2008): 81; Reutter, "Who's Afraid of Angela Merkel?" 215.

54. Reutter, "Who's Afraid of Angela Merkel?" 215.

55. Reutter, "Who's Afraid of Angela Merkel?" 215, 216.

56. Wiliarty, "Angela Merkel's Path to Power."

57. Wiliarty, "Angela Merkel's Path to Power," 83.

58. Wiliarty, "Angela Merkel's Path to Power," 84.

59. Wiliarty, "Angela Merkel's Path to Power," 84.

60. Wiliarty, "Angela Merkel's Path to Power," 85.

61. Wiliarty, "Angela Merkel's Path to Power," 85.

62. Wiliarty, "Angela Merkel's Path to Power," 86–87.

63. Wiliarty, "Angela Merkel's Path to Power," 81.

64. Ruth Wittlinger, "The Merkel Government's Politics of the Past," *German Politics and Society* 89, no. 4 (Winter 2008): 9–27.

65. Wittlinger, "The Merkel Government's Politics of the Past," 13.

66. Ruth Wittlinger and Martin Larose, "No Future for Germany's Past? Collective Memory and German Foreign Policy," *German Politics* 16, no. 4 (December 2007): 481–95.

67. Wittlinger, "The Merkel Government's Politics of the Past," 13.

68. Wittlinger, "The Merkel Government's Politics of the Past," 14.

69. Angela Merkel, "Honorary Degree Acceptance Speech," *Social Research* 76, no. 3 (Fall 2009): 782.

70. Merkel, "Honorary Degree Acceptance Speech," 786.

71. Merkel, "Honorary Degree Acceptance Speech," 786.

72. Merkel, "Honorary Degree Acceptance Speech," 786.

73. Merkel, "Honorary Degree Acceptance Speech," 784.

74. Hermann, "Explaining Foreign Policy Behavior," 12.

75. Juergen Baetz and Melissa Eddy, "German Chancellor Confident that Euro Will Survive Debt Crisis," *Washington Post*, November 26, 2010, A18; "Brussels Meeting Focuses on EU Debt Crisis," National Public Radio, *Morning Edition*, December 16, 2010.

76. "European Debt Crisis," *New York Times*, *Times Topics*, December 20, 2012, http://topics.nytimes.com/top/reference/timestopics/subjects/e/european_sovereign_debt_crisis/index.html.

77. Noah Barkin and Stephen Brown, "Europe in 'Toughest Hour since World War Two'; Germany Fears EU Will Collapse if Euro Fails, Calls for Closer Continental Political Union," *The Gazette* (Montreal), November 15, 2011, B8.

78. Ian Traynor and Kate Connolly, "Germany and France Head towards Showdown on Austerity," *Guardian (London)*, April 28, 2012, 14.

79. Laurence Knight, "Has Europe Rediscovered Its Mojo?" BBC News, December 13, 2012, http://www.bbc.co.uk/news/business-20679152.

# 4. DECISION UNITS, SMALL GROUPS, AND AUTONOMOUS GROUPS

1. Margaret G. Hermann and Charles F. Hermann, "Who Makes Foreign Policy Decisions and How: An Empirical Inquiry," *International Studies Quarterly* 33, no. 4 (December 1989): 362. See also Ryan K. Beasley, Juliet Kaarbo, Charles F. Hermann, and Margaret G. Hermann, "Leaders, Groups, and Coalitions: Understanding People and Processes in Foreign Policymaking," *International Studies Review* 3, no. 2 (Summer 2001): 217–50.

2. Robert L. Jervis, "Hypotheses on Misperception," *World Politics* 20, no. 3 (April 1968): 467.

3. Hermann and Hermann, "Who Makes Foreign Policy Decisions and How," 363.

4. Hermann and Hermann, "Who Makes Foreign Policy Decisions and How," 366.

5. Hermann and Hermann, "Who Makes Foreign Policy Decisions and How," 365.

6. Hermann and Hermann, "Who Makes Foreign Policy Decisions and How," 363.

7. Charles F. Hermann, Janice Gross Stein, Bengt Sundelius, and Stephen G. Walker, "Resolve, Accept, or Avoid: Effects of Group Conflict on Foreign Policy Decisions," *International Studies Review* 3, no. 2 (Summer 2001): 134.

8. Hermann, Stein, Sundelius, and Walker, "Resolve, Accept, or Avoid," 134.

9. Irving L. Janis, *Victims of Groupthink* (Boston: Houghton Mifflin, 1972); Irving L. Janis, *Groupthink: Psychological Studies of Foreign Policy Decisions and Fiascoes*, rev. ed. (Boston: Houghton Mifflin, 1982).

10. Janis, *Groupthink*, 176.

11. Mark Schafer and Scott Crichlow, "Antecedents of Groupthink: A Quantitative Study," *Journal of Conflict Resolution* 40, no. 3 (September 1996): 429.

12. Hermann, Stein, Sundelius, and Walker, "Resolve, Accept, or Avoid," 140.

13. Hermann, Stein, Sundelius, and Walker, "Resolve, Accept, or Avoid," 140.

14. International Crisis Group, "Conflict History: Iran," March 2006, http://www.crisisgroup.org (accessed November 8, 2007).

15. Ray Takeyh, "Time for Détente with Iran," *Foreign Affairs*, March–April 2007, online version, http://www.foreignaffairs.com/articles/62444/ray-takeyh/time-for-d%C3%83%C2%A9tente-with-iran (accessed March 1, 2013).

16. Gareth Smyth, "Fundamentalists, Pragmatists, and the Rights of the Nation: Iranian Politics and Nuclear Confrontation," 16, report by the Century Foundation (New York and Washington, D.C.: Century Foundation, 2006).

17. Takeyh, "Time for Détente with Iran."

18. Takeyh, "Time for Détente with Iran"; see also Smyth, "Fundamentalists, Pragmatists, and the Rights of the Nation."

19. Takeyh, "Time for Détente with Iran."

20. Smyth, "Fundamentalists, Pragmatists, and the Rights of the Nation," 17.

21. Takeyh, "Time for Détente with Iran."

22. Javier Blas, "Sanctions Take Heavy Toll on Iran," *Financial Times*, November 28, 2012.

23. David E. Sanger, "Iran Offers Plan, Dismissed by U.S., on Nuclear Crisis," *New York Times*, October 4, 2012, http://www.nytimes.com/2012/10/05/world/middleeast/iranians-offer-9-step-plan-to-end-nuclear-crisis.html; Helene Cooper and Mark Landler, "U.S. Officials Say Iran Has Agreed to Nuclear Talks," *New York Times*, October 20, 2012, http://www.nytimes.com/2012/10/21/world/iran-said-ready-to-talk-to-us-about-nuclear-program.html.

24. Kenneth Katzman, "Iran: U.S. Concerns and Policy Responses," Congressional Research Service report for Congress, September 5, 2012, 3, http://fpc.state.gov/c18185.htm.

25. Katzman, "Iran: U.S. Concerns and Policy Responses," 13.

26. Katzman, "Iran: U.S. Concerns and Policy Responses," 13.

27. Hermann and Hermann, "Who Makes Foreign Policy Decisions and How," 364.

28. Hermann and Hermann, "Who Makes Foreign Policy Decisions and How," 368.

29. Hermann and Hermann, "Who Makes Foreign Policy Decisions and How," 368.

30. Graham Allison and Philip Zelikow, *Essence of Decision: Explaining the Cuban Missile Crisis*, 2nd ed. (New York: Longman, 1999), 256.

31. Allison and Zelikow, *Essence of Decision*, 256.

32. Allison and Zelikow, *Essence of Decision*, 256.

33. Hermann and Hermann, "Who Makes Foreign Policy Decisions and How," 368.

34. Esra Çuhadar-Gürkaynak and Binnur Özkeçeci-Taner, "Decisionmaking Process Matters: Lessons Learned from Two Turkish Foreign Policy Cases," *Turkish Studies* 5, no. 2 (Summer 2004): 43–78.

35. Çuhadar-Gürkaynak and Özkeçeci-Taner, "Decisionmaking Process Matters," 50.

36. Çuhadar-Gürkaynak and Özkeçeci-Taner, "Decisionmaking Process Matters," 51.

37. Çuhadar-Gürkaynak and Özkeçeci-Taner, "Decisionmaking Process Matters," 52.

38. Çuhadar-Gürkaynak and Özkeçeci-Taner, "Decisionmaking Process Matters," 53.

39. "War Powers Act of 1973," *New York Times*, *Times Topics*, December 13, 2012, http://topics.nytimes.com/top/reference/timestopics/subjects/w/war_powers_act_of_1973.

40. Hermann and Hermann, "Who Makes Foreign Policy Decisions and How," 368.

41. Scott Shane, "Election Spurred a Move to Codify U.S. Drone Policy," *New York Times*, November 24, 2012, http://www.nytimes.com/2012/11/25/world/white-house-presses-for-drone-rule-book.html.

# 5. NATIONAL SELF-IMAGE, CULTURE, AND DOMESTIC INSTITUTIONS

1. Ulf Hedetoft, "National Identity and Mentalities of War in Three EC Countries," *Journal of Peace Research* 30, no. 3 (1993): 295.

2. Hedetoft, "National Identity," 292.

3. Hedetoft, "National Identity," 295.

4. Peter R. Baehr, "Trials and Errors: The Netherlands and Human Rights," in *Human Rights and Comparative Foreign Policy*, ed. David P. Forsythe (New York: United Nations University Press, 2000), 52.

5. James N. Rosenau, "Pre-theories and Theories of Foreign Policy," in *Approaches to Comparative and International Politics*, ed. R. Barry Farrell (Evanston, Ill.: Northwestern University Press, 1966), 133.

6. Maurice A. East and Charles F. Hermann, "Do Nation-Types Account for Foreign Policy Behavior?" in *Comparing Foreign Policies: Theories, Findings, and Methods*, ed. James N. Rosenau (New York: John Wiley and Sons for Sage, 1974), 272.

7. East and Hermann, "Do Nation-Types Account for Foreign Policy Behavior?" 299.

8. "The Globalization Index," *Foreign Policy*, November–December 2007, 68–76.

9. "The Failed States Index 2012," *Foreign Policy*, http://www.foreignpolicy.com/failed_states_index_2012_interactive.

10. Vision of Humanity, "The Global Peace Index 2012," June 16, 2012, http://www.visionofhumanity.org/gpi_data.

11. Vision of Humanity, "The Global Peace Index 2012," 11–12.

12. Vision of Humanity, "The Global Peace Index 2012," 7.

13. Vision of Humanity, "The Global Peace Index 2012," 9.

14. Matthew S. Hirshberg, "The Self-Perpetuating National Self-Image: Cognitive Biases in Perceptions of International Interventions," *Political Psychology* 14, no. 1 (1993): 78.

15. Steven Erlanger, "Racial Tinge Stains World Cup Exit in France," *New York Times*, June 23, 2010, http://www.nytimes.com/2010/06/24/world/europe/24france.html.

16. Erlanger, "Racial Tinge."

17. Alastair Ian Johnston, "Realism(s) and Chinese Security Policy in the Post-Cold War Period," in *Unipolar Politics: Realism and State Strategies after the Cold War*, ed. Ethan B. Kapstein and Michael Mastanduno (New York: Columbia University Press, 1999), 288.

18. Hirshberg, "Self-Perpetuating National Self-Image," 78.

19. Hirshberg, "Self-Perpetuating National Self-Image," 87.

20. Hirshberg, "Self-Perpetuating National Self-Image," 96.

21. Daniel Bar-Tal and Dikla Antebi, "Beliefs about Negative Intentions of the World: A Study of Israeli Siege Mentality," *Political Psychology* 13, no. 4 (1992): 634.

22. Bar-Tal and Antebi, "Beliefs about Negative Intentions of the World," 643.

23. Jodi Rudoren, "Israeli Identity Is at the Heart of a Debate on Service," *New York Times*, July 5, 2012, http://www.nytimes.com/2012/07/06/world/middleeast/national-identity-at-heart-of-debate-on-israeli-military-service.html.

24. Rudoren, "Israeli Identity."

25. Geoffrey Wiseman, *Concepts of Non-Provocative Defense* (New York: Palgrave, 2002), 58.

26. Wiseman, *Concepts of Non-Provocative Defense*, 57–58.

27. Laura Neack, *Elusive Security: States First, People Last* (Lanham, Md.: Rowman & Littlefield, 2007), 106–11.

28. Peter J. Katzenstein and Nobuo Okawara, "Japan's National Security: Structures, Norms, and Policies," *International Security* 17, no. 4 (1993): 87.

29. Yozo Yokota and Chiyuki Aoi, "Japan's Foreign Policy toward Human Rights: Uncertain Changes," in Forsythe, ed., *Human Rights and Comparative Foreign Policy*, 127.

30. Katzenstein and Okawara, "Japan's National Security," 92.

31. Katzenstein and Okawara, "Japan's National Security," 97.

32. Yukiko Miyagi, "Foreign Policy Making under Koizumi: Norms and Japan's Role in the 2003 Iraq War," *Foreign Policy Analysis* 5 (2009): 351.

33. Miyagi, "Foreign Policy Making under Koizumi," 354.

34. Paul Wiseman, "Nationalism Gains Strength in Japan; Candidates Push to Rearm Country and Rewrite History," *USA Today*, July 27, 2007, A6.

35. Anthony Faiola, "Japan Upgrades Its Defense Agency; New Laws Widen Mission, Require Schools to Foster Patriotism," *Washington Post*, December 16, 2006, A15; Norimitsu Onishi, "Japanese Lawmakers Pass Two Laws That Shift Nation Away from Its Postwar Pacifism," *New York Times*, December 16, 2006, A10; Joseph Coleman, "Japan Brings Back Patriotic Education, Upgrades Defense Agency to Full Ministry," Associated Press, December 15, 2006.

36. Ruth Wittlinger and Martin Larose, "No Future for Germany's Past? Collective Memory and German Foreign Policy," *German Politics* 16, no. 4 (December 2007): 483.

37. Wittlinger and Larose, "No Future for Germany's Past?" 485.

38. Wittlinger and Larose, "No Future for Germany's Past?" 486.

39. Wittlinger and Larose, "No Future for Germany's Past?" 488–90.

40. Wittlinger and Larose, "No Future for Germany's Past?" 490.

41. Ruth Wittlinger, "The Merkel Government's Politics of the Past," *German Politics and Society* 89, no. 4 (Winter 2008): 10.

42. Jeffrey Herf, "Berlin Ghosts: Why Germany Was against the Libya Intervention," *New Republic*, March 24, 2011, http://www.tnr.com; Judy Dempsey, "Berlin's Diplomacy under a Dark Cloud," *International Herald Tribune*, April 5, 2011, 4; Klaus-Dieter Frankenberger, "Germany in Flux," *International Herald Tribune*, April 18, 2011, 9.

43. Herf, "Berlin Ghosts."

44. Judy Dempsey, "Germany Would Join Aid Effort for Libyans," *International Herald Tribune*, April 9, 2011, 3.

45. Dempsey, "Berlin's Diplomacy under a Dark Cloud."

46. Michael Doyle, "Kant, Liberal Legacies, and Foreign Affairs," *Philosophy and Public Affairs* 12, no. 3 (1983): 205–35.

47. T. Clifton Morgan, "Democracy and War: Reflections on the Literature," *International Interactions* 18, no. 3 (1992): 198.

48. Brett Ashley Leeds and David R. Davis, "Beneath the Surface: Regime Type and International Interaction, 1953–78," *Journal of Peace Research* 36, no. 1 (1999): 7.

49. Leeds and Davis, "Beneath the Surface," 8; Morgan, "Democracy and War," 199.

50. David P. Forsythe, "Democracy, War, and Covert Action," *Journal of Peace Research* 29 (1992): 385–95; Laura Neack, "Linking State Type with Foreign Policy Behavior," in *Foreign Policy Analysis*, ed. Laura Neack, Jeanne A. K. Hey, and Patrick J. Haney (Englewood Cliffs, N.J.: Prentice Hall, 1995), 220–21.

51. Bruce Russett, *Grasping the Democratic Peace: Principles for a Post–Cold War World* (Princeton, N.J.: Princeton University Press, 1993).

52. Bruce Russett, "Bushwacking the Democratic Peace," *International Studies Perspectives* 6, no. 4 (November 2005): 396.

# 6. DOMESTIC POLITICS

1. Laura Neack, *Elusive Security: States First, People Last* (Lanham, Md.: Rowman & Littlefield, 2007), 98.

2. Peter F. Trumbore and Mark A. Boyer, "International Crisis Decisionmaking as a Two-Level Process," *Journal of Peace Research* 37, no. 6 (November 2000): 680.

3. Trumbore and Boyer, "International Crisis Decisionmaking," 680.

4. Joe D. Hagan, "Domestic Political Explanations in the Analysis of Foreign Policy," in *Foreign Policy Analysis*, ed. Laura Neack, Jeanne A. K. Hey, and Patrick J. Haney (Englewood Cliffs, N.J.: Prentice Hall, 1995), 122.

5. Hagan, "Domestic Political Explanations," 137, fig. 8.1.

6. Hagan, "Domestic Political Explanations," 128.
7. Hagan, "Domestic Political Explanations," 131.
8. Hagan, "Domestic Political Explanations," 129.
9. David Rose, "The Gaza Bombshell," *Vanity Fair*, April 2008, http://www.vanityfair.com/politics/features/2008/04/gaza200804.
10. Evan Harris, "Cheney: Mistake for Bush Administration to Push for 2006 Palestinian Elections," ABC News, *Political Punch*, June 6, 2010, http://abcnews.go.com/blogs/politics/2010/06/cheney-mistake-for-bush-admin-to-push-for-2006-palestinian-elections.
11. Rose, "The Gaza Bombshell."
12. Rose, "The Gaza Bombshell."
13. Edward D. Mansfield and Jack Snyder, "Democratization and the Danger of War," *International Security* 20, no. 1 (1995): 13–15.
14. Edward D. Mansfield and Jack Snyder, "Incomplete Democratization and the Outbreak of Military Disputes," *International Studies Quarterly* 46, no. 4 (December 2002): 532.
15. Mansfield and Snyder, "Democratization and the Danger of War," 26.
16. Mansfield and Snyder, "Democratization and the Danger of War," 33.
17. Mansfield and Snyder, "Incomplete Democratization," 530.
18. Mansfield and Snyder, "Incomplete Democratization," 531.
19. Mansfield and Snyder, "Incomplete Democratization," 532.
20. Mansfield and Snyder, "Incomplete Democratization," 532.
21. Mansfield and Snyder, "Democratization and the Danger of War," 90.
22. Neil MacFarlane, "Realism and Russian Strategy after the Collapse of the USSR," in *Unipolar Politics: Realism and State Strategies after the Cold War*, ed. Ethan B. Kapstein and Michael Mastanduno (New York: Columbia University Press, 1999), 236.
23. Rajan Menon, "In the Shadow of the Bear: Security in Post-Soviet Central Asia," *International Security* 20, no. 1 (1995): 149–81.
24. Menon, "In the Shadow of the Bear," 157.
25. Menon, "In the Shadow of the Bear," 160.
26. Menon, "In the Shadow of the Bear," 158–59.
27. Maria Persson Lofren, "Russia: Mothers for Peace Oppose Sons in War," Inter Press Service, October 2, 1996.
28. "Putin Flies into Grozny in Fighter Bomber," Deutsche Presse-Agentur, March 20, 2000.

# 7. PUBLIC OPINION AND MEDIA

1. Jill Mahoney, "Canadians Rank Arctic Sovereignty as Top Foreign-Policy Priority," *Globe and Mail*, January 24, 2011, http://www.theglobeandmail.com/news/politics/canadians-rank-arctic-sovereignty-as-top-foreign-policy-priority/article563348.
2. Jill Mahoney, "In the Arctic, Canada Willing to Fight to Keep the True North Free," *Globe and Mail*, January 25, 2011, http://www.theglobeandmail.com/news/politics/in-the-arctic-canada-willing-to-fight-to-keep-the-true-north-free/article1881683.
3. "Harper on Arctic: 'Use It or Lose It,'" Canada.com, July 10, 2007, http://www.canada.com/topics/news/story.html?id=7ca93d97-3b26-4dd1-8d92-8568f9b7cc2a.
4. "The Globe's Election Endorsement: Facing Up to Our Challenges," *Globe and Mail*, April 27, 2011, http://www.theglobeandmail.com/commentary/editorials/the-globes-election-endorsement-facing-up-to-our-challenges/article585060.
5. "Globe Election Endorsements through History," *Globe and Mail*, March 30, 2011, http://www.theglobeandmail.com/commentary/editorials/globe-election-endorsements-through-history/article636344.
6. "Rethinking the Top of the World: Arctic Security Public Opinion Survey," Canada Centre for Global Security Studies at the Munk School of Global Affairs, January 2011, http://munkschool.utoronto.ca/wp-content/uploads/2012/07/ArcticCouncil_GordonFoundation_2011.pdf, iv.

7. "Rethinking the Top of the World," iv.
8. "Rethinking the Top of the World," v.
9. "Rethinking the Top of the World," v.
10. "Rethinking the Top of the World," vii.
11. "Rethinking the Top of the World," viii.
12. Gabriel Almond, *The American People and Foreign Policy* (New York: Praeger, 1950), as quoted in Ulf Bjereld and Ann-Marie Ekengren, "Foreign Policy Dimensions: A Comparison between the United States and Sweden," *International Studies Quarterly* 43, no. 3 (September 1999): 504.
13. Bjereld and Ekengren, "Foreign Policy Dimensions," 504–5.
14. Thomas Risse-Kappen, "Public Opinion, Domestic Structure, and Foreign Policy in Liberal Democracies," *World Politics* 43, no. 4 (1991): 480.
15. Risse-Kappen, "Public Opinion," 481.
16. Ole Holsti, *Public Opinion and American Foreign Policy* (Ann Arbor: University of Michigan Press, 1996), 31.
17. Holsti, *Public Opinion*, 110.
18. Steven Kull and Clay Ramsay, "The Myth of the Reactive Public," in *Public Opinion and the International Use of Force*, ed. Philip Everts and Pierangelo Isnernia (London: Routledge, 2001), 205.
19. Matthew A. Baum, "How Public Opinion Constrains the Use of Force: The Case of Operation Restore Hope," *Presidential Studies Quarterly* 34, no. 2 (June 2004): 191.
20. Baum, "How Public Opinion Constrains the Use of Force," 188.
21. Baum, "How Public Opinion Constrains the Use of Force," 200.
22. Baum, "How Public Opinion Constrains the Use of Force," 206.
23. Baum, "How Public Opinion Constrains the Use of Force," 203.
24. Risse-Kappen, "Public Opinion," 510.
25. Risse-Kappen, "Public Opinion," 510.
26. Risse-Kappen, "Public Opinion," 511.
27. Justin Vaïsse, "Making Sense of French Foreign Policy," Brookings Institution, July 2, 2003, http://www.brookings.edu/research/opnions/2003/07/02france-vaisse.
28. Paul Belkin, "France: Factors Shaping Foreign Policy, and Issues in U.S.-French Relations," Congressional Research Service report for Congress, April 14, 2011, http://fpc.state.gov/c18185.htm.
29. Joseph S. Nye Jr., "Redefining NATO's Mission in the Information Age," *NATO Review* (Winter 1999): 13.
30. Baum, "How Public Opinion Constrains the Use of Force," 204.
31. Baum, "How Public Opinion Constrains the Use of Force," 204.
32. Jonathan Mermin, "Television News and American Intervention in Somalia: The Myth of a Media-Driven Foreign Policy," *Political Science Quarterly* 112, no. 3 (1997): 387.
33. Mermin, "Television News," 386.
34. Mermin, "Television News," 387.
35. Mermin, "Television News," 387.
36. Mermin, "Television News," 388.
37. Mermin, "Television News," 388.
38. Mermin, "Television News," 389.
39. Tony Shaw, "The British Popular Press and the Early Cold War," *History* 83, no. 269 (1998): 66–85.
40. Shaw, "British Popular Press," 78.
41. Robert Booth, "WikiLeaks Cables Claim al-Jazeera Changed Coverage to Suit Qatari Foreign Policy," *Guardian* (London), December 5, 2010, http://www.guardian.co.uk/world/2010/dec/05/wikileaks-cables-al-jazeera-qatari-foreign-policy.
42. Alexander Kühn, Christoph Reuter, and Gregor Peter Schmitz, "Al-Jazeera Losing Battle for Independence," *Spiegel*, February 15, 2013, http://www.spiegel.de/international/world/al-jazeera-criticized-for-lack-of-independence-after-arab-spring-a-883343.html.
43. Warren P. Strobel, *Late-Breaking Foreign Policy: The News Media's Influence on Peace Operations* (Washington, D.C.: US Institute for Peace Press, 1997), 6.

44. Strobel, *Late-Breaking Foreign Policy*, 211.
45. Strobel, *Late-Breaking Foreign Policy*, 5.
46. Strobel, *Late-Breaking Foreign Policy*, 212.
47. Robert M. Entman, *Projections of Power: Framing News, Public Opinion, and US Foreign Policy* (Chicago: University of Chicago Press, 2004), 2.
48. Entman, *Projections of Power*, 13.
49. Entman, *Projections of Power*, 5.
50. Entman, *Projections of Power*, 6.
51. Entman, *Projections of Power*, 15.
52. Entman, *Projections of Power*, 29.
53. Entman, *Projections of Power*, 29.
54. Entman, *Projections of Power*, 31.
55. Entman, *Projections of Power*, 20.

# 8. GREAT POWERS IN GENERAL, THE UNITED STATES SPECIFICALLY

1. National Intelligence Council, *Global Trends 2030: Alternative Worlds*, December 2012, http://www.dni.gov/nic/globaltrends, iii.
2. National Intelligence Council, *Global Trends 2030*, iv.
3. National Intelligence Council, *Global Trends 2030*, x.
4. National Intelligence Council, *Global Trends 2030*, x.
5. National Intelligence Council, *Global Trends 2030*, xii.
6. Kenneth N. Waltz, *Man, the State and War* (New York: Columbia University Press, 1959), 159.
7. Waltz, *Man, the State, and War*, 160.
8. Charles Kindleberger, "Dominance and Leadership in the International Economy: Exploitation, Public Goods, and Free Rides," *International Studies Quarterly* 25, no. 2 (1981): 249–50.
9. Robert Gilpin, *U.S. Power and the Multinational Corporation: The Political Economy of Foreign Direct Investment* (New York: Basic, 1975), 24, as quoted in James E. Dougherty and Robert L. Pfaltzgraff Jr., *Contending Theories of International Relations: A Comprehensive Survey*, 5th ed. (New York: Longman, 2001), 72.
10. One of the classic treatments of this is in Thomas C. Schelling, *Arms and Influence* (New Haven, Conn.: Yale University Press, 1966).
11. Graham Evans and Jeffrey Newnham, *The Penguin Dictionary of International Relations* (New York: Penguin Putnam, 1998), 210.
12. Evans and Newnham, *Penguin Dictionary of International Relations*, 209.
13. Edward N. Luttwak, "Where Are the Great Powers? At Home with the Kids," *Foreign Affairs* 73, no. 4 (1994): 26.
14. Luttwak, "Where Are the Great Powers?" 26.
15. Luttwak, "Where Are the Great Powers?" 23.
16. Luttwak, "Where Are the Great Powers?" 23.
17. As quoted in Ian Lustick, "The Absence of Middle Eastern Great Powers: Political 'Backwardness' in Historical Perspective," *International Organization* 51, no. 4 (1997): 659.
18. Lustick, "Absence of Middle Eastern Great Powers," 657.
19. Robert J. Art, *A Grand Strategy for America* (Ithaca, N.Y.: Cornell University Press, 2003), 1.
20. Christopher Layne, "From Preponderance to Offshore Balancing: America's Future Grand Strategy," *International Security* 22, no. 1 (1997): 87.
21. John Gerard Ruggie, "Multilateralism: The Anatomy of an Institution," in *Multilateralism Matters: The Theory and Praxis of Institutional Form*, ed. John Gerard Ruggie (New York: Columbia University Press, 1993), 25.

22. Anne-Marie Burley, "Regulating the World: Multilateralism, International Law, and the Projection of the New Deal Regulatory State," in Ruggie, ed., *Multilateralism Matters*, 130–31.

23. Walter A. McDougall, "Back to Bedrock: The Eight Traditions of American Statecraft," *Foreign Affairs* 76 (1997): 140.

24. Ruggie, "Multilateralism: The Anatomy of an Institution," 25, emphasis added.

25. Burley, "Regulating the World," 131–32.

26. Steve Weber, "Shaping the Postwar Balance of Power: Multilateralism in NATO," *International Organization* 46, no. 3 (1992): 639.

27. G. John Ikenberry, "Is American Multilateralism in Decline?" *Perspectives on Politics* 1, no. 3 (September 2003): 543.

28. Peter F. Cowhey, "Elect Locally—Order Globally: Domestic Politics and Multilateral Cooperation," in Ruggie, ed., *Multilateralism Matters*, 159–60.

29. John Gerard Ruggie, "Third Try at World Order? America and Multilateralism after the Cold War," *Political Science Quarterly* 109, no. 4 (Autumn 1994): 562.

30. Ruggie, "Third Try at World Order?" 562.

31. Weber, "Shaping the Postwar Balance of Power," 635.

32. Weber, "Shaping the Postwar Balance of Power," 635.

33. Weber, "Shaping the Postwar Balance of Power," 636.

34. Ruggie, "Multilateralism: The Anatomy of an Institution," 8.

35. Burley, "Regulating the World," 145.

36. Miles Kahler, "Multilateralism with Small and Large Numbers," *International Organization* 46, no. 3 (Summer 1992): 681.

37. James A. Caporaso, "International Relations Theory and Multilateralism: The Search for Foundations," *International Organization* 46, no. 3 (Summer 1992): 601.

38. Anne-Marie Slaughter, "Does Obama Have a Grand Strategy for His Second Term?" *Washington Post*, January 18, 2013, http://articles.washingtonpost.com/2013-01-18/opinions/36474186_1_grand-strategy-national-security-strategy-foreign-policy.

39. Joseph S. Nye Jr., *Soft Power: The Means to Success in World Politics* (New York: PublicAffairs, 2005).

40. Josef Joffe, "How America Does It," *Foreign Affairs* 76, no. 5 (1997): 16.

41. Joffe, "How America Does It," 24.

42. Dana Priest, *The Mission: Waging War and Keeping Peace with America's Military* (New York: Norton, 2004).

43. Joffe, "How America Does It," 16.

44. Margaret P. Karns and Karen A. Mingst, *The United States and Multilateral Institutions* (Boston, Mass.: Unwin Hyman, 1990), 6.

45. David G. Haglund, "Trouble in Pax Atlantica? The United States, Europe, and the Future of Multilateralism," in *U.S. Hegemony and International Organizations*, ed. Rosemary Foot, S. Neil MacFarlane, and Michael Mastanduno (New York: Oxford University Press, 2003), 215–38; Ikenberry, "Is America Multilateralism in Decline?"

46. Ikenberry, "Is America Multilateralism in Decline?" 534.

47. Stephen W. Walt, "A Grand Strategy for American Foreign Policy," *Boston Review*, February–March 2005, http://www.bostonreview.net/BR30.1/walt.php.

48. David E. Sanger, "Pursuing Ambitious Global Goals, but Strategy Is More," *New York Times*, January 20, 2013, http://www.nytimes.com/2013/01/21/us/politics/obamas-foreign-policy-goals-appear-more-modest.html.

49. Sanger, "Pursuing Ambitious Global Goals."

50. Slaughter, "Does Obama Have a Grand Strategy."

51. Daniel W. Drezner, "Does Obama Have a Grand Strategy?" *Foreign Affairs* (July–August 2011), http://www.foreignaffairs.com/articles/67919/daniel-w-drezner/does-obama-have-a-grand-strategy.

52. Barack Obama, "National Security Strategy of the United States," May 2010, http://www.whitehouse.gov/sites/default/files/rss_viewer/national_security_strategy.pdf, 3.

53. Obama, "National Security Strategy," ii.

54. Obama, "National Security Strategy," i.

55. J. T. Mathews, "The World in 2013," in *Global Ten: Challenges and Opportunities for the President in 2013*, ed. J. T. Mathews (Washington, D.C.: Carnegie Endowment for Peace, 2012) http://www.cargnegiendowment.org/files/global_ten.pdf, 5–16.

56. Obama, "National Security Strategy," ii.

57. Obama, "National Security Strategy," 1. Obama references the "Report of the High-Level Panel on Threats, Challenges and Change," *A More Secure World: Our Shared Responsibility*, United Nations, 2004, http://www.un.org/secureworld/report2.pdf.

58. Obama, "National Security Strategy," 2–3.

59. Obama, "National Security Strategy," 3.

60. "Remarks by the President in Address to the Nation on Libya," March 28, 2011, http://www.whitehouse.gov/the-press-office/2011/03/28/remarks-president-address-nation-libya.

61. "Remarks by the President in Address to the Nation on Libya."

62. "Remarks by the President in Address to the Nation on Libya," emphasis added.

63. Nick Squires, "Europe Backs French Mali Mission with Strong Words," *Christian Science Monitor*, January 17, 2013, http://www.csmonitor.com/World/Europe/2013/0117/Europe-backs-French-Mali-mission-with-strong-words-modest-means; Carlo Muñoz, "US Has 'Responsibility' to Support French Offensive in Mali, Says Panetta," *The Hill, Defcon*, January 14, 2013, http://thehill.com/blogs/defcon-hill/operations/277063-us-has-responsibility-to-support-french-offensive-in-mali-says-panetta-; Elisabeth Bumiller, "Leon Panetta Says U.S. Has Pledged to Help France in Mali," *New York Times*, January 14, 2013, http://www.nytimes.com/2013/01/15/world/africa/leon-panetta-says-us-has-pledged-to-help-france-in-mali.html.

64. G. John Ikenberry, Michael Mastanduno, and William C. Wohlforth, "Introduction: Unipolarity, State Behavior, and Systemic Consequences," *World Politics* 61, no. 1 (January 2009): 1.

65. Ikenberry, Mastanduno, and Wohlforth, "Introduction," 14.

66. Ikenberry, Mastanduno, and Wohlforth, "Introduction," 14–15.

67. Ikenberry, Mastanduno, and Wohlforth, "Introduction," 15.

# 9. COMPETITORS, RISING POWERS, AND ALLIES

1. "UK-France Summit 2010 Declaration on Defence and Security Co-operation," November 2, 2010, http://www.number10.gov.uk/news/uk%E2%80%93france-summit-2010-declaration-on-defence-and-security-co-operation.

2. "UK-France Summit 2010 Declaration."

3. "UK-France Summit Press Conference," November 2, 2010, http://www.number10.gov.uk/news/uk-france-summit-press-conference.

4. Stephen M. Walt, "Alliances in a Unipolar World," *World Politics* 61, no. 1 (January 2009): 107.

5. Walt, "Alliances in a Unipolar World," 107; Christopher Layne, "The Unipolar Illusion Revisited: The Coming End of the United States' Unipolar Moment," *International Security* 31, no. 2 (Fall 2006): 7–41.

6. Walt, "Alliances in a Unipolar World," 97.

7. G. John Ikenberry, Michael Mastanduno, and William C. Wohlforth, "Introduction: Unipolarity, State Behavior, and Systemic Consequences," *World Politics* 61, no. 1 (January 2009): 15.

8. Walt, "Alliances in a Unipolar World," 99.

9. Walt, "Alliances in a Unipolar World," 93.

10. Laura Neack, *Elusive Security: States First, People Last* (Lanham, Md.: Rowman & Littlefield, 2007), 75–84.

11. Dinah Walker, "Trends in U.S. Military Spending," Council on Foreign Relations, August 23, 2012, http://www.cfr.org/geoeconomics/trends-us-military-spending/p28855.

12. Stockholm International Peace Research Institute, "Military Expenditure," in *SIPRI Yearbook 2012: Armaments, Disarmament and International Security*, http://www.sipri.org/yearbook/2012/04.

13. "World's Largest Economies," CNNMoney, http://money.cnn.com/news/economy/world_economies_gdp (accessed February 10, 2013).

14. National Intelligence Council, *Global Trends 2030: Alternative Worlds*, December 2012, http://www.dni.gov/nic/globaltrends, iv.

15. Julie Boland, "Ten Years of the Shanghai Cooperation Organization: A Lost Decade? A Partner for the United States?" Brookings Institution, June 2011, http://www.brookings.edu/research/papers/2011/06/shanghai-cooperation-organization-boland.

16. National Intelligence Council, *Global Trends 2025: A Transformed World*, November 2008, http://www.dni.gov/nic/NIC_2025_project.html, 38–39.

17. National Intelligence Council, *Global Trends 2030*.

18. Boland, "Ten Years of the Shanghai Cooperation Organization."

19. Walt, "Alliances in a Unipolar World," 102.

20. Walt, "Alliances in a Unipolar World," 96.

21. Walt, "Alliances in a Unipolar World," 103.

22. Walt, "Alliances in a Unipolar World," 97.

23. "India Official Says Will Co-ordinate with Shanghai Bloc on Over Terror Threats," BBC Worldwide Monitoring, December 6, 2012.

24. Walt, "Alliances in a Unipolar World," 104.

25. Walt, "Alliances in a Unipolar World," 105.

26. Toumas Forsberg, "Germany Foreign Policy and the War on Iraq: Anti-Americanism, Pacifism or Emancipation," *Security Dialogue* 36, no. 2 (2005): 215.

27. Eric Westervelt, "NATO's Intervention in Libya: A New Model?" National Public Radio, *Morning Edition*, September 12, 2011, http://www.npr.org/2011/09/12/140292920/natos-intervention-in-libya-a-new-model; Jeffrey Herf, "Berlin Ghosts: Why Germany Was against the Libya Intervention," *New Republic*, March 24, 2011, http://www.tnr.com.

28. Steven Erlanger, "The French Way of War," *New York Times*, January 19, 2013, http://www.nytimes.com/2013/01/20/sunday-review/the-french-way-of-war.html.

29. Saibal Dasgupta, "Copenhagen Conference: India, China Plan Joint Exit," *Times of India*, November 28, 2009, http://articles.timesofindia.indiatimes.com/2009-11-28/india/28074806_1_rich-nations-india-and-china-copenhagen-conference.

30. Andrew C. Revkin and David M. Broder, "A Grudging Accord on Climate Talks," *New York Times*, December 19, 2009, http://www.nytimes.com/2009/12/20/science/earth/20accord.html.

31. "U.S., Brazil 'Disagree More Than They Agree,' Analyst Says," *PBS Newshour*, April 9, 2012, http://www.pbs.org/newshour/bb/world/jan-june12/brazil_04-09.html.

32. Alexei Barrionuevo and Sebnem Arsu, "Brazil and Turkey Near Nuclear Deal with Iran," *New York Times*, May 16, 2010, http://www.nytimes.com/2010/05/17/world/middleeast/17iran.html.

33. "U.S. Says Iran Sanctions Effort Must Continue," *Voice of America*, May 27, 2010, http://www.voanews.com/content/irans-fm-says-consideration-of-nuclear-plan-is-positive-95121019/172036.html.

34. "Brazil Reveals Obama Letter in Spat over Iran Nuclear Deal," *Today's Zaman*, May 29, 2010, http://www.todayszaman.com/news-211443-brazil-reveals-obama-letter-in-spat-over-iran-nuclear-deal.html.

35. Dilma Rousseff, "Statement by H. E. Dilma Rousseff, President of the Federative Republic of Brazil, at the Opening of the General Debate of the 66th Session of the United Nations General Assembly," New York, September 21, 2011.

36. "Letter Dated 9 November 2011 from the Permanent Representative of Brazil to the United Nations Addressed to the Secretary-General," November 11, 2011, A/66/551-S/2011/701.

37. Thomas Wright, "Brazil Hosts Workshop on 'Responsibility While Protecting,'" *Foreign Policy*, *Multilateralist Blog*, August 29, 2012, http://bosco.foreignpolicy.com/posts/2012/08/29/brazil_backs_responsibility_while_protecting.

38. Eduardo J. Gómez, "Brazil's European Dream: Why Brasilia Sees the Euro Crisis as a Once-in-a-Generation Opportunity," *Foreign Policy*, March 20, 2012, http://www.foreignpolicy.com/articles/2012/03/20/brazils_european_dream.

39. K. Alan Kronstadt, Paul K. Kerr, Michael F. Martin, and Bruce Vaughn, "India: Domestic Issues, Strategic Dynamics, and U.S. Relations," Congressional Research Service report for Congress, September 1, 2011, http://fpc.state.gov/documents/organization/174187.pdf, 11.

40. Kronstadt et al., "India," summary; Geoffrey Pyatt, "Taking Stock of the U.S.-India Nuclear Deal," Mumbai, India, September 30, 2011, http://www.state.gov/p/sca/rls/rmks/2011/174883.htm.

41. Simon Denyer and Rama Lakshmi, "U.S.-India Nuclear Deal Drifts Dangerously," *Washington Post*, July 15, 2011, http://articles.washingtonpost.com/2011-07-15/world/35267081_1_nuclear-weapons-reactors-nuclear-accident.

42. Denyer and Lakshmi, "U.S.-India Nuclear Deal Drifts Dangerously."

43. Yogesh Joshi, "Paying Dividends: The U.S.-India Nuclear Deal Four Years On," *The Diplomat*, December 28, 2012, http://thediplomat.com/2012/12/28/americas-strategic-bet-on-india-is-paying-off.

44. Kronstadt et al., "India," 4.

45. Neeta Lal, "India's Copenhagen Conundrum," *World Politics Review*, December 10, 2009, http://www.worldpoliticsreview.com/articles/4789/indias-copenhagen-conundrum.

46. "Tawang Is Part of India: Dalai Lama," *Times of India*, July 4, 2008, http://articles.timesofindia.indiatimes.com/2008-06-04/india/27742278_1_tawang-dalai-lama-tibetan-spiritual-leader.

47. "A Dalai Lama Dilemma: This Small Region May One Day Thrust Itself Back into the Headlines," *Economist*, October 20, 2012, http://www.economist.com/news/asia/21564878-small-region-may-one-day-thrust-itself-back-headlines.

48. Frank Jack Daniel, "Special Report: In Himalayan Arms Race, China One-Ups India," Reuters, July 30, 2012, http://www.reuters.com/article/2012/07/30/us-india-china-idUSBRE86T00G20120730.

49. Daniel, "Special Report."

50. Daniel, "Special Report."

51. Steven Rattner, "India Is Losing the Race," *New York Times, Opinionator*, January 19, 2013, http://opinionator.blogs.nytimes.com/2013/01/19/india-is-losing-the-race.

52. Charalampos Efstathopoulos, "Reinterpreting India's Rise through the Middle Power Prism," *Asian Journal of Political Science* 19, no. 1 (April 2011): 74–95.

53. Andrew F. Cooper, Richard A. Higgott, and Kim Richard Nossal, *Relocating Middle Powers: Australia and Canada in a Changing World Order* (Vancouver: University of British Columbia Press, 1993), 19.

54. John W. Holmes, *The Shaping of Peace: Canada and the Search for World Order, 1943–1975* (Toronto: University of Toronto Press, 1982); Bernard Wood, *The Middle Powers and the General Interest* (Ottawa: North-South Institute, 1988).

55. J. L. Granatstein, "Peacekeeping: Did Canada Make a Difference? And What Difference Did Peacekeeping Make to Canada?" in *Making a Difference: Canada's Foreign Policy in a Changing World Order*, ed. John English and Norman Hillmer (Toronto: Lester, 1992), 224–25.

56. Cooper, Higgott, and Nossal, *Relocating Middle Powers*.

57. Carsten Holbraad, *Middle Powers in International Politics* (New York: St. Martin's, 1984).

58. "Canada's International Policy Statement: A Role of Pride and Influence in the World," Department of Foreign Affairs and International Trade, 2005, http://publications.gc.ca/site/eng/274692/publication.html, 5.

59. "Canada's International Policy Statement," 2.

60. "Canada's International Policy Statement," 3.

61. "Canada's International Policy Statement," 26.

62. Myles Higgins, "The Politics of Arctic Sovereignty," *The Independent.ca*, August 15, 2011, http://theindependent.ca/2011/08/15/the-politics-of-arctic-sovereignty.

63. "Does Harper Really Care about the Arctic?" *Macleans*, May 13, 2011, http://www2.macleans.ca/2011/05/13/does-harper-really-care-about-the-arctic.

64. "Canada Uncertain about Joining NATO's Arctic War Games," CBC News, August 24, 2012, http://www.cbc.ca/news/politics/story/2012/08/24/pol-cp-arctic-military-nato-pco.html.

65. Efstathopoulos, "Reinterpreting India's Rise through the Middle Power Prism," 78.

66. "Building a Better World: The Diplomacy of Ubuntu," white paper on South Africa's foreign policy, May 13, 2011, http://www.info.gov.za/view/DownloadFileAction?id=149749.

67. Efstathopoulos, "Reinterpreting India's Rise through the Middle Power Prism," 88.

68. Efstathopoulos, "Reinterpreting India's Rise through the Middle Power Prism," 78.

69. Evan A. Laksmana, "Indonesia's Rising Regional and Global Profile: Does Size Really Matter?" *Contemporary Southeast Asia* 33, no. 2 (2011): 170, 171.

70. Maria Papadakis and Harvey Starr, "Opportunity, Willingness, and Small States: The Relationship between Environment and Foreign Policy," in *New Directions in the Study of Foreign Policy*, ed. Charles F. Hermann, Charles W. Kegley, and James N. Rosenau (Winchester, Mass.: Unwin Hyman, 1987).

71. Davis B. Bobrow and Steve Chan, "Simple Labels and Complex Realities: National Security for the Third World," in *National Security in the Third World: The Management of Internal and External Threats*, ed. Edward E. Azar and Chung-in Moon (Aldershot, UK: Edward Elgar, 1988), 56–57.

72. Mary Ann Tétreault, "Autonomy, Necessity, and the Small State: Ruling Kuwait in the Twentieth Century," *International Organization* 45, no. 4 (1991): 567.

73. Walt, "Alliances in a Unipolar World," 98.

# 10. CONCLUSION: A NESTED GAME WITH MANY PLAYERS

1. This case can be studied in detail, including issues of British, Chilean, and international law, in Human Rights Watch, "Discreet Path to Justice? Chile, Thirty Years after the Coup," September 9, 2003, http://www.hrw.org/reports/2003/09/09/discreet-path-justice.

2. "U.K. House of Lords: Regina v. Bartle and the Commissioner of Police for the Metropolis, Ex parte Pinochet," International Law in Brief, November 16–27, 1998, http://www.asil.org/ilib0111.cfm.

3. Andrew Sparrow and Bruce Johnston, "Pope Backs Call to Free Pinochet," *Daily Telegraph* (London), February 19, 1999, 1. See also "Vatican Plea on Pinochet's Behalf Prompts Outrage," *Boston Globe*, February 20, 1999, A20.

4. Human Rights Watch, "The Case against Hissène Habré," http://www.hrw.org/node/93175 (accessed February 28, 2013).

5. Margaret E. Keck and Kathryn Sikkink, "Transnational Advocacy Networks in International Politics: Introduction," in *Essential Readings in World Politics*, ed. Karen Mingst and Jack Snyder (New York: Norton, 2001), 335.

6. Karen Mingst, "Uncovering the Missing Links: Linkage Actors and Their Strategies," in *Foreign Policy Analysis*, ed. Laura Neack, Jeanne A. K. Hey, and Patrick J. Haney (Englewood Cliffs, N.J.: Prentice Hall, 1995), 231.

7. Mingst, "Uncovering the Missing Links," 237, quoting Peter Haas, "Introduction: Epistemic Communities and International Policy Coordination," *International Organization* 46, no. 1 (1992): 3.

8. Jonathan Curiel, "The Rise of Global Anger: Why They Hate the U.S. So Fiercely," *San Francisco Chronicle*, September 16, 2001, D4.

9. Sam Dillon with Donald G. McNeil Jr., "Spain Sets Hurdle for Extraditions," *New York Times*, November 24, 2001, A1.

10. James K. Glassman, "Alliance for Youth Movements Summit at Columbia University in New York, December 3–5, 2008," Washington, D.C., November 24, 2008, http://2002-2009-fpc.state.gov/112321.htm.

11. Samantha M. Shapiro, "Revolution, Facebook-Style," *New York Times*, January 25, 2009, http://www.nytimes.com/2009/01/25/magazine/25bloggers-t.html.

12. "April 6 Youth Movement," *PBS Frontline*, http://www.pbs.org/wgbh/pages/frontline/revolution-in-cairo/inside-april6-movement (accessed February 28, 2013).

13. Shapiro, "Revolution, Facebook-Style."

14. Glassman, "Alliance for Youth Movements."

15. Glassman, "Alliance for Youth Movements."

16. "08CAIRO2572, April 6 Activist on His U.S. Visit and Regime," December 30, 2008, http://wikileaks.ch/cable/2008/12/08CAIRO2572.html. See also, David Wolman, "The Idealism Clinic: On the Origins of Egypt's Revolution," *The Atlantic*, February 11, 2011, http://www.theatlantic.com/technology/archive/2011/02/the-idealism-clinic-on-the-origins-of-egypts-revolution/71132.

17. Helene Cooper and Robert F. Worth, "In Arab Spring, Obama Finds a Sharp Test," *New York Times*, September 24, 2012, http://www.nytimes.com/2012/09/25/us/politics/arab-spring-proves-a-harsh-test-for-obamas-diplomatic-skill.html.

# Glossary

**accommodation strategy** a strategy in which leaders attempt to bargain with a vocal opposition, accommodating or adopting some of its demands, in order to avoid controversy; associated with a restrained, noncontroversial foreign policy

**aggressive leader** a leadership personality profile with the following traits: high nationalism, high need to control others, high need for power, high distrust in others, and low integrative complexity; expects international interactions to be on his or her own terms

**anarchy** the general condition of the international system in which no ultimate authority (such as a world government) exists to govern relations between states and other international actors

**attribution bias** a cognitive error in which one assumes that one's own group is good by nature and only does bad things when forced to do so, while the opponent does bad things because it is inherently bad

**austerity** a policy designed to reduce government debt by severely cutting government spending; intended to shock an economy into course-correction and diminish the government's involvement in it especially during difficult economic periods

**autocratic** a form of government in which a leader (an autocrat) wields unlimited power

**balance of power** the distribution of power among the great power states in the international system or in a regional system

**balancing** the effort by a state or group of states to build a counterweight against the power of another state or group of states in order to achieve a new balance of power; hard balancing involves constructing a military counterweight; *see also* soft balancing

**bandwagoning** joining a powerful state or group of states in order to appease it and lessen the threat it poses; sometimes done in anticipation of a future pay-off for joining

**belief set** an organized, relatively integrated, and persistent set of perceptions that an individual, group, or state holds about a particular universe

**bipolar international system** an international system in which power is fairly evenly distributed between two significant powers (states) or two power blocs (groups of states)

**civilian protection** the notion that the international community should protect people from mass atrocity crimes when a state cannot or will not protect them; a civilian protection mandate by the UN Security Council authorizes the use of all necessary measures (including force) to render such protection

**civil society** the public realm "located" between households and government in which interest groups of all sorts protect individuals from the government (and from the free market)

**client state** a weak state that maintains the support of a powerful state, or patron, by playing on the patron's concerns that the client regime may be overthrown if not given sufficient support; *see also* patron-client relationship

**CNN effect** an explanation of the media's role in foreign policy making that posits that media broadcasts of unsettling international images incite the public to demand foreign policy action by the government; foreign policy makers, then, must take under consideration issues that they may not have otherwise considered and/or they must make foreign policy decisions without full and appropriate deliberation

**coalition building** the bringing together of diverse actors and groups who share an interest in a common policy outcome; because the coalition is loosely built on a narrow issue-base, it requires constant maintenance and rebuilding by coalition leaders

**coalition building strategy** a linkage actor strategy that involves the building of a transnational coalition of diverse linkage actors who share an interest in a common outcome

**coalition government** in a parliamentary system, an arrangement to govern between two or more political parties that together control sufficient votes to be the majority group in parliament; the leader of the party with the greatest number of seats in parliament is typically the head of the government formed

**cognition** the study of the mental process or faculty of knowing

**cognitive consistency** the idea that the images in a belief set must be logically connected and fairly well integrated

**cognitive miser** the idea that individuals are assumed to be limited cognitive managers (lazy thinkers) who rely on shortcuts to interpret and understand new information

**collective good** a common good—such as international peace and security—that is available to all members of a group and cannot be denied to any based on contributions; in international relations, collective goods are said to be provided by a hegemon or through multilateral arrangements built on diffuse reciprocity

**conciliatory leader** a leadership personality profile with the following traits: low nationalism, low need to control others, low distrust of others, high need for affiliation, and high integrative complexity; such a leader is more responsive to the international environment and cooperative

**constructive engagement** a policy of long-term involvement meant to change or influence the policy and behavior of a target state through offering incentives rather than threats and punishments

**constructivism** a view that proposes that our understanding of world politics is a social creation (construction); for instance, constructivism holds that the international system is not anarchic but is *understood* and accepted to be anarchic

**crisis** a circumstance in which a threat exists that requires immediate action by decision makers

**democracy** a type of government in which power is exercised by the people through freely contested, open, and regularly held elections in which representatives are selected for government office; a central feature of a democracy is decentralized political authority

**democratic peace** the theory that democracies are less likely to go to war with other democracies

**democratization** the process in which constitutional limits are placed on the exercise of power by central authorities while free and openly contested elections for political office, with universal suffrage and mass political participation, are regularized as the norm

**deterrence** a situation in which the opponent is stopped from initiating an action—such as a military attack—because of the threat of disproportionate retaliation and/or punishment

**diplomatic immunity** the principle that heads of state are not personally liable for actions made on behalf of the state; related to the fundamental notion that all actions are necessary and proper for the security of the state and no one has the right to question what a state (or regime) does for its own security

**dual game** *see* **nested game**

**elite** individuals who exercise great influence in the policy-making process either in the role of government officials, domestic opponents or as individuals who have greater access to decision makers

**enemy image** a belief set that portrays the opponent as inherently evil and strategically cunning with nearly unlimited capacity for causing harm

**Eurozone** the group of seventeen states within the European Union who use a single currency (the euro) and agree to limit government debt and deficits to commonly set targets; not all EU members are members of the Eurozone

**framing** the act of explaining a problem in such a way as to promote a certain solution to it; a successful "frame" is culturally resonant and repeated with great frequency so that competing frames are shut out

**game theory** a mathematically based method for evaluating interactive choices that assumes that each player in the "game" (1) operates under the same assumptions and rules for interaction, (2) is aware of the payoff system, and (3) holds a clear understanding of "winning"

**globalization** the internationalization of culture and economics, accompanied by increased interdependence between individuals, states, and nonstate international actors

**global south** the countries that were at one time colonies, possessions, or subordinate parts of empires that have political and economic development issues often associated with under- and uneven development; also called the "Third World"

**governance** the act, process, or power of governing

**grand strategy** a global vision and set of operating principles that frame the foreign policy of a great power with special emphasis on the harnessing of military force to achieve global goals

**grassroots mobilization** a linkage actor strategy in which public education and publicity efforts create widespread public engagement in favor of a cause or policy outcome

**groupthink** a distortion of small group decision making in which the members' desires for maintaining group cohesion are prioritized over problem solving; associated with premature closure around a solution advocated by a strong group member

**hegemon** the preponderant power in the international system as determined by military and economic power

**hegemonic order** the international system created by the hegemon to suit its global goals and objectives

**humanitarian intervention** military involvement in the internal affairs of a state by another state, group of states, or international organization for the purpose of stopping mass killings and/or preventing a humanitarian disaster such as widespread famine

**insulation strategy** a strategy in which leaders deflect attention from and otherwise protect their foreign policy through suppressing, overriding, or co-opting the opposition

**integrative complexity** a measure of information processing based on the simplicity to complexity of words used and reasoning expressed; higher integrative complexity is typically associated with more cooperative international behavior; measured complexity falls for all decision makers in crises

**international organization (IO)** a formal organization created by an agreement among states in order to facilitate cooperation on matters of mutual concern; may be regionally based or global

**international system** as a descriptive term (rather than as a level of analysis), refers to the totality of international actors, distribution of resources, and the (written and unwritten) rules and (formal and informal) institutions that govern relations among the actors

**internationalist** a foreign policy orientation that favors cooperation and mutual empowerment over the narrow pursuit of immediate national interests

**intifada** uprising or public resistance; associated in this book with the Palestinian uprisings in Israeli-occupied contested territories

**leader** a person, usually the head of a government, who makes policy choices affecting the international and domestic environments

**leadership** the top decision makers in a national government; regime

**legitimacy** the recognition or acceptance by citizens and/or international actors, including other states, that a government has the right to exercise power and make decisions on behalf of the country

**liberal international order** the American hegemonic order constructed after World War II and built on the foundations of free trade and multilateral, institutionalized problem solving;

associated with the construction of numerous multilateral organizations designed to facilitate international cooperation and prevent world war

**linkage** the direct or indirect interconnectedness of two policies, groups, ideas, and so on

**linkage actors** individuals, government representatives, and nonstate actors who work across national boundaries to influence public policy

**mobilization strategy** a strategy in which leaders use assertive, sometimes risky and aggressive foreign policy behaviors, and calls to nationalism to assert their government's legitimacy against a vocal opposition

**most favored nation (MFN)** refers to the extension of beneficial trade terms (usually in the form of lowered tariffs) to a country that reflect the best terms extended to third parties in the past or in the future

**multilateralism** called the "international governance of the many"; participation in institutionalized arrangements of more than three states on specific issue areas; the arrangements codify obligations and benefits of membership and punishments for noncompliant behavior

**multipolar international system** an international system in which power is fairly evenly distributed among four or five major powers (states)

**mutual assured destruction (MAD)** the idea that because both the Americans and Soviets possessed nuclear second-strike capability (the ability to sustain a first attack and retaliate in kind), any war between the two initiated by either side would destroy both

**national interest** the interests of a state that are of primary importance for protection and enhancement

**national self-image** the concept or image of the country that is shared among a country's elite and public and guides the country's foreign and domestic policies and behaviors

**nationalism** strong, positive feelings about a group that are shared among its members and lead the members to want to preserve the group at all costs; once mobilized can become aggressive and bellicose

**negotiation** the process through which international actors interact with and engage one another in order to achieve common objectives

**neoconservativism** a political philosophy associated with the idea of maintaining American primacy in international affairs through the muscular and/or militarized promotion of what are claimed to be American values; typically associated with the George W. Bush administration

**neoimperialism** the idea that the Western, or advanced industrialized states, use indirect means—usually with some moral justification—to impose their political and economic structures on less-developed countries

**neoliberal institutionalism** a variant on liberalism that proposes that international cooperation occurs because self-interested states understand the long-term benefits of common or collective action through multilateralism

**nested game** the concept that national leaders must divide their attention between the domestic and international environments, sometimes using one arena to further agendas in the other; also called a dual or two-level game

**neutrality** a policy that a country will not take sides in international disputes or form military alliances of any sort

**nongovernmental organization (NGO)** an international actor whose members are not states, and whose membership and interests transcend national boundaries

**nonprovocative defense** a defense posture in which a country only maintains weapons that can be used for national territorial defense and cannot be easily reconfigured for outward force projection; intended to cause no fear in others about the state's intentions

**nonstate actor** an international actor that is not a state or a representative of a state

**normal power** a state with both military and economic power; phrase is applied to the aspirations of some in postwar Japan and Germany who want their countries to shed antimilitaristic restrictions in order to achieve full great-power status

**nuclear deterrence** the condition in which opposing nuclear-weapons states refrain from using such weapons against one another because of the mutual threat of unacceptable damage

**operational code** a cognitive map of an individual's normative and behavioral beliefs; indicates a leader's predisposition toward action

**patron-client relationship** a reciprocal and strategic relationship between a strong state and a weak one (or between a great power and a small power)

**peace enforcement operation** a multinational military force tasked with creating secure conditions in a conflict zone; in the post–Cold War era such an operation is typically approved by UN Security Council but not under UN command; commanded by a lead state heading a coalition of the willing; a peace enforcement operation mandate is a mandate to conduct a war for limited purposes

**peacekeeping** the use of a neutral, noncombatant multinational armed force for the purpose of enforcing a cease-fire, maintaining a demilitarized zone, overseeing the return to normal politics and other postconflict tasks; typically authorized by the UN Security Council and under UN command and control

**pluralist model** the theory that public policy results from bargaining, negotiating, and politicking among many distinct and autonomous interests within a society

**policy coalition** a group composed of diverse interests formed by political leaders in order to get a certain policy program accepted and executed

**power approach** a linkage actor strategy in which the highest diplomatic circles or ultimate power resources are tapped in order to influence a policy outcome

**primacy** a term referring to the preponderance of power in the international system; the state with preponderant power is said to have primacy

**public** the populace of a country; often differentiated into the mass public and the attentive public; distinct from the elite

**public opinion** the general views of the majority of individuals about some idea, person, policy, or action

**rational decision making** an approach to studying the behavior of actors in the international system that assumes that all actors will select the course of action that they perceive as most likely to bring about the preferred outcome while maximizing benefits and minimizing costs

**regime** the central, primary decision makers within a national government

**rule of law** the authority of law in a society that acts to constrain unlimited, antisocial behavior by individuals or groups and arbitrary exercises of power by governing officials

**scapegoating** attributing the blame for some bad or negative condition on others, particularly foreigners; typically performed by elites attempting to mobilize the mass public

**security dilemma** a cyclic situation in which actions undertaken by a state to increase its security ultimately decrease overall security because other states (mis)perceive the defensive actions to be hostile and threatening and so they respond in kind

**siege mentality** when members of a group, nation, or state share the belief that the outside world holds hostile behavioral intentions toward the group

**soft balancing** an effort to build a counterweight against the dominant state on specific policies or issues without challenging the dominance of the state or the current international system

**soft power** the ability to persuade others to pursue common goals; also understood as the "pull" of an attractive culture and/or society

**sovereignty** the ultimate decision-making and decision-enforcing authority within a defined territory; only states are sovereign in the international system

**state** a legal-political concept denoting a sovereign actor in the international system with a recognized territory, population, and effective government

**state building** the historical process whereby the institutions of government are constructed and the authority of the government is extended over territory and population

**technocratic approach** a linkage actor strategy in which expert knowledge is utilized to influence a policy outcome

**terrorism** the use or threatened use of violence against noncombatants for the purpose of intimidating governments and societies in pursuit of political and/or social objectives

**transnational actors** individuals or organizations in the international system that conduct activities across national borders

**two-level game** *see* **nested game**

**ultimate decision unit** the set of authorities that has the final say on policy direction and the commitment of national resources; the decision made by the unit cannot be easily reversed by any other actor in the government

**unilateralism** when a state acts alone in its pursuit of its own narrowly defined foreign policy goals

**unipolar international system** an international system in which one state holds a preponderance of political, military, and economic power

**unipole** the state that holds preponderant power in a unipolar international system

# Index

# About the Author

Laura Neack is professor of political science at Miami University, Oxford, Ohio. She teaches courses in world politics, foreign policy analysis, and national, international, and human security. Professor Neack is the author of *Elusive Security: States First, People Last* (2007) and the first and second editions of *The New Foreign Policy* (2003, 2008), and she is coeditor of two books, *Global Society in Transition* (2002) and *Foreign Policy Analysis: Continuity and Change in Its Second Generation* (1995). Professor Neack is also the author of numerous journal articles and book chapters on human security, foreign policy analysis, and UN peacekeeping. She received her doctorate in political science in 1991 from the University of Kentucky.